Building BACKYARD STRUCTURES

Sheds, Barns, Bins, Gazebos & Other Outdoor Construction

Paul Levine, Tom Begnal & Dan Thornton

Sterling Publishing Co., Inc.
New York

Acknowledgments

Our thanks to the following people and organizations for their valuable assistance: *American Wood Preservers' Association,* Woodstock, Maryland; *American Wood Preservers' Institute,* Vienna, Virginia; *APA–the Engineered Wood Association,* Tacoma, Washington; *Cedar Shake and Shingle Bureau,* Bellevue, Washington; *Southern Pine Inspection Bureau,* Pensacola, Florida; and *Mr. Timm Locke,* product publicity manager, *Western Wood Products Association,* Portland, Oregon.

Library of Congress Cataloging-in-Publication Data

Levine, Paul, 1943–
    Building backyard structures : sheds, barns, bins, gazebos & other outdoor construction / Paul Levine, Tom Bengal & Dan Thornton.
       p. cm.
    Includes index.
    ISBN 0-8069-4216-9
    1. Garden structures—Design and construction. I. Bengal, Tom.
II. Thornton, Dan. III. Title.
TH4961.L48 1997
690′.89—dc21   96-53254
                                  CIP

10 9 8 7 6 5 4 3 2 1

Published by Sterling Publishing Company, Inc.
387 Park Avenue South, New York, N.Y. 10016
© 1997 by Paul Levine, Tom Bengal, and Dan Thornton
Distributed in Canada by Sterling Publishing
c/o Canadian Manda Group, One Atlantic Avenue, Suite 105
Toronto, Ontario, Canada M6K 3E7
Distributed in Great Britain and Europe by Cassell PLC
Wellington House, 125 Strand, London WC2R 0BB, England
Distributed in Australia by Capricorn Link (Australia) Pty Ltd.
P.O. Box 6651, Baulkham Hills, Business Centre, NSW 2153, Australia
Printed and bound in Hong Kong
All rights reserved

Sterling ISBN 0-8069-4216-9

Contents

Introduction

What could be better than to escape from today's stressful world by building objects that are beautiful, practical, and fun to use? It's a real joy to be able to stand back after building something and admire it.

In the following pages, you will learn how to build a variety of different useful outdoor structures. You can share in both the building of these structures and their use with family and friends. I greatly enjoyed working on these projects with Tom and Dan, two people who have my respect and admiration after years of association.

Tom's uncanny ability to provide the proper information is found on every page. His contribution of facts such as that burning pressure-treated wood or just breathing the fine dust from it is dangerous because it contains arsenic will be appreciated by everyone.

Dan's efforts can be seen in the deceptively simple line drawings used to convey woodworking information. Without drawings such as Dan's, any book on woodworking can quickly become a wordy bore. His delicate hand can also be seen in the choice of colors for some of the projects. Too often, this is an overlooked aspect. Dan is a first-rate colorist.

It was fun to work on these projects. I hope that you will find similar pleasure when you read the information on how to build outdoor structures and then tackle specific ones. They include a utility shed, a pole barn, a woodshed, a garbage house, a pool or patio shed, a gazebo, and a playhouse for children.

Remember, the whole point of life is to enjoy it. Whether you're spending time with your family and friends while making these buildings or while using them, enjoy yourself!

Paul Levine

General Safety Instructions

Before beginning any of the woodworking or construction techniques described in this book, review the following safety instructions:

1. Don't attempt any procedure you are not comfortable with or properly equipped to perform.
2. Always use safety glasses when using hand or power tools.
3. Wear a dust mask if your work is generating dust.
4. Know your power tool. Read the owner's manual and understand the limitations and potential hazards of the tool before you use it.
5. Don't use power tools in wet locations.
6. Always use blade guards on power tools that are equipped with them.
7. Unplug power tools before making adjustments or changing saw blades, bits, cutters, etc.
8. Make sure the switch is in the ''off'' position before connecting the power plug.
9. Always use power tools that are double-insulated and grounded.
10. Don't try to force a tool to do an operation that it is not designed to do.
11. When using a power tool, use clamps or other means to ensure that the workpiece is held securely in place.
12. Keep your hands well away from saw blades, cutters, bits, etc.
13. Dress properly. Don't wear loose clothing or jewelry that can get caught in moving parts.
14. Keep your work area clean. Clutter often causes accidents.
15. Keep children away from work areas.
16. Don't work when you are fatigued or under the influence of medication, drugs, or alcohol.
17. When working outside, use extension cords designed for outside applications.
18. Construct sturdy scaffolding before installing roofing shingles.
19. When using ladders, make sure they stand on ground that is firm and level. Position them close to your work, so that you avoid overreaching.
20. Before walking on a roof, make sure the underlayment is firmly attached.
21. Remove or bend over any protruding nails at the work site.
22. When using toxic finishes, carefully follow the manufacturer's safety instructions. Make sure that there is adequate ventilation and, if necessary, wear an appropriate respirator.

Chapter 1.
Building Materials

Although the outdoor storage projects in this book differ in size, shape, and utility, each one is constructed using many of the same basic building materials. Lumber, plywood, nails, screws, hardware, and other such products are common to many of the projects. This chapter provides some basic information about the construction materials mentioned throughout the book.

LUMBER

Wood is one of our oldest materials. It is also one of our most valued natural resources. When wood is cut to specific thicknesses, widths, and lengths, it is called *lumber*. There are two basic types of lumber: softwood and hardwood.

SOFTWOOD

Wood cut from conifers, the cone-bearing trees, is classified as softwood. Typically, the leaves are needle-shaped and remain attached throughout the year. Examples include sugar pine, shortleaf pine, Douglas fir, spruce, western hemlock, and redwood.

Softwood lumber has many applications in general building construction. It is used for joists, plates, studs, headers, beams, rafters, fascias, siding, flooring, paneling, molding, and much more. More than 15 species of softwoods are used for general building construction.

HARDWOOD

Wood cut from deciduous trees is classified as hardwood. Deciduous trees have broad leaves that usually fall off in the colder months. They include such species as oak, ash, maple, walnut, rosewood, and mahogany.

Almost all hardwoods are, indeed, harder than softwoods. Of course, there are always ex-

ceptions. For example, balsa is classified as a hardwood because it comes from a deciduous tree, but it is considerably softer than most softwoods. Shortleaf pine is another exception, as this southern pine is harder than some of the hardwoods.

Most hardwoods not only have a hard surface, they also offer a good measure of strength and beauty. That makes hardwoods ideal for furniture, flooring, millwork, paneling, interior trim, and much more. But, because hardwoods are both heavy and expensive, they are rarely used to frame houses or the small outdoor storage structures that are found in this book. Softwoods, which provide adequate strength at an economical price, are used almost exclusively for such construction. Since hardwoods are not required for any of the projects in this book, the discussion of lumber is limited to the softwoods.

MOISTURE CONTENT

A tree is made up of tiny elongated cells. A typical softwood species has about four million cells in a cubic inch. In a living tree, the cells are saturated with water. Indeed, water can account for half the weight of a living tree.

The amount of water in the cells is called the *moisture content* of the wood. Moisture content is the weight of the water in wood expressed as a percentage of the weight of the wood from which all water has been removed. Wood with a moisture content greater than 19 percent is called *unseasoned lumber* or *green lumber*. Wood with a moisture content that's 19 percent or less is called *seasoned* or *dry*.

Once a tree is harvested, the water begins to evaporate and the wood slowly dries. Cutting a tree into boards exposes more surface area, and the drying process speeds up somewhat. Little dimensional change occurs in the wood until the moisture content reaches about 30 percent. As the moisture content starts to drop below 30 percent, the wood begins to shrink in both width and thickness. Indeed, a 2 × 8-inch board dried to a moisture content of 15 percent can shrink ¼ inch in width and ⅟₁₆ inch in thickness. The actual amount of shrinkage varies somewhat depending upon the wood species and how the board was oriented when still part of the tree.

Wood changes little in length as it dries. The amount is small enough to be considered insignificant for general construction projects.

When wood dries and shrinks, it is subject to checking, splitting, and warping (see Lumber Characteristics sidebar). To minimize such problems, much of the lumber at the mills is dried under controlled conditions before it is shipped to lumberyards and building supply centers.

Lumber dried under controlled conditions is either *air-dried* or *kiln-dried*. As the name suggests, air-dried lumber is allowed to dry simply by exposing it to the outside air. The lumber is protected from the weather, and spacers are placed between the boards to allow plenty of air circulation. Air-drying is a relatively slow process.

Kiln-dried lumber is dried in a huge oven called a kiln. Both the temperature and humidity are carefully controlled during the drying process. Kiln-drying is a much faster process than air-drying.

Not all lumber is air-dried or kiln-dried by the mills. Lumber that has a nominal thickness of 4 inches and greater is generally shipped unseasoned. In addition, some lumber with a nominal thickness of less than 4 inches is also shipped unseasoned. (Nominal size is the size the lumber is known at and sold in the market. The nominal size is different from the lumber's actual size.)

KEEPING LUMBER DRY

Wood either gains or loses moisture in an effort to be in balance with the relative humidity of the surrounding air. When the surrounding air is dry, an unseasoned board loses moisture through evaporation. A seasoned board that is stored in a damp basement absorbs moisture from the air. If the board remains in the basement long enough, its moisture content may increase to over 19 percent. That means the board no longer meets the moisture standards for sea-

soned lumber. Storing lumber in a dry environment can help keep moisture problems to a minimum.

Lumber that has too much moisture is going to dry after it is installed, and that sometimes causes problems. For example, a window casing might be installed with a perfectly tight miter joint, but as the casing dries and shrinks in width, the joint is likely to open.

FRAMING AND APPEARANCE LUMBER

Lumber to be used as structural members (joists, rafters, etc.) is called *framing lumber*. Lumber that is to be used for appearance applications (siding, flooring, paneling, molding, etc.) is classified as *appearance lumber*.

Framing lumber is inspected under somewhat different standards than appearance lumber. Strength characteristics are of prime importance for framing lumber, with appearance a secondary consideration. Appearance lumber must meet appearance standards first, and, in most instances, strength standards are not considered.

Framing Lumber

There are two classifications of framing lumber: *dimension lumber* and *timber*. Most structural lumber for general building construction falls under one of these two classifications. Dimension lumber is milled to 2- to 4-inch nominal thickness, and to widths of more than 2 inches. Dimension lumber is divided into four categories: light framing, structural light framing, structural joists and planks, and studs. Each category is then further divided into specific grades.

Appearance Lumber

Lumber that's graded primarily for appearance is often called *board lumber* or *boards*. Depending upon the grade category, boards can measure from ⅜ to 4 inches in nominal thickness and have nominal widths that are 2 inches or greater. However, most appearance boards found in lumberyards or building supply centers have 1- or 1¼-inch nominal thicknesses. The three board categories you are most likely to use are select, finish, and common.

NOMINAL VS. DRESSED DIMENSIONS

Mills cut lumber to *nominal dimensions*. That

means when they are cutting a 2 × 4 stud, the lumber is cut to 2 inches thick and 4 inches wide. At this stage, the lumber is said to be *in the rough* because the big, fast-cutting mill saw blades produce very rough surfaces.

After rough-cutting, some lumber is either air- or kiln-dried, to reduce its moisture content. Once dry, the rough surfaces are planed smooth and the lumber is ready to be shipped. Lumber that has been planed smooth is called *dressed* or *surfaced lumber*. But this smooth lumber is now noticeably thinner and narrower than the original nominal dimensions. This final size is called the *dressed dimension* of the lumber. A seasoned 2 × 4 dressed stud is 1½ inches thick × 3½ inches wide. Standard nominal and dressed dimensions (thickness and width) for most lumber sizes can be found in Table 1-1. Keep in mind that lumberyard and building-supply-center employees almost always use nominal dimensions when discussing lumber size.

THE BOARD FOOT

Most lumber is priced and sold by the *board foot*. The board foot is a measure of volume, and it is equal to 144 cubic inches. Therefore, a 1 × 12-inch board that is 1 foot long is equal to one board foot. So, too, is a 2 × 6-inch board that is 1 foot long.

Various formulas are used to calculate board footage. The one most often used is as follows:

$$\frac{\text{thickness (in.)} \times \text{width (in.)} \times \text{length (ft.)}}{12} =$$

the number of board feet. Remember, you must use nominal dimensions for the length and width.

LUMBER SIZES
Nominal vs. Actual (dressed) Dimensions

Nominal	Actual (dressed)
1 × 2	¾ × 1½
1 × 3	¾ × 2½
1 × 4	¾ × 3½
1 × 6	¾ × 5½
1 × 8	¾ × 7¼
1 × 10	¾ × 9¼
1 × 12	¾ × 11¼
2 × 2	1½ × 1½
2 × 3	1½ × 2½
2 × 4	1½ × 3½
2 × 6	1½ × 5½
2 × 8	1½ × 7¼
2 × 10	1½ × 9¼
2 × 12	1½ × 11¼
4 × 4	3½ × 3½
6 × 6	5½ × 5½

Table 1-1. Nominal versus actual (dressed) dimensions of lumber.

LUMBER CHARACTERISTICS

Bow: Any flatwise deviation from a straight line extending from end to end on a piece of lumber.

Check: A relatively shallow lengthwise crack in the grain, usually formed as the lumber shrinks during the drying process. A check does not extend through the wood to the opposite or adjoining surface.

Crook: Any edgewise deviation from a straight line extending from end to end on a piece of lumber.

Cup: Any deviation from a straight line extending from edge to edge across the face of a piece of lumber.

Decay: A breakdown of wood structure, caused by the action of fungi, that reduces the strength of lumber. Also called rot or dote.

Hole: Often caused by wood-boring insects or worms. Holes can extend either partially or entirely through the lumber.

Knot: The remains of a branch or limb, embedded in a tree, which is exposed when the tree is cut into lumber. Knots are classified according to shape, size, quality, and location.

LUMBER CHARACTERISTICS (continued)

Knothole: A hole through lumber created when a knot falls out.

Pitch: A concentration of resinous material.

Pitch Pocket: A gap between the growth rings of the wood. The gap may be filled with resin, or the resin may be gone, leaving an empty gap.

Pitch Streak: A well-defined accumulation of pitch in the shape of a streak.

Pith: The small, soft core in the center of a log.

Shake: A lengthwise crack in the grain that runs between or through the growth rings.

Split: A lengthwise crack that extends completely through the wood to an opposite or adjoining surface.

Stain: Any discoloration on the exterior or interior of the wood.

Torn Grain: Grain that is torn from the surface when the wood is planed (dressed) at the mill.

Wane: The presence of bark, or lack of wood, from any cause (except eased edges) on the edge or corner of a piece of lumber.

Warp: Any deviation of lumber from a flat, straight surface. Various types of warp include cup, bow, and crook.

PRESSURE-TREATED LUMBER

Lumber that remains dry and free from wood-boring insects can last indefinitely. However, wood exposed to moisture for long periods of time can be subject to fungi attack that causes decay. Also, termites, carpenter ants, and other wood-boring insects can weaken wood to the point that it has little strength.

The pressure-treating process forces wood preservative chemicals deep into the cells of the wood. The result is a lumber product that offers resistance to fungus growth and insect attack. Yet, the addition of the chemicals does not change the strength of the wood or its ability to expand or contract with changes in moisture content. Pressure-treated wood is generally sold as either ''wet'' or ''kiln-dried after treatment'' (KDAT).

Many building codes require the use of pressure-treated wood (or naturally decay-resistant wood species) for construction lumber that come in contact with concrete, masonry, or exposed soil. This code requirement sometimes includes floor joists and crawl-space members within 12 to 18 inches of exposed soil.

Most of the pressure-treated lumber produced for residential construction uses waterborne preservatives. Waterborne preservatives use water as the solvent or carrier. Chromated copper arsenate (CCA) and ammoniacal copper zinc arsenate (ACZA) are two commonly used waterborne preservative chemicals.

Preservation Retention

The level of resistance to fungus growth and insect attack is directly related to the amount of preservative chemical that is added to the wood. Chemical retention is expressed as the number of pounds of chemical retained in each cubic foot (pcf) of wood after treatment. The higher the number, the greater the resistance of the wood to fungi and insects. Some common examples of retention values are as follow:

0.25 pcf—For above-ground applications, such as deck components not in contact with the ground.

0.40 pcf—For lumber in contact with soil or freshwater. Landscaping timber usually requires this retention value. Some lumber with a 0.40 (or higher) retention value is notched (incised) to improve the chemical saturation.

0.60 pcf—For permanent wood foundations, and also for any wood that is buried in the ground, such as signposts or pole barn support posts.

The American Wood Preservers' Association (AWPA) has developed standards for pressure-treated wood. Most companies manufacture pressure-treated wood in conformance with AWPA standards.

The Quality Mark

Manufacturers label pressure-treated wood with a *quality mark*. The quality mark, which is applied as either an ink stamp or an end tag, provides useful information about the pressure-treated product. It includes: 1, the year of treatment; 2, the preservative used; 3, the proper exposure condition; 4, the retention level; 5, the trademark of the inspection agency; 6, the applicable AWPA standard; 7, the treating company and plant location (Illus. 1-1).

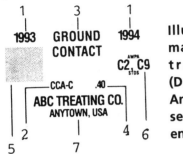

Illus. 1-1. A quality mark for pressure-treated lumber. (Drawing courtesy of American Wood Preservers Institute, Vienna, Virginia.)

Working Safely with Pressure-Treated Wood

Throughout this century, billions of board feet of pressure-treated lumber have been safely used. However, the chemicals CCA and ACZA contain inorganic arsenic, so it makes good sense to keep a few safety tips in mind whenever you use this product.

When working with pressure-treated lumber, or any wood product for that matter, always wear a dust mask, safety glasses, and gloves. After construction, any sawdust from pressure-treated wood should be cleaned up and disposed of. Clothes covered with sawdust from pressure-treated wood should be washed separately from other household clothing.

Don't use pressure-treated wood where the preservative could become a component of food or animal feed, or where it could come into direct or indirect contact with drinking water (except for incidental contact such as when used on docks or bridges). Don't use pressure-treated wood to make kitchen cutting boards or countertops. And, finally, don't burn pressure-treated wood because toxic chemicals could be produced as part of the smoke and ashes.

It is a good idea to treat pressure-treated lumber with a water-repellent finish as soon as the wood is installed. The high moisture content of pressure-treated wood can cause the wood to split as it dries, which can lead to early failure.

NATURALLY DECAY-RESISTANT WOODS

Some wood species have a natural resistance to decay and insects. Redwood, cedar, and cypress are excellent choices for outdoor projects. They might even outlast pressure-treated lumber, and look considerably better, too.

PLYWOOD

There are two different types of plywood. One is made primarily to be used for general construction, and the other is intended for purposes such as furniture construction. This discussion is limited to general-construction plywood.

Plywood used for general construction is manufactured in accordance with United States Product Standard PS 1-83, which was developed cooperatively between the United States Department of Commerce and the construction and general plywood industry. This plywood is widely used as subflooring, wall and roof sheathing, siding, and other applications.

APA—the Engineered Wood Association is a nonprofit trade association. Its member mills produce about 80 percent of the structural wood-panel products made in the United States. The APA works to ensure that its member mills manufacture products in accordance with APA performance standards and/or United States Product Standard PS 1-83 for Construction and General Plywood.

HOW PLYWOOD IS MADE

To make the type of plywood that's used for construction, a log is cut to length and mounted on a machine that operates like an oversized lathe. Spindles at each end of the log allow it to rotate as a long cutting blade slices a continuous thin sheet of wood from the spinning log. The thin sheets, called *veneers* or *plies,* are dried and cut to size and then are glued at right angles to each other. The outer veneers make up the front and back faces (Illus. 1-2).

Special cutters are used to remove any small defects in the veneer, such as splits and knotholes. The cut area is repaired with a wood or synthetic plug, sometimes called a patch. Plywood used for general construction is almost always made with an odd number of veneers, usually three, five, or seven. Using an odd number allows the grain of the front and back faces to run in the same direction. The cross-grain construction gives plywood its excellent strength. The construction also results in exceptional dimensional stability, so there is little expansion or contraction with changes in relative humidity.

Most plywood is made into 4 × 8-foot panels, although other sizes are also available.

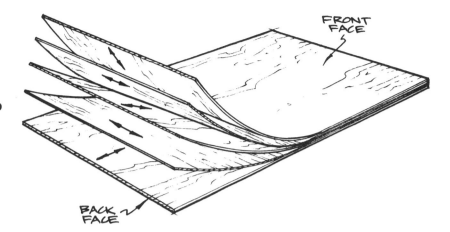

Illus. 1-2. Plywood is made up of thin sheets of wood.

GRADES OF PLYWOOD

When discussing plywood used for general construction, the term *grade* is used in a couple of different ways. For APA-sanded panels, it refers to the quality of the front and back face veneers. For example, the plywood could be stamped grade A-C. Such a designation indicates that the front face has an A-quality veneer while the back face has a C-quality veneer. A variety of grade combinations are possible, including A-A, A-B, A-C, B-B, B-C, C-D, etc. The various veneer grades, as defined by the APA, are shown in Illus. 1-3. (Although not shown in Illus. 1-3, some manufacturers also produce an N grade, which is the highest quality veneer and is available only on special order.)

For APA performance-rated panels, the grade can also refer to the suggested final use of the plywood. The APA performance-rated grades are APA-rated Sheathing, APA-rated Underlayment, APA-rated Sturd-I-Floor, and APA-rated Siding.

EXPOSURE DURABILITY

The exposure durability of plywood found on the grade stamp refers to the strength of the glue bond. There are four classifications as follows:

1. *Exterior.* Plywood in this classification has a fully waterproof bond. It is designed for permanent exposure to weather or moisture.
2. *Exposure 1.* Plywood in this classification also has a fully waterproof bond. However, this plywood is designed for applications where high moisture conditions might be encountered in service, or where long construction delays are expected before the plywood can be protected from the weather.
3. *Exposure 2.* This plywood is intended for protected applications when only moderate delays are expected before the plywood is protected from moisture.
4. *Interior.* This plywood is manufactured with interior glue and is intended for interior applications only.

Illus. 1-3. Plywood veneer grades. (Drawing courtesy of APA–the Engineered Wood Association.)

A	Smooth, paintable. Not more than 18 neatly made repairs, boat, sled, or router type, and parallel to grain, permitted. Wood or synthetic repairs permitted. May be used for natural finish in less demanding applications.
B	Solid surface. Shims, sled or router repairs, and tight knots to 1 inch across grain permitted. Wood or synthetic repairs permitted. Some minor splits permitted.
C Plugged	Improved C veneer with splits limited to 1/8-inch width and knotholes or other open defects limited to 1/4 x 1/2 inch. Wood or synthetic repairs permitted. Admits some broken grain.
C	Tight knots to 1-1/2 inch. Knotholes to 1 inch across grain and some to 1-1/2 inch if total width of knots and knotholes is within specified limits. Synthetic or wood repairs. Discoloration and sanding defects that do not impair strength permitted. Limited splits allowed. Stitching permitted.
D	Knots and knotholes to 2-1/2-inch width across grain and 1/2 inch larger within specified limits. Limited splits are permitted. Stitching permitted. Limited to Exposure 1 or Interior panels.

SPAN RATING

Span ratings are stamped on APA-rated Sheathing, APA-rated Sturd-I-Floor, and APA-rated Siding. On APA-rated Sheathing, the span ratings are shown as two numbers separated by a slash, for example $^{32}/_{16}$ or $^{48}/_{24}$. The left-hand number indicates the maximum support spacing (in inches) when the plywood is used for roof sheathing; the right-hand number indicates the maximum support spacing (in inches) when the plywood is used for subflooring. On APA-rated Sturd-I-Floor and Siding, the span rating is shown as a single number.

FASTENERS

When building your outdoor storage project, it's important to use the correct fastener for the job at hand. Do-it-yourselfers are fortunate to have a wide range of fasteners from which to choose, a fact that can be quickly confirmed by visiting any hardware store or building supply center. We'll discuss a few of the common fasteners here.

NAILS

The nail is by far the most commonly used fastener in construction today. While nails come in many types, shapes, and sizes, only a few are used to build the kinds of small outdoor storage structures found in this book.

The term *penny,* indicated by the lowercase letter d, is used to specify the length of common, finishing, casing, and several other types of nails. The lower the number, the shorter the nail. A 2d nail, the smallest size, is 1 inch long.

The *common nail* (Illus. 1-4) is used for general framing, while finishing and casing nails (Illus. 1-5) are used mostly for light-duty work such as trim. Size for size, the casing nail has a slightly larger diameter than the finishing nail. Also, the casing nail has a conical-shaped head. Other specialty nails you might use include siding, flooring, and roofing nails.

Nails exposed to the weather or moisture should be resistant to rust. Galvanized steel, copper, and aluminum nails all offer good rust resistance. If you are uncertain about the best nail

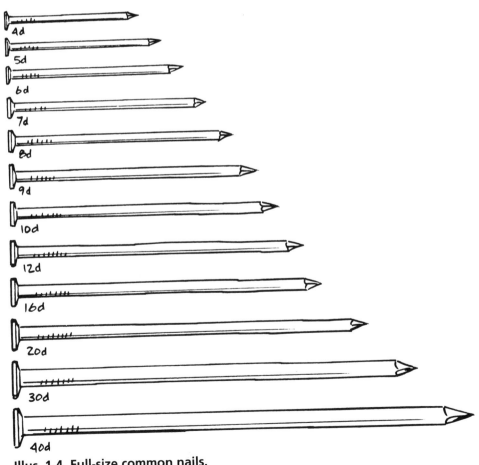

Illus. 1-4. Full-size common nails.

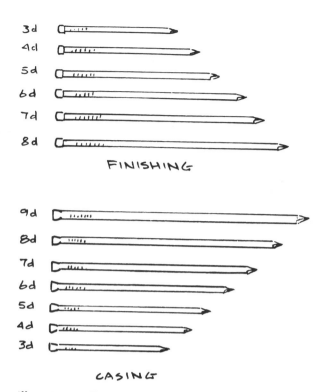

Illus. 1-5. Full-size casing and finishing nails.

for a specific application, don't be afraid to ask for help at your local lumberyard. Most lumberyards have a staff of knowledgeable salespersons who are more than willing to help you out.

Despite modern technology, the nails we use today have changed very little over the years. While some new shapes and coatings help nails do their job better, the nails used to build the projects in this book are basically the same type of nails that have been made for over 100 years.

Nail Guns

The revolutionary changes at the job site affect not the actual fasteners, but rather how they are driven. Pneumatic, impulse, and powder-actuated nail guns not only make work go quicker, they allow tasks not possible before.

The most popular nail delivery system is the *pneumatic nail gun*. These guns drive anything from a ⅝-inch-long brad to a good-sized common nail. And they drive nails as fast as you can pull the trigger.

Pneumatic guns require an air supply such as an air tank or an electricity- or gasoline-driven compressor. The air drives a piston which, in turn, drives the nail. An electric compressor can run a pneumatic gun indefinitely, but the compressor must always be within an extension-cord length of the power source. A gasoline-driven compressor can operate a gun all day long at a remote site without the need for any electricity. Pneumatic guns have one drawback: you need to cart along the air hose.

Impulse guns use a cartridge to drive the fasteners, so there is no need for an external power source. The cartridge also eliminates the need for the cumbersome hose line that binds the pneumatic gun to the compressor. The types of fasteners available for impulse guns are similar to the fasteners available for pneumatic guns.

Impulse guns are very helpful, especially when you are working at a remote site. However, these guns are usually much heavier than their air-driven counterparts. Also, the cartridges don't have a very long life.

Powder-activated guns use an explosive charge to drive the fastener. These guns are not fast or nearly as safe as the others. Their one saving grace is that they have the capacity to drive fasteners into difficult material like concrete. Powder-activated guns are of limited use when you are building small outdoor structures.

Many rental places rent nail guns and compressors, and they also sell the fasteners. Fasteners for these guns come in a variety of coatings suitable for exposure to weather. Once you use one of these neat tools, it's hard to go back to swinging a hammer. Indeed, a nail gun can make quick work of a framing or roofing job.

To run a pneumatic nail gun, you need an air source, an air hose that's sufficiently long to get the compressed air to the site, a nail gun, and the appropriate nails. If you are building a backyard shed, it won't do any good to have the compressor in the basement if the air line is too short to reach the site. If you use an extension cord to get the compressor closer to the shed, make sure the cord is grounded and the proper size. Also, the extension cord must be suitable for outdoor use.

The air source can be quite small. A simple tank can be used for a limited period of time. A small pancake-type compressor can run multiple guns (Illus. 1-6).

A nail gun makes a great addition to your tool collection. If you are buying one, make sure that it can handle the size and type of fasteners you use most often. Also, make sure it has a safety shoe. The safety shoe sits under the tip of the gun (Illus. 1-7). The trigger is locked out until the shoe has been pressed tight up to the tip.

Illus. 1-6. A small pancake-type compressor can be used to operate a pneumatic nail gun.

Illus. 1-7. The safety shoe is an important feature on a nail gun. The trigger won't function until the shoe is seated.

The trigger can't function until the shoe is seated. The safety shoe prevents the user from accidentally firing a fastener before the gun is properly positioned.

Pneumatic nail guns can do things that are not possible with a hammer. Many new guns drive the fastener below the surface, making it unnecessary to set the fastener with a nail set. And, since nail guns drive the nails so fast, the pieces being fastened don't have a chance to shift out of position. This feature can be a great plus, especially when you are making jigs.

If you are considering buying a nail gun, try to first rent or borrow one. Using one for a while might help you determine the type that's best for your needs.

Some Tips on Hammering Technique

Many carpenters still use hammers to drive nails. While hammering is usually a simple task, there are some techniques that can make the work go faster and with less stress on the worker.

Driving a nail sends a shock along the arm, so take some precautions if you are not in the habit of using a hammer. Also, use some common sense. If it is cold outside, wear a warm, comfortable sweater or jacket. Exposing your arm to both the shock of driving nails and the cold can do lasting damage to your arm. Warm up properly, and keep your arm from getting cold. Don't use too large a hammer for the first time. Start off with a light hammer until your arm gets used to the abuse.

Always wear eye protection when hammering. The hammer, and what it hits, can shatter and send small objects flying at your face. And, of course, be careful with your fingers. We all know how easy it is to hit a finger instead of the nail.

When using the hammer, don't hold it close to its head. The farther down the handle it is

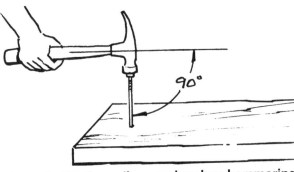

Illus. 1-8. Hit the nail squarely when hammering it.

held, the more force it delivers to the nail. This grip might feel awkward at first, but your arm is going to benefit in the long run.

Try to hit the nail squarely when hammering (Illus. 1-8). If you bend the nail, it means you are hitting the nail at an angle.

In some instances, it is necessary to toenail two pieces together (Illus. 1-9). Since the nail must be driven at an angle to the surface of the lumber, it can be difficult to start nailing. The nail often slips out of position. To start nailing, hold the nail square to the wood and tap it in slightly. Then push the nail to the desired angle and finish driving it in.

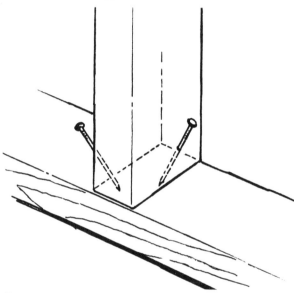

Illus. 1-9. Toenailing technique. This consists of driving the nails in at an angle.

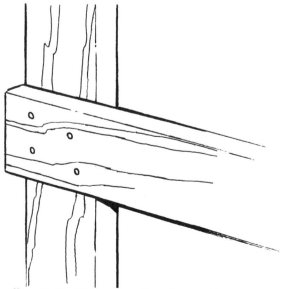

Illus. 1-10. Stagger nails when adding several to a joint, so they will not split the wood.

Increasing Holding Power of Nails

One way to increase the holding power of nails is to use more of them. However, there is a limit to the number of nails that can be used to fasten two parts. When adding several nails to a joint, stagger the nails so they are less likely to split the wood (Illus. 1-10).

You can also increase the holding power of nails by slightly angling them while driving them into the wood. When using this technique, drive two nails at opposing angles (Illus. 1-11).

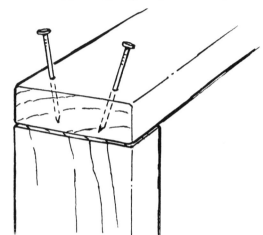

Illus. 1-11. Driving two nails into wood at opposing angles will increase their holding power.

Coated nails and nails with specially designed shanks also have greater holding power. Among the latter types of nail are ringed (Illus. 1-12), spiral (Illus. 1-13), and barbed nails (Illus. 1-14).

A nail can be "clinched" to increase its resistance to withdrawal. To clinch a nail, drive it through the parts to be fastened, allowing the nail point to extend out the other side. Then, flatten the protruding point back across the grain (Illus. 1-15).

SCREWS

Screws have greater holding power than nails. You'll often find screws used in applications where nails aren't strong enough. Also, screws are used to mount many types of hardware. Screws also offer an advantage in that they can be removed and reinstalled. However, they usually take more time to install than nails, and are more expensive.

You can choose from three common head types: flat, round, or oval. *Flathead* wood screws can be driven flush with the surface when coun-

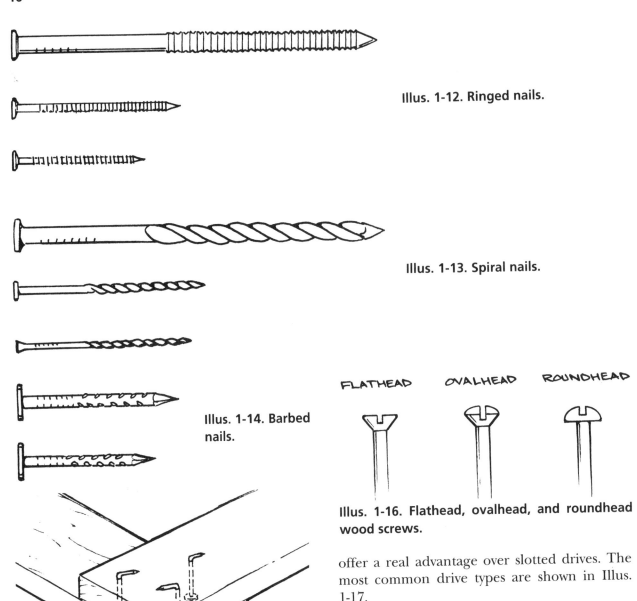

Illus. 1-12. Ringed nails.

Illus. 1-13. Spiral nails.

Illus. 1-14. Barbed nails.

FLATHEAD   OVALHEAD   ROUNDHEAD

Illus. 1-16. Flathead, ovalhead, and roundhead wood screws.

Illus. 1-15. Clinching a nail. First, drive it through the parts that are being fastened, and then flatten its protruded point back across the grain.

offer a real advantage over slotted drives. The most common drive types are shown in Illus. 1-17.

SLOTTED   PHILLIPS   SQUARE

Illus. 1-17. Shown here are screw heads with the most common drive types: slotted, Phillips, and square.

tersunk. *Roundhead* wood screws are handy when you want the extra holding power created by the flat area under the head. *Ovalhead* wood screws are generally used for decorative applications (Illus. 1-16).

Unlike nails, screws have changed over the years. At one time, only screws with slotted-drive heads were commonly available. Today many drive types can be found, including Phillips-head, Pozi-drive, square-head and Torx-head, to name a few. Almost all the new drive designs

All the new drive-type screws have less of a tendency to slip when you drive them. Some, like the screws with square-tip drives, can be easily held before you drive, even when you hold the screw upside down. Despite the many advances, the slotted-drive screw remains the most common type, followed by the Phillips-head screw.

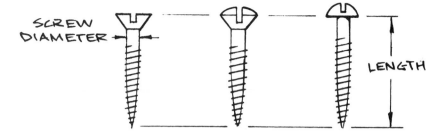

Illus. 1-18. The diameter of a screw is measured across its shank. The length of a screw is measured from its tip to the widest portion of its head.

Wood screws are manufactured in lengths from ¼ inch to 6 inches. The diameter is specified as a screw number, the numbers ranging from 0 to 24. About two-thirds of the wood screw length is threaded.

The screw diameter is measured across the *shank,* which is the unthreaded portion of a wood screw. The length of a screw is measured from its tip to the widest portion of its head (Illus. 1-18). Commonly used screw lengths (¼ through 4 inches) and the corresponding screw-number sizes are shown in Table 1-2.

In order to minimize the chances of splitting the wood and to provide proper holding power, it's important to drill a pilot hole and a shank hole before driving a wood screw. If the screw must be countersunk flush with the surface of the wood, you'll also need to use a countersink bit. The holes can be bored using individual bits, or you can use a combination bit that bores the pilot, shank, and countersink holes in one operation. Table 1-3 lists suggested wood-screw shank and pilot holes for both hardwood and softwood.

While there are very specific types of screws designed for joining wood, the common Sheetrock screw has found favor with many carpenters and woodworkers. The Sheetrock screw's hardened body make it useful, although it tends to be brittle. The hardening process also makes Sheetrock screws resistant to rust.

Sheetrock screws can usually be driven without drilling shank, pilot, or countersink holes, and that can be a real timesaver.

By far the greatest advance in the use of screws is in the power tools that drive them. An electric drill equipped with the appropriate driving bit can drive all the new types of screws. However, screws with slotted heads do not drive well with power drivers. The tip of the driver slips off the screw too easily.

The most popular drill/drivers are the cordless and the electric drill/drivers. These power tools come with a clutch that allows you to adjust the force that drives the screws. The cordless types are easier to use than regular electric drill/drivers. That's because you don't have to drag the electric cord around, which always seems to get tangled up.

A 12-volt driver can supply enough force to sink a drywall screw head below the surface of most construction material without the need to

SCREW SIZES MOST OFTEN USED

Length (inches)	Length (centimeters)	Commonly Available Screw Numbers
¼	.64	0, 1, 2, 3
⅜	.95	2, 3, 4, 5, 6, 7
½	1.3	2, 3, 4, 5, 6, 7, 8
⅝	1.6	3, 4, 5, 6, 7, 8, 9, 10
¾	1.9	4, 5, 6, 7, 8, 9, 10
⅞	2.2	6, 7, 8, 9, 10, 12
1	2.5	6, 7, 8, 9, 10, 12, 14
1¼	3.2	6, 7, 8, 9, 10, 12, 14, 16
1½	3.8	6, 7, 8, 9, 10, 12, 14, 16, 18
1¾	4.4	7, 8, 9, 10, 12, 14, 16, 18
2	5.1	8, 9, 10, 12, 14, 16, 18, 20
2¼	5.7	10, 12, 14, 16, 18, 20
2½	6.4	12, 14, 16, 18, 20
2¾	7.0	14, 16, 18, 20
3	7.6	16, 18, 20
3½	8.9	16, 18, 20
4	10.2	18, 20

Table 1-2. Shown here are the commonly used lengths of screws and the corresponding screw-number sizes.

WOOD SCREW SHANK AND PILOT HOLE DRILL SIZES
(For Softwood and Hardwood)

Screw Number	Shank Diameter (inches)	Shank Hole Drill Size (inches)	Softwood Pilot Hole Drill Size (inches)	Hardwood Pilot Hole Drill Size (inches)
0	.060	1/16	—	1/32
1	.073	5/64	1/32	1/32
2	.086	3/32	1/32	3/64
3	.099	7/64	3/64	1/16
4	.112	7/64	3/64	1/16
5	.125	1/8	1/16	5/64
6	.138	9/64	1/16	5/64
7	.151	5/32	1/16	3/32
8	.164	11/64	5/64	3/32
9	.177	3/16	5/64	7/64
10	.190	3/16	3/32	7/64
12	.216	7/32	7/64	1/8
14	.242	1/4	7/64	9/64
16	.268	7/64	9/64	5/32
18	.294	19/64	9/64	3/16
20	.320	21/64	11/64	13/64

Table 1-3. Shank and pilot-hole drill sizes for wood screws when used in softwood and hardwood.

predrill or countersink. Predrilling is advisable when working with most hardwoods.

Screw Materials

Screws are made from many metals (Illus. 1-19). The most common screw material seems to be white metal. This material is soft and easily distorted. Hardened Sheetrock screws are usually available. These screws are made to drive into steel studs. The coarse-thread type of Sheetrock screw is very satisfactory for joining wood parts.

Brass screws are also common. Brass won't rust and can be used for decorative work. The ultimate material for rust resistance is stainless steel. Stainless steel screws are more expensive than other screws, but it's an option you might want to consider when mounting outdoor hardware or for any other application where small quantities of screws are needed.

BOLTS

Bolts have many times the holding power of screws and nails (Illus. 1-20). The most commonly used bolts for outdoor storage work are the *hex-head bolt* and the *carriage bolt*. As the name suggests, hex-head bolts have a hexagonal head. The shaft of the bolt is threaded. Used with a nut and washers, bolts can be tightened with wrenches. Bolts are available in steel, galvanized steel, and stainless steel.

To use a hex-head bolt, first position the

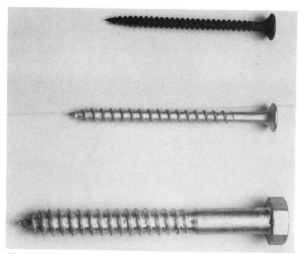

Illus. 1-19. Sheetrock screw (top) and lag screws.

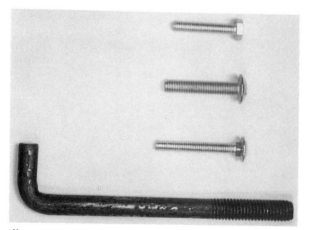

Illus. 1-20. Hex-head bolts (top) and J-Bolt.

A carriage bolt has an advantage in that only one wrench is needed to tighten the bolt. Also, the round, low-profile head is less obtrusive than a hexagonal head—something that might be important for certain applications.

If the wood under the head of a carriage bolt gets chewed up and can no longer hold the bolt, there is no practical way to continue using a carriage bolt. In all likelihood, it will need to be replaced with a hex-head bolt.

FINISHES

Moisture and sunlight take their toll on unprotected outdoor lumber. The wood surface expands as it absorbs moisture from a rainstorm or morning dew and then the surface contracts as it dries. This constant process of swelling and shrinking eventually causes the wood to develop cracks and splits. In addition, moisture helps create an environment that is friendly to decay-causing fungi. Sunlight is also a problem, as it causes wood to darken.

A good outdoor finish can help keep moisture and sunlight problems to a minimum. These finishes usually fall into one of three general categories: paint, stain, and varnish. Each is described below.

PAINT

For certain outdoor projects, the deep, rich color of a solid paint is hard to beat. A high-quality exterior latex paint is your best choice. First, though, apply a coat or two of primer to the bare wood. Ask your paint dealer to recommend a primer that's going to be compatible with the latex you use.

Unfortunately, even top-quality paints eventually peel and flake. When that happens, you'll need to scrape and sand the old paint before new paint can be applied. Few homeowners welcome that job. For this reason we usually try to avoid painting outdoor projects.

STAIN

A good-quality transparent wood stain can add color to your project, yet still allow the grain of the wood to show. We like the oil-based stains that are used to finish outdoor decks. These deck stains are easy to apply and are available in

wood parts that are to be bolted together. Drill a hole just large enough to accept the threads. For a ⅜-inch-diameter bolt, a ⅜-inch-diameter hole usually works fine. Slip a washer on the bolt and pass the shaft through the hole. Add another washer on the other side, and then thread a nut onto the shaft. Tighten the bolt with wrenches.

Carriage bolts are made especially to be used with wood. These bolts have round, smooth heads that cannot be grabbed by a wrench. There is a square flange under the head. The shaft is much like that on a hex-head bolt.

To use a carriage bolt, drill a hole just large enough to accept the thread, and then install the carriage bolt through the hole without a washer. Now, tap the head until the square flange begins to seat in the surface of the wood. Add a washer and nut, and then tighten the nut firmly. The tightening action drives the flange into the wood until the round head is fully seated.

a wide assortment of colors. The stain penetrates the wood and won't peel or flake. You'll have to reapply a coat or two every few years, but the job is considerably less of a chore than scraping and sanding paint.

VARNISH

Marine (exterior) spar varnish is often used when a clear finish is desired. Keep in mind, however, that it's not going to be a quick job. Spar varnish dries slowly and most manufacturers recommend at least three coats on bare wood. Always follow the manufacturer's instructions carefully.

Chapter 2.
Planning Your Project

By doing some early planning, you can go a long way toward ensuring the success of your outdoor project. You must make sure that the project meets all applicable building codes and zoning laws, and that you have the necessary permits. Also, you should try to choose a project design that is going to complement your home and its surroundings. Then, too, you need to locate the project where it is going to best serve your needs. This chapter offers some suggestions to help get you started.

BUILDING CODES, ZONING LAWS, AND PERMITS

In order to make sure your project is going to meet all applicable building codes and zoning laws, it's important to check with your local building and zoning departments early in the planning stage. Building codes serve to ensure that structures meet all safety and construction standards. Zoning laws generally specify the minimum distance that a structure is allowed to be located from property lines (also called the setback requirement), buildings, utility lines, septic systems, etc. In addition, zoning laws can dictate the maximum height of a structure and the allowable lot coverage (the percentage of your property that the structure covers).

In many communities, you are going to need a building permit (issued by the building department) before any construction can begin. If you intend to include plumbing or electricity, additional permits are likely to be required. In some communities, a building permit isn't required for small (under 100 square feet) outdoor structures that are not built on a permanent foundation.

Keep in mind that other regulations might also have to be considered. If your house is in a subdivision that has deed restrictions, make sure

your new structure is going to conform to the deed requirements. And, if your house is in a designated historic district, special requirements might apply to your new project.

DESIGN CONSIDERATIONS

Consider the appearance of your outdoor project, and how it's going to influence the look of your house and property. You don't want to unintentionally create an eyesore in the backyard, so make every effort to choose a project design that's not going to take away from the visual appeal of your property.

An attractive project usually starts with an attractive design. Beyond that, it often helps to incorporate a design element of your house into the project. If your project is a shed, you might use a siding that matches the siding on your house. Or perhaps the shed can be painted a color that matches or complements the house color. If your project is unattractive, try to hide it behind shrubs or locate it out of sight as much as possible.

It's best to avoid project designs that conflict with the style of your house. For example, a rustic country-style shed probably won't work well if the house is in the English Tudor style.

By the way, to keep on good terms with your neighbors, it's a good idea to tell them about your project plans before starting construction.

CHOOSING THE SITE

It is important to give some thought as to where you are going to locate the project on your property. Indeed, the project's usefulness and longevity might well depend upon where it's put. There are several factors that will help you determine where to locate the project. They are discussed below.

MAXIMIZING THE PROJECT'S USEFULNESS

Consider how you plan to use the project and try to locate it where its intended use can be maximized. A garden shed belongs near the garden. For the sake of convenience, a woodshed probably should be close to the house, but hidden from view as much as possible. A handsome gazebo is going to be the focal point of your property, so its location should allow for plenty of visibility. A kid's playhouse should be within easy view of Mom and Dad's watchful eyes.

ACCESS TO THE PROJECT

If your project gets regular use, you'll want to locate it in an area that's easily accessible. A long trek to the woodshed won't be welcomed on an icy, cold winter morning. If you expect to regularly load and unload heavy items from a utility shed, locate the shed for easy access to a pickup truck or other vehicle. For some projects, it might be worth adding a path or walkway to help improve access.

Also, consider how your project location is going to affect current use of your property. If your kids have a backyard baseball field, you won't want to put the gazebo on second base.

WATER, SLOPE, AND SOIL

Wood exposed to moisture for extended periods of time can rot surprisingly quickly, so avoid locating your project in areas that drain poorly. If possible, grade the site to direct water away from the project. A steep slope can complicate the foundation work, so always try to locate the project on a level area. Also, look for firm soil around the site, because loose soil can lead to uneven settling.

SUNLIGHT

The type of project you are building may determine how much of it should be exposed to direct sunlight, and, consequently, where to locate it. Firewood in a woodshed can benefit from the drying effects of direct sunlight, but a playhouse might best be located under a shady tree to protect kids from the hot summer sun. The south side of your structure is exposed to the most sunlight, something to keep in mind if your project

has windows. Also, be mindful of the shadows that your project casts—you don't want your project to shade the flower garden.

THE SITE PLAN

Before making a final decision on the location of your outdoor project, it often helps to create a site plan on paper. A site plan provides a bird's-eye view of your property, and it can go a long way towards helping you find the best spot to put the project. In some communities, depending upon the project, you might need to submit a site plan to the building department before you can get a building permit.

A good site plan offers a number of advantages. It allows you to study the project location in relation to your house, other structures, property and utility lines, fences, walkways, shrubbery, etc. It also helps you to consider such factors as accessibility, line of sight, sunlight, and shade. Once the site plan is drawn, it's an easy matter to move the project around, on paper, until you find the location that best serves your needs.

In order to draw the plan, you are going to need an $8\frac{1}{2} \times 11$-inch sheet of graph paper (with $\frac{1}{4}$-inch squares), several sheets of tracing paper, a pencil, and a ruler. Graph and tracing paper are available at almost any store that sells school supplies. A scale of $\frac{1}{4}$ inch equaling 5 feet works well for most projects, but any convenient scale can be used.

Following are the steps for drawing a site plan:

Step 1: Mark the Property Line and Structures Outline the perimeter of your property on the graph paper, and then indicate the setback requirement with a dotted line. Draw in the location of your house and any other structures. Show the location of all doors and windows that are going to face your project (Illus. 2-1).

Step 2: Mark the Utilities Mark the location of utilities that could be affected by your plan, including water, gas, or electric lines. If you live in the country, mark the location of your well, water line, septic tank, and fields (Illus. 2-2).

Step 3: Mark the Trees, Shrubs, and Gardens Add to your plan the location of any trees, shrubs, and gardens that could be affected by your project. Also, to help determine the effects of sunlight and shade, mark the four com-

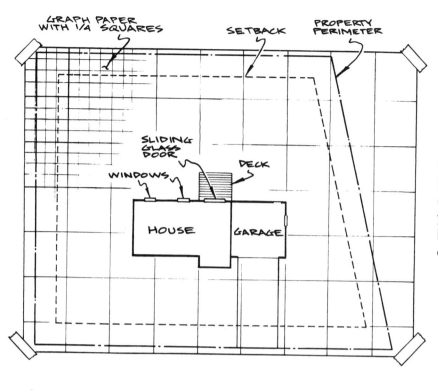

Illus. 2-1. The first step in drawing a site plan is to mark the outline of the perimeter of your property and draw in the location of your house and any other structures.

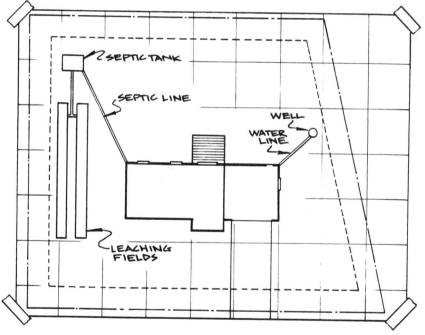

Illus. 2-2. The next step is to mark the location of the utilities.

pass points (north, south, east, and west) on the plan (Illus. 2-3).

Step 4: Experiment with Locations Using masking tape temporarily attach a sheet of tracing paper to the graph paper plan. Sketch your proposed project location on the tracing paper and then consider the project's effects on your house and property (Illus. 2-4). Is the line of sight acceptable when viewed through various windows in your house? Does its location inter-

fere with the well, septic system, or any other utilities? Are you going to need to remove any trees or shrubs? Is it necessary to add shrubs to hide the project from view? What are the effects of sun and shade on the location? Is the project easily accessible? A good site plan can go a long way towards answering these and other questions you are likely to have.

Tracing paper works well here because it allows you to try all kind of ideas. Don't be afraid to experiment. To sketch a new idea, simply remove the tracing paper from the graph paper plan, add another sheet, and go to work.

The finalized version of your tracing paper, along with your graph paper plan, serves as a master plan for your project location, so keep it in a safe place. Also, as mentioned earlier, you might need to submit the site plan to your building department in order to get your building permit.

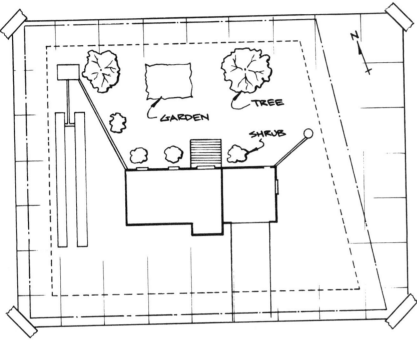

Illus. 2-3. The next steps are to add the location of any trees, shrubs, and gardens that will be affected by the project and to mark the four compass points.

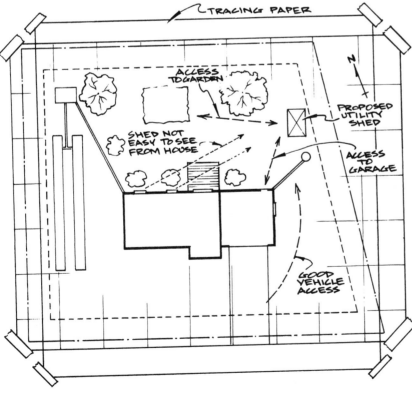

Illus. 2-4. Next, sketch the project location on tracing paper on the graph paper plan, and determine how it will affect your house and property.

Chapter 3. Foundations

This chapter covers the basic information for constructing a foundation for an outdoor structure. A foundation serves several important functions. It supports the weight of the outdoor structure, keeps it level and square, helps it settle evenly, and protects it from moisture and other problems.

Various types of foundations can be constructed, but the one that's best for your project is going to depend upon the size of the structure, its intended use, the soil conditions, and the climate. Also, cost is likely to be a factor, since some types of foundations are more expensive than others. A few commonly used foundation types are shown in Illus. 3-1. They include skid, concrete-post, perimeter, slab, and pole foundations.

Check your building codes before starting. Local codes often dictate the types of foundations that are acceptable. In many regions, codes

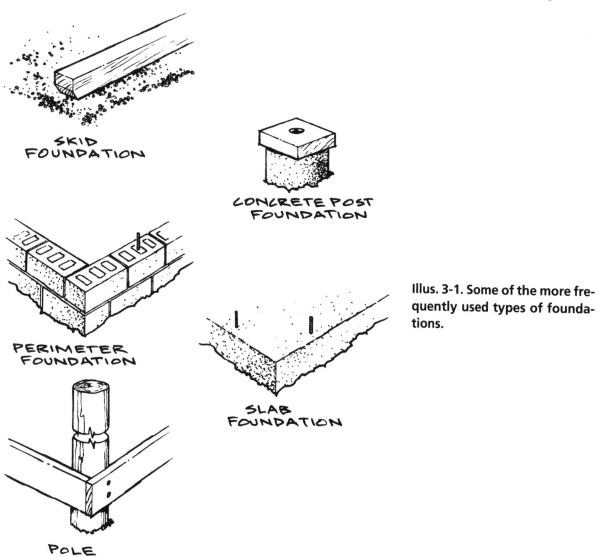

SKID
FOUNDATION

CONCRETE POST
FOUNDATION

PERIMETER
FOUNDATION

SLAB
FOUNDATION

POLE
FOUNDATION

Illus. 3-1. Some of the more frequently used types of foundations.

specify that the foundation footing must be below the frost line. In areas that suffer bitterly cold winters, the frost line can be more than four feet. Also, before starting to dig the foundation, call your local utilities to find out the location of water, gas, or electrical lines.

The step-by-step instructions that follow explain how to make a wooden skid foundation and a concrete post foundation. Both of these foundations are often used in conjunction with small structures.

Perimeter and slab foundations are somewhat more complicated. Indeed, a discussion of their construction is beyond the scope of this book. Slab foundations might not be acceptable in regions subject to heavy frost heaves. If you don't have a lot of experience with perimeter or slab foundations, consider having the work done by a professional foundation contractor.

Pole foundations are used in conjunction with pole-frame construction. The poles are embedded in the ground and extend up to the structure's roof. Horizontal members between the posts support the siding, so it isn't necessary to frame the walls and tie them together. If you are trying to keep costs to a minimum, pole-frame construction might be the best way to go. For more information, refer to the instructions for making the pole barn project.

BUILDING A WOODEN SKID FOUNDATION

Skid foundations are acceptable for many small outdoor structure designs. The skids should be made from pressure-treated lumber suitable for ground contact (see Chapter 1). (The skids are the wooden planks that elevate the foundation above the ground.) Also, the soil must be firm and well drained. Before laying the skids, remove the soil to a depth of 4 inches. Then fill the area with compacted gravel and level it off. Following are the steps for building a wooden skid foundation:

Step 1: Cut the Skids to Length Check your shed plans to determine the length of the skids. The skids should be cut from stock that is straight and true. Measure and mark each one, and then use a circular saw to cut them to length. It's important for the skids to be exactly the same length, so measure, mark, and cut them with care.

Step 2: Position the First Skid Place the first skid in approximate position on the gravel base, making sure that it is aligned according to your site plan as discussed in Chapter 2. Add or remove gravel as needed so that the skid is level along its length (Illus. 3-2).

Step 3: Position the Second Skid Place the second skid in approximate position, and then adjust it to establish the width of the shed. Once the two skids are properly spaced, select a pair of straight and true 2 × 4's and temporarily tack them near the ends of each skid (Illus. 3-3). The 2 × 4's serve to maintain the correct width of the shed during the leveling and squaring steps that follow.

Step 4: Level the Skids Add or remove gravel as needed to level the second skid relative to the first one. To do this, use a level to first check that the second skid is level along its length as you did in Step 2. Then, check along the 2 × 4's to ensure that the skids are level in relation to each other. Finally, make sure both skids are level across their widths (Illus. 3-4).

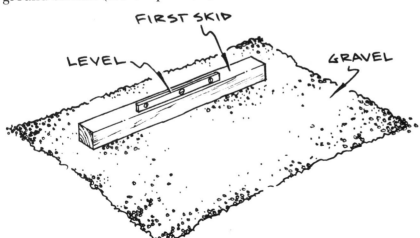

Illus. 3-2. After cutting the skids to length, place the first skid in the gravel base.

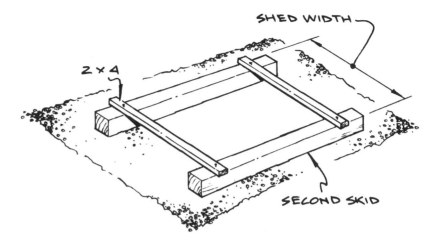

Illus. 3-3. Next, place the second skid in position, adjust it, and temporarily tack a pair of 2 × 4's near the ends of each skid.

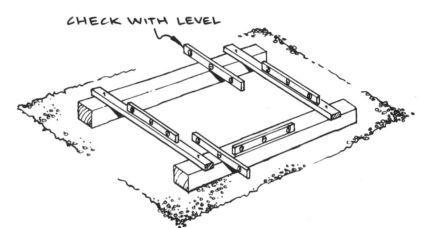

Illus. 3-4. Align the second skid with the first one.

Step 5: Check the Skids for Squareness
Once both skids are level, measure across their diagonals, from corner to corner. If the measurements are the same, the skids are square to each other. If not, push or pull on one of the skids as needed to get equal diagonal measurements (Illus. 3-5). When the skids are square, the two 2 × 4's can be removed. The skid foundation is now ready to receive the floor framing (see Chapter 4).

BUILDING A CONCRETE POST FOUNDATION

Cardboard tube forms, sold at most lumberyards and building supply centers, help simplify the construction of concrete post foundations. The forms are available in a variety of diameters and lengths. They are sold under such brand names as Sonotube and Handi-Man forms. The step-by-step instructions that follow are based on using

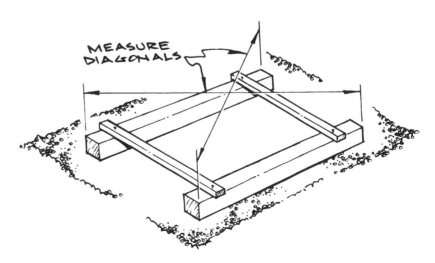

Illus. 3-5. Make sure the skids are square to one another. This is done by measuring across their diagonals.

an 8-inch-diameter form, but the same procedure applies to forms of any diameter. Some building codes require a footing under the post.

Our concrete post design incorporates a wooden cap (see Illus. 3-1). An *anchor bolt,* also called a *J-bolt,* attaches the cap to the top of the concrete post. The floor frame is then nailed to each of the post caps as described in Chapter 4.

Try to have a couple of helpers on hand for this job. You sometimes need to be in two places at the same time, so the extra hands are going to make the process a lot easier. Following are the steps for building a concrete post foundation:

Step 1: Drive Stakes for the First Two Corners

Drive a stake in the ground to mark one corner of the structure, and then drive a nail into the center of the stake. Hook your tape measure on the nail and measure the exact length of the shed. Be sure to align the shed according to the site plan as discussed in Chapter 2. Drive a second stake at this point, again adding a nail at its center. Tie a line (mason's line works well here) to one of the nails, pull the line tightly, and secure it to the nail on the other stake (Illus. 3-6). Double-check to make sure the distance between the nails equals the length of the shed.

Step 2: Drive a Stake for the Third Corner

Some right-angle geometry, based on the Pythagorean theorem, is used to ensure that the lines are going to be square to each other. Measure along the mason's line and mark a point exactly 8 feet from the centerpoint of the second stake. A piece of masking tape makes it easier to mark the point. Label this point A.

Tie mason's line to the nail on the second stake and pull it tightly. Hook your measuring tape to the nail and measure the width of the shed along the line. Mark the shed width on the line using masking tape and label it point B. At the same time, use masking tape to mark a point

6 feet from the centerpoint of the stake. Label this point C.

Now, while pulling the line tightly, swing it either left or right until the distance between points A and C (the hypotenuse of the triangle) measures exactly 10 feet. When it does, the lines are square to each other. To establish the width of the shed, drive a third stake at point B. Add a nail to the center of the stake (Illus. 3-7).

Step 3: Drive a Stake for the Fourth Corner

Repeat the basic procedure used in Step 2 to locate the fourth stake. As a final layout check, it's a good idea to measure across the diagonals (corner-to-corner). If the diagonal measurements are the same, the lines are square to each other.

Step 4: Construct the Batter Boards

The *batter boards,* each one made up of two posts and a ledger, are now assembled at the corners of the shed (Illus. 3-8). (The batter boards are temporary wood frames used with a mason's line to lay out foundation corners.) To allow room for the post excavations, locate the batter boards about 18 inches from the stakes. Since a mason's line is going to be stretched tightly between the boards, use sturdy stock here. We generally use scrap 2 × 4's for all the batter board parts.

Cut the 16 posts to 36-inch lengths, and then sharpen one end of each piece. Use a band saw to sharpen the posts to a point. Next, cut the ledger stock to about 30 inches long. (The ledgers are the horizontal parts of the batter boards.) Nail a pair of posts to each ledger, spacing the posts about 20 inches apart. Drive the posts a foot or so into the ground (or until secure), roughly centering the ledger on the stake.

Step 5: Level the Batter Boards

All eight of the batter board ledgers should be level and at approximately the same height. Getting the ledgers to the same height can be done with a "leveling post" made from 2 × 4 stock. First,

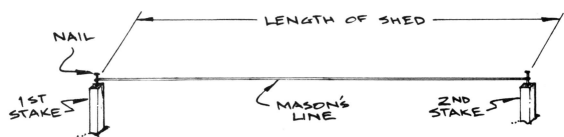

Illus. 3-6. The first step in building a concrete post foundation is driving stakes for the first two corners.

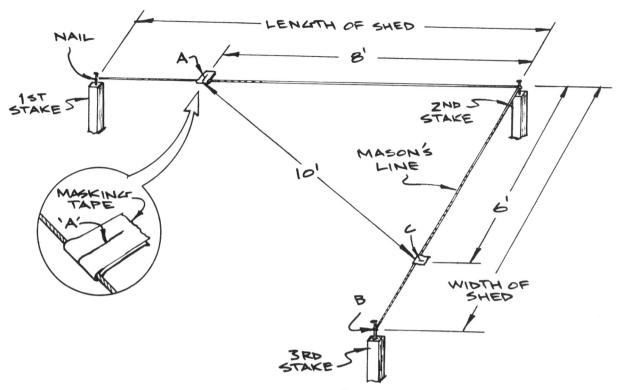

Illus. 3-7. Driving a stake for the third corner.

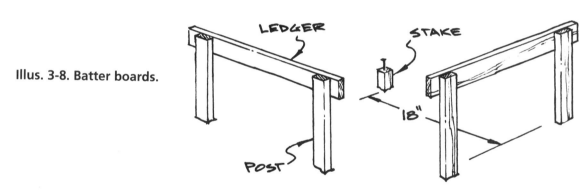

Illus. 3-8. Batter boards.

level each of the ledgers along their length, and then drive a leveling post midway between each of the four corner stakes. Now, select a flat board and place one end of the board on a leveling post, and the other end on a ledger (Illus. 3-9). Raise or lower the post until the board is perfectly level. Next, using the same leveling post, place the board on the opposite ledger. Raise or lower the ledger until it is level with the leveling post. When it is, the two opposing ledgers are at the same height. Continue this procedure for all remaining ledger boards.

Step 6: Establish the First Batter Board Lines Pull a length of mason's line across the top edges of the ledgers so that the line extends over stakes 1 and 2. Use a plumb bob to make sure the line is directly over the centerpoint of each stake. Once the line is properly positioned,

mark the point where it crosses the top edge of the ledger boards and then make a shallow (1/8–3/16-inch) saw kerf cut at the marked points. Now, pull the line tight, insert it into the saw kerf, and then secure the line to a nail driven into the back of the ledger (Illus. 3-10).

Step 7: Add the Remaining Lines Repeat the basic procedure used in Step 6 to establish the remaining three batter board lines. When the procedure is completed, the points where the lines cross represent the four corners of the shed (Illus. 3-11)

Step 8: Determine the Concrete Post Centerpoints As shown in Illus. 3-12, each concrete post is going to be capped with pressure-treated lumber that measures 1½ inches thick × 8 inches square. The outside corner of the cap is going to be located at the corner of

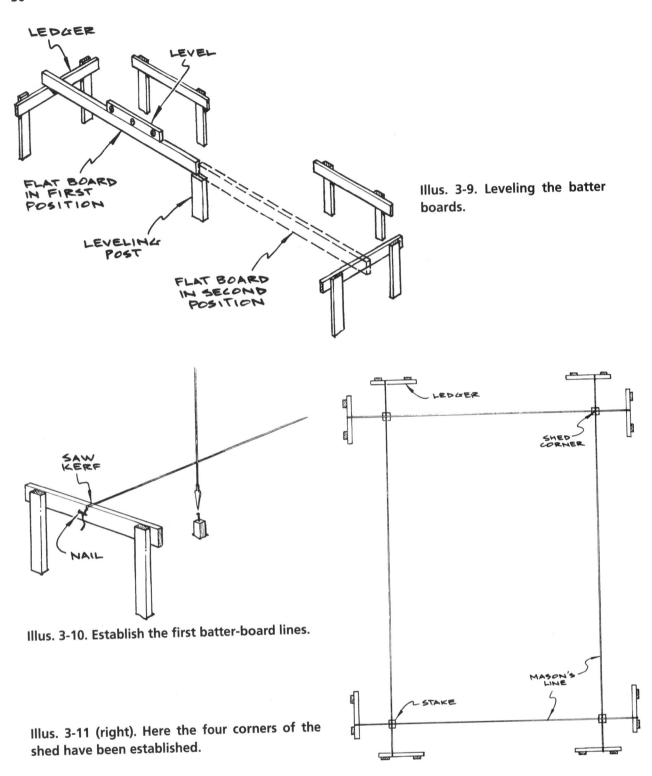

Illus. 3-9. Leveling the batter boards.

Illus. 3-10. Establish the first batter-board lines.

Illus. 3-11 (right). Here the four corners of the shed have been established.

the shed. An anchor bolt, washer, and nut will secure the cap to the post. The shed floor frame is then nailed to the wooden caps.

However, before the holes for the concrete posts can be dug, you need to locate and drive stakes for each of the post centerpoints. That means the batter board lines must be relocated.

For our 8-inch-diameter post with an 8-inch-square wooden cap, each batter board line must be moved 4 inches (half the diameter) towards the center of the shed. Measure and mark the 4-inch dimension on each ledger board, cut a shallow saw kerf at the mark, move the batter board lines, and resecure them with nails. The

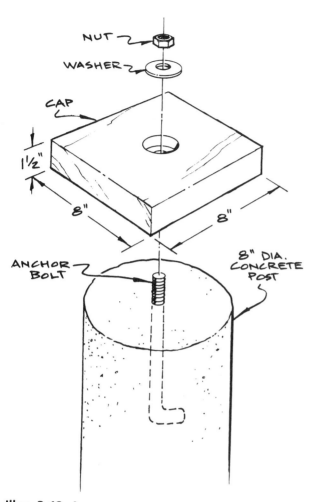

NUT

WASHER

CAP

1½"

8"

8"

ANCHOR BOLT

8" DIA. CONCRETE POST

Illus. 3-12. A concrete post.

points where the lines cross now represent the centerpoints of the four concrete posts at each corner of the shed.

Using a *plumb bob* at each point the lines cross, mark the post centerpoints at ground level. Hammer in a short stake to mark each spot. If your shed has any intermediate posts, you'll also want to mark them at this time.

Step 9: Dig the Post Holes The batter board lines must be removed before you can start digging. Keep the lines handy, though, because they are going to be used again soon.

Shallow holes can be easily dug with a shovel. But, if the holes must be three or four feet deep, a post hole digger makes the job considerably easier. If you have a lot of holes, a power auger might be the best way to go. You can rent a post hole digger or power auger at most tool rental stores. (A post hole digger is a specially designed double-handled shovel used to dig holes.)

Remove the stake that marks the post center-point and start digging. The hole should be a few inches bigger than the diameter of the cardboard form. As mentioned earlier, the hole depth is going to be based on the requirements of your local building code. To help provide drainage under the post, it's a good idea to add 2 to 3 inches of loose gravel to the bottom of the hole.

Step 10: Install the Cardboard Tube Forms Place the cardboard tubes in the hole, allowing them to stick out several inches above the ground. Add a couple of pieces of masking tape across the top of the tubes, and then measure and mark the centers of the tubes on the masking tape.

Replace the batter board lines, using the ledger saw kerfs that represent the post center-points. At the points where the lines cross each other, use a plumb bob to position the tubes so that they are centered, using the centerpoint on the masking tape as a guide (Illus. 3-13). Check

Illus. 3-13. Installing the cardboard tube form. Use a plumb bob to position the tube so that it is centered.

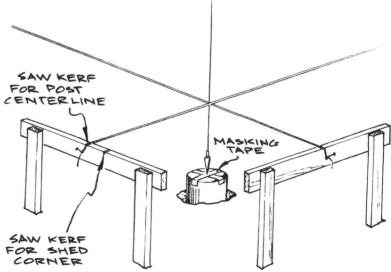

SAW KERF FOR POST CENTERLINE

MASKING TAPE

SAW KERF FOR SHED CORNER

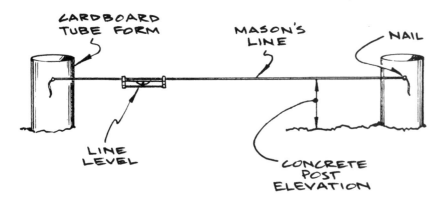

Illus. 3-14. Marking level points on the tubes.

that the tops of the tubes are level, and then carefully fill in the hole around the outside of the tubes with gravel. Remove the masking tape and the batter board lines.

Step 11: Mark Level Points on the Tubes
Determine how high above the ground you want the tops of the concrete posts (to minimize moisture problems, they should be at least 3 inches), and then mark that point on the outside of one of the cardboard tubes. Bore a small hole at the mark and insert a long nail. Tie a mason's line to the nail and extend the line the length of the shed to another cardboard tube. Add a line level to the mason's line, and then pull the line tight. Adjust the line until it is level, and then mark the point on the other tube (Illus. 3-14).

Repeat this procedure until the level point is marked on all the tubes. Make sure a nail is inserted into each tube at the mark. Once all the level marks have been made, use a handsaw to trim the tubes an inch or so above the nails.

Step 12: Add the Concrete Fill each tube with concrete to the level of the nail. As you add the concrete, tamp it with a long stick to eliminate air pockets. Remove the nail, and then use a small (about 6-inch-long) block of wood to smooth the top surface of the concrete.

Step 13: Install the Bolts Slowly lower an anchor bolt into the center of the wet concrete. To prevent air pockets, wiggle the bolt as it is lowered. Install each bolt so that it extends 1¼ to 1⅜ inches above the concrete. Also, check to make sure the bolt is square to the surface.

Once again, replace the batter board lines using the post centerpoint saw kerfs on the ledger boards. Use the plumb bob to position each bolt so that it is exactly centered on the post (Illus. 3-15). Allow the concrete to cure, and then remove the exposed portion of the cardboard tubes.

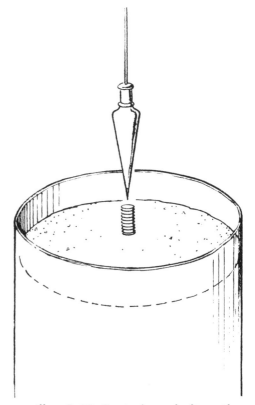

Illus. 3-15. Centering a bolt on the post.

Step 14: Add the Wooden Caps Using 2 × 10 pressure-treated lumber, cut the post caps to 8 inches square. (Be sure to use pressure-treated wood that's rated for ground contact.) You'll need one cap for each of the concrete posts. At the center of each cap, drill and counterbore for a washer and nut. Make the drill hole a bit oversized to allow for some adjustment. If you don't have a large enough bit to drill the counterbore, use a chisel to chop out a square mortise.

Once more, replace the batter board lines, but this time use the ledger board saw kerfs that represent the corners of the shed (as established in Steps 5 and 6). Add the post cap, washer, and nut to each post. Use the plumb bob to check that the outside corner of the cap is perfectly

Text Continues on Page 41

The utility shed provides plenty of storage capacity. It can also be put to use as a gardening shed or wood-working shop. See Chapter 8 for information on how to build the utility shed.

Wood shutters and a flower box add charm to the utility shed.

Leveling the skids on the utility shed.

Nailing the subfloor.

Raising the back wall.

Tying the side wall to the back wall.

Nailing the side wall to the back wall and floor.

The roof stringers are
partially complete.

Nailing the roof stringers.

Sturdy scaffolding makes the roofing job
safer and easier.

The cedar shingles are dipped into a wood waterproofer before installation.

Shingling the roof.

An inside view of the shed shows staggered blocking, fill-in bracing, tongue-and-groove siding, and the roof framing.

This inside view of the shed shows the window framing.

This inside view reveals the ridge board, rafters, spaced wood sheathing, and shingles.

Above left: Installing the board-and-batten doors on the utility shed. Above right: This view of the gabled end shows eaves covered with plywood.

Applying stain to the doors.

The shed ready for doors.

aligned with the corner lines of the batter board. The oversized drill hole should allow you to adjust the cap as needed. When all looks okay, tighten each nut securely (Illus. 3-16). Removing the batter boards completes work on the foundation. The posts are now ready for the floor frame.

Illus. 3-16 (right). After you have determined that the outside corner of the cap is aligned perfectly with the corner lines of the batter board, tighten each nut on the post securely.

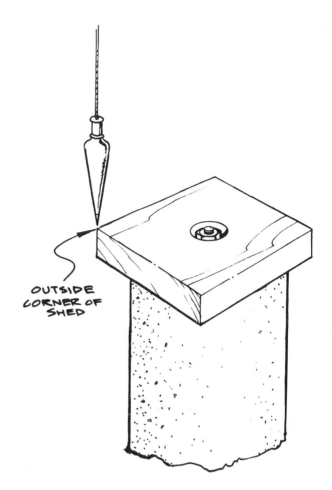

OUTSIDE CORNER OF SHED

Chapter 4. Framing

This chapter covers the basic techniques for framing a small outdoor structure. For our purposes here, this is defined as a single-story building with a floor area that is under 100 square feet.

The chapter is divided into three sections: floor framing, exterior wall framing, and roof framing. Step-by-step instructions explain each section, and several construction options are provided. Taken one step at a time, framing a small outdoor structure in not an especially complicated or difficult procedure. Indeed, you'll probably be surprised at how quickly the framing goes together. Keep in mind, however, that accurate layout, cutting, and assembly are important to the success of the project.

FLOOR FRAMING

The floor framing creates a solid base for the wall and roof framing that follow. A well-constructed floor is strong, rigid, square, and level. Work carefully here, because a floor that's poorly made is going to create problems throughout the entire construction of the structure. The step-by-step instructions that follow explain how to frame a floor for three different types of foundations: wooden skid, concrete post, and perimeter. (See Chapter 3 for details on how to build wooden skid and concrete post foundations.) The procedures described and shown are commonly used, but keep in mind that there can be other ways to frame each foundation type. Check your plans and local building codes before starting.

Slab foundations, briefly mentioned in the previous chapter, don't require floor framing because the slab serves as the shed floor. A few special considerations for slab foundations are discussed in the Exterior Wall Framing section of this chapter.

FLOOR FRAMING TERMINOLOGY

Several components are common to just about all floor frames (Illus. 4-1 and 4-2). The *floor joists* are the horizontal boards, installed on edge, that serve as the primary supporting members of the frame. To keep the floor joists from twisting or turning, *header joists* are secured at each end of the floor joists. The floor joists located at each end of the frame are called the *end joists* or *stringer joists*.

The *subfloor* consists of plywood panels secured to the floor joists. The assembled subfloor is often called a *platform* or *deck*. *Blocking* is sometimes installed between the floor joists to strengthen the frame and to provide additional nailing surfaces for the subfloor. Perimeter foundations require a *sill plate* (sometimes called a *mudsill*) to secure the floor framing to the foundation. The sill plate is attached to the foundation with *anchor bolts*, also called *J-bolts*.

Floor framing for concrete post foundations often incorporate a *beam* at each end of the joists. When that occurs, the joists can be secured to the beams with *joist hangers*. Some concrete post foundations incorporate wooden *post caps*. A cap is secured to each concrete post with an anchor bolt. The beams are then nailed to the wooden caps, effectively securing the floor framing to the concrete posts.

BUILDING A FLOOR FRAME

Your outdoor structure plans, in conjunction with local building codes, are going to dictate the size and spacing of the floor joists and other floor frame members. Some codes require the use of pressure-treated lumber for floor joists, beams, sill plates, and other subfloor members. Check the plans and building codes before starting.

Plywood is the material most often used for

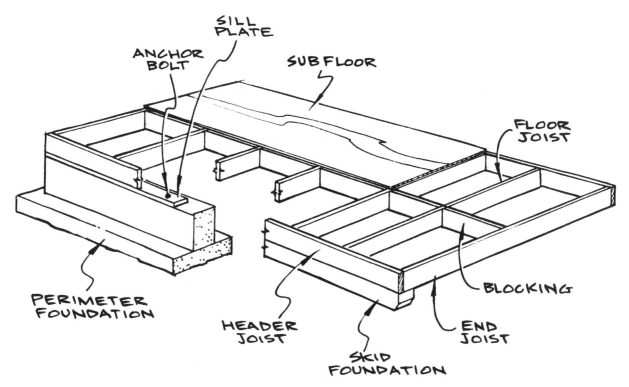

Illus. 4-1. Floor framing for skid and perimeter foundations.

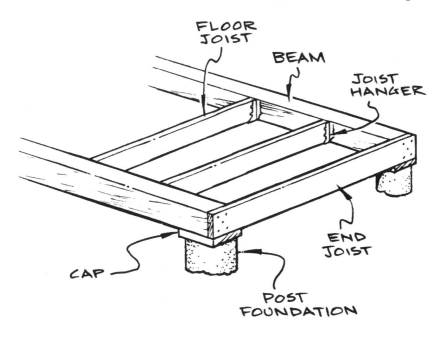

Illus. 4-2. Floor framing for a post foundation.

subfloors. It is available in various thicknesses in 4 × 8-foot panels. See Chapter 1 for more information about plywood.

A plywood subfloor has several advantages. It can be installed quickly, holds nails effectively, and adds rigidity to the floor frame. Also, because of its cross-grain construction, plywood is dimensionally stable. That means it changes little in length and width, even as the relative humidity changes.

Be sure to select plywood that is sold specifically for use as a subfloor. Also, check your plans to determine the specified subfloor thickness. The proper subfloor thickness is going to depend upon the joist spacing.

Most outdoor storage floors are framed with joists spaced either 16 or 24 inches on-center. Both these floor joist spacings facilitate the use of 4 × 8-foot plywood panels. When a floor is framed with joists that are 16 or 24 inches on-

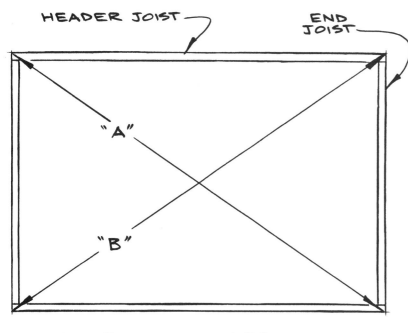

HEADER JOIST

END JOIST

"A"

"B"

BOX IS SQUARE
WHEN "A" EQUALS "B"

Illus. 4-3. The box for a skid foundation is square when the measurements diagonally across the box are the same.

center, the end edges of adjoining 4 × 8 sheets of plywood are located in the center of a joist. This allows the plywood to be nailed securely in place. The step-by-step instructions that follow are based on a 24-inch joist spacing, but the basic procedure applies just as well to a 16-inch spacing.

Floor Framing for a Skid Foundation
Step 1: Assemble the End and Header Joists

Cut the two end joists and the two header joists to length. Make the cuts with care to ensure the ends are square. Overlap the ends (see Illus. 4-1) and assemble each joist with nails. Use three 16d galvanized common nails for 2 × 6 and 2 × 8 lumber, and four 16d nails for 2 × 10 lumber. Drive the nails through the header joists and into the end joists.

Step 2: Check the End and Header Joists for Squareness

When assembled, the end and header joists create a box. This box must be square before you attach it to the skids.

Place the box on the skids. The outside face of each header should be flush with the outside faces of the skids. Also, the ends of the header should be flush with the ends of the skids. To check for squareness, measure diagonally across the box, corner to corner (Illus. 4-3). If the two measurements are the same (A in Illus. 4-3 is the exact length as B), the wall is square. If not, temporarily secure one of the header joists and then

push or pull the other header joist as needed to get equal diagonal measurements.

Step 3: Fasten the Box to the Skids

Once the box is square, toenail the ends of the end joists to the skid with three 10d galvanized common nails (two nails driven from the outside face, one nail driven from the inside face). Then, toenail the header joist to the skid using 16d galvanized

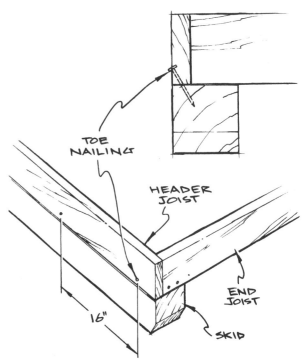

TOE NAILING

HEADER JOIST

END JOIST

SKID

16"

Illus. 4-4. Toenailing the header joist to the skid.

common nails spaced 16 inches on-center (Illus. 4-4).

Step 4: Lay Out the Floor Joists Scribe a line 23¼ inches from one end of a header joist and mark an X to show at which side of the line the floor joist is located. Then, measuring from the marked line, scribe a line every 24 inches across the full length of the header joist. Mark all the floor joist locations with an X after each line (Illus. 4-5). It's acceptable for the last floor joist to measure less than 24 inches from the end.

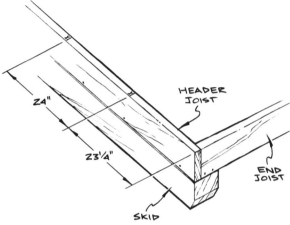

Illus. 4-5. Mark all the floor joist locations with an X.

Next, use a square to mark the locations of the floor joists on the inside face of the header joists (Illus. 4-6). To complete the floor joist layout, repeat the above procedures on the other header joist.

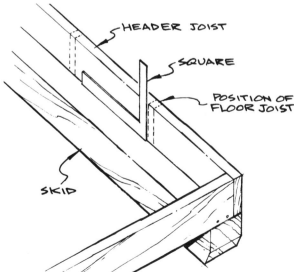

Illus. 4-6. Use a square to mark the locations of the floor joists on the inside face of the header joists.

Step 5: Install the Floor Joists Measure the distance between the inside faces of the header joists and cut each of the floor joists to the measured dimension. Place the first floor joist in position between the header joists. Use the lines marked in Step 4 to ensure that the floor joist is square.

Secure the floor joist by driving nails through the header joists and into the ends of the floor joist. Use three 16d common nails for 2 × 6 and 2 × 8 lumber, and four 16d nails for 2 × 10 lumber (Illus. 4-7). Also, toenail each end of the floor joist to the skids with three 10d nails (two nails on one side, one nail on the other). Before driving any of the nails, make sure the top edge of the floor joist is flush with the top edge of the header. Repeat this procedure for all the remaining floor joists.

As you prepare to add each floor joist, keep in mind that most lumber has a bowed edge. You can spot the bow by sighting down the edge of the joist. It's best to install the joists so that the bowed edge faces upward. By doing so, any weight on the shed floor will act to straighten the joist.

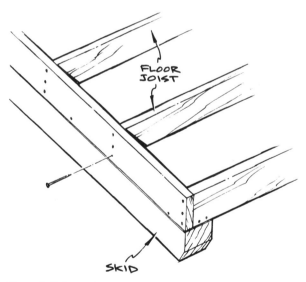

Illus. 4-7. Installing the floor joists.

Step 6: Add the Blocking Some shed designs specify blocking in order to provide additional strength and rigidity to the floor. Also, when installed at 4-foot intervals (as it sometimes is), the blocking serves to support the edges of the 4-foot-wide plywood subfloor. The blocking can be installed either staggered or in-line (Illus. 4-8). As a general rule, blocking is made from the same size lumber as the joist material.

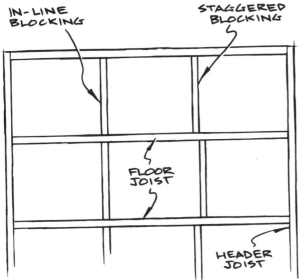

Illus. 4-8. The blocking can be installed in-line or staggered.

It's easier to install staggered blocking because all the ends can be face-nailed. However, if the blocking is used to support the edges of the plywood subfloor, the blocking must be installed in-line. That means one end of the blocking is face-nailed and the other end is toenailed. Snap a chalk line across the floor joists to keep the blocking properly aligned.

Step 7: Install the Subfloor Starting at any corner of the floor frame, position a 4 × 8-foot sheet of plywood so that it's flush with header and end joists. Make sure that the plywood end is centered on a floor joist. Note from Illus. 4-9 that the long grain of the plywood runs perpendicular to the direction of the joists.

Use 6d nails to secure plywood that's ½ inch thick or less in place. Use 8d nails for ⅝-, ¾-, and ⅞-inch-thick plywood. Space the nails 6 inches apart along all edges and 12 inches apart along the floor joists. It's helpful to scribe lines across the width of the plywood, spacing the lines 24 inches on-center (some plywood comes with premarked lines). The lines make it considerably easier to locate the center of the floor joists when driving the nails.

Continue installing panels along the floor frame. To prevent the panels from buckling should any expansion occur, allow a space of ⅛ inch between their edges and ends, unless otherwise specified by the manufacturer. (You can use an 8d nail as a gauge, as it has a diameter of very nearly ⅛ inch.) For maximum strength, the subfloor joints should be staggered, so start the second row with a half sheet of plywood. After all the panels are installed, use a handsaw or circular saw to trim any overhang flush with the outside edge of the box.

Check along the perimeter of the subfloor or platform to make sure the floor remains level. If adjustments are required, raise or lower the skids as necessary by adding or removing gravel.

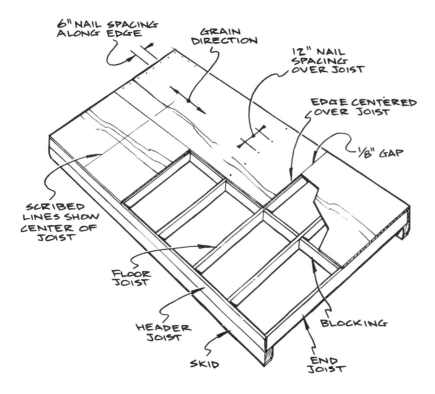

Illus. 4-9. Installing the subfloor.

Floor Framing for a Concrete Post Foundation

Step 1: Attaching the End Joists and Beams
Cut the two end joists and the two beams to length. Make the cuts with care to ensure the ends are square. Place the beams on the caps. Then butt the beams to the end joists and assemble each joint with five 16d galvanized common nails. Note from Illus. 4-10 that the nails are driven through the end joists and into the ends of the beams.

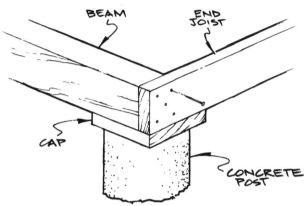

Illus. 4-10. Attaching the end joists and beams for a concrete post foundation.

Step 2: Check to Ensure That the Box Is Square and Level
See Floor Framing for a Skid Foundation, Step 2, for an explanation about how to square the box. Once it's square, check it to make sure that it is level all around its perimeter. If the box isn't level, use light hammer taps to insert tapered shims as needed between the joists/beams and the caps (Illus. 4-

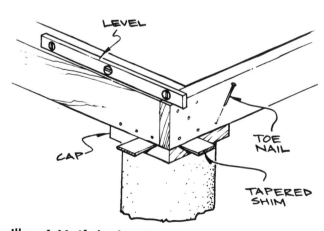

Illus. 4-11. If the box is not level all around its perimeter, insert tapered shims between the joists/beams and the caps.

11). You can buy shim stock at most lumberyards, or simply use cedar shingles.

Once the box is square and level, toenail the beams and end joists to the caps with 12d galvanized common nails. Avoid driving the nails into the concrete post. Add three nails to each face of the beam. Also toenail the end joist—three nails to the outside face, two nails to the inside face. If shims were used, trim them flush with the beams or joists.

Step 3: Lay Out the Floor Joists
Scribe a line 23¼ inches from the outside face of an end joist and mark an X to show on which side of the line the floor joist is located. Then, measuring from the marked line, scribe a line every 24 inches across the full length of the beam. Mark all the floor joist locations with an X after each line (Illus. 4-12). It's acceptable for the last floor joist to measure less than 24 inches from the end. Repeat the procedure on the other header beam.

Step 4: Attach the Joist Hangers
Using a square, extend the floor joist lines from the top of each beam to its inside face. Attach the joist hangers to the beams at the marked lines. Use a nail size that's recommended by the hanger manufacturer. Locate the hangers so that when the floor joists are added later, the top edge of each joist is going to be flush with the top edge of the beam.

Step 5: Install the Floor Joists
Measure the distance between the inside faces of the beams and cut each of the floor joists to the measured dimension. Place the joists into the joist hangers and secure each one with nails recommended by the hanger manufacturer.

When installing the joists, make sure the bowed edge faces upward. (See Skid Foundations, Step 5 for details.)

Step 6: Add the Blocking and Subfloor
See Skid Foundations, steps 6 and 7 for details.

Floor Framing for a Perimeter Foundation

Step 1: Cut the Sill Plate
For a small outdoor structure, sill plates are typically made from 2 × 4 or 2 × 6 lumber. As a general rule, the sill plates are installed so that the outside edges of the plates are flush with the outside faces of the foundation. In some areas, building codes specify that sill plates must be made from pressure-treated lumber. Select straight and true lumber for your sill plate stock. Then cut the plates to

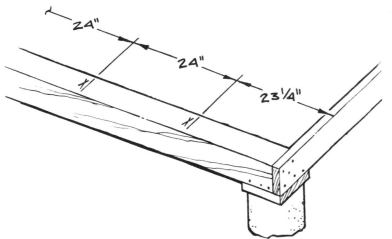

Illus. 4-12. Laying out the floor joists.

length and lay them in their approximate positions on the foundation.

Step 2: Bore the Bolt Holes Butt the inside edges of the sill plates against the anchor bolts and use a square to mark the anchor bolt locations on each of the plates. Next, measure the distance from the edge of the foundation to the centerpoint of each bolt and mark that location on the sill plates (Illus. 4-13). Bore a through hole at each centerpoint location, making the hole ¼ inch larger than the diameter of the anchor bolt. (For example, bore a ¾-inch-diameter hole for a ½-inch-diameter bolt.) The oversized holes allow for some adjustment of the sill plate during installation.

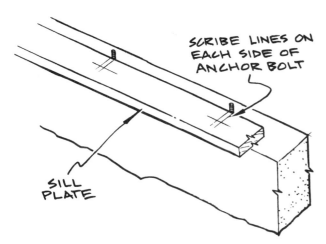

SCRIBE LINES ON EACH SIDE OF ANCHOR BOLT

SILL PLATE

Illus. 4-13. Boring the bolt holes in the sill plate.

Step 3: Install the Sill Plates Place the sill plates onto the bolts and then add a washer and nut to each bolt. Make sure the plates are flush with the edge of the foundation. Hand-tighten the nuts and then check that the sills are square.

(See Skid Foundations, Step 2 for details on how to square the parts.)

Step 4: Level the Sill Plates Check to make sure the sill plates are level all around the perimeter. If any area isn't level, insert tapered shims as needed between the foundation and the sill plates (see Concrete Post Foundations, Step 2). Shim stock is available at most lumberyards, or you can simply use cedar shingles. When all looks okay, tighten the nuts firmly.

Step 5: Assemble the End and Header Joists Cut the two end joists and the two header joists to length. Make sure the ends are square. Overlap the ends and assemble each joint with nails. Use three 16d galvanized common nails for 2 × 6 and 2 × 8 lumber, and four 16d nails for 2 × 10 lumber. Note from Illus. 4-1 that the nails are driven through the header joists and into the end joists.

Step 6: Check the Box for Squareness When assembled, the end and header joists create a box. This box must be square before it is secured to the sill plates. Place the box on the sill plates. The outside faces of the end joists and header joists should be flush with the outside edges of the sill plates.

To check for squareness, measure diagonally across the box from corner to corner (see Floor Framing for a Skid Foundation, Step 2, for details on how to square the parts). If the two measurements are the same, the wall is square. If not, temporarily secure one of the header joists and then push or pull the other header joist as needed to get equal diagonal measurements.

Step 7: Attach the Box to the Sill Plate After squaring the box, toenail the end and header joists to the sill plate using 16d common nails spaced 16 inches on-center.

Step 8: Add the Floor Joists and Subfloor

See Floor Framing for a Skid Foundation, steps 4 through 7, for details.

EXTERIOR WALL FRAMING

The exterior wall framing supports the roof and provides a surface for attaching the siding material. Framed walls are constructed one at a time, usually on the subfloor of the structure. Once a wall is assembled, it is raised and secured in place. The typical components of a framed exterior wall with a door and window are shown in Illus. 4-14.

WALL FRAMING TERMINOLOGY

The *bottom plate*, also called the *sole plate*, provides a base for attaching all the vertical members. At the top of the wall, the vertical members are secured to the *top plate*. Generally a *top cap* is added to the top plate to provide additional support for the roof and to help tie the wall frames together. When joined together, the top cap and the top plate form a *double plate*. The *studs* are the vertical members of the wall that extend from the bottom plate to the top plate. Studs located on each side of a door or window rough opening are called *king studs*. The single stud at the end of a wall is sometimes called the *end stud*. *Corner posts* are used when it is necessary to create inside corners for finishing the interior of the walls with Sheetrock, sheathing, paneling or other materials.

The *header* (also called a *lintel*) supports the weight of the structure over an opening such as a door or window. Two header members nailed together are called a *double-header*. The *rough sill* is a horizontal member that creates a base for the window. Short studs, called *cripples*, are located between the header and the top plate or between the rough sill and the bottom plate. Other short studs, called *trimmers*, are located on either side of a door or window rough opening to support the header.

When vertical, horizontal, or diagonal siding is used, *blocking* is sometimes installed between

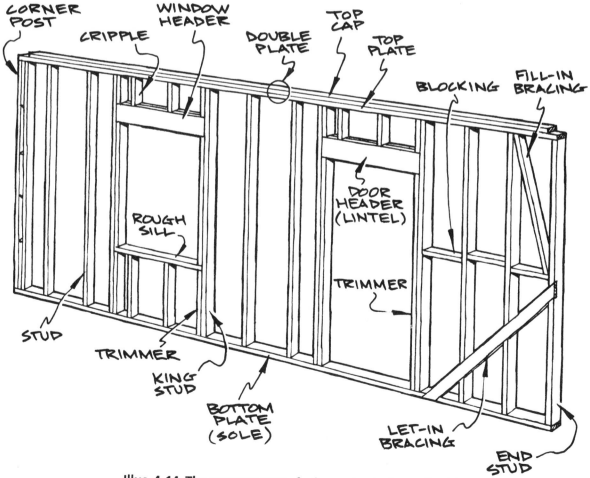

Illus. 4-14. The components of a framed exterior wall with a door and window.

the studs to create additional nailing surfaces for the siding. Walls with vertical, horizontal, or diagonal siding also require *let-in bracing* or *fill-in bracing* to help keep them square.

WALL FRAMING TECHNIQUES

The following step-by-step instructions show basic procedures for constructing, raising, plumbing, and squaring exterior walls for a small shed. Keep in mind that the floor platform must be square before you start (see the Floor Framing section in this chapter).

Except for the headers, the walls of a small structure are usually framed using 2 × 4 stock. Depending upon the design of the structure, the headers can be made from 2 × 4, 2 × 6, 2 × 8, or 2 × 12 lumber.

Local codes and the structure's design will dictate the stud spacing. Most walls are framed with studs spaced either 16 or 24 inches on-center. Both these stud spacings facilitate the use of 4 × 8-foot plywood sheathing or siding. When a wall is framed with studs that are 16 or 24 inches on-center, the vertical edges of adjoining 4 × 8 sheets of plywood are located in the center of a stud. This allows the plywood to be nailed securely in place. The step-by-step instructions that follow are based on a 24-inch stud spacing, but the basic procedure applies just as well to 16-inch spacing.

Corner posts create an inside corner for finishing the inside of the walls with sheathing, Sheetrock, paneling, or other materials. Since most outdoor storage structures have unfinished inside walls, the plans in this book do not include corner posts. However, if you are going to finish the inside of the walls, add the corner posts as discussed in Step 7.

Following are the step-by-step instructions for wall framing:

Step 1: Mark the Wall Locations Select the straightest stock you can find for the bottom and top plates. Plates made from straight stock help ensure that the walls are going to be straight and true. (If you have a slab foundation, use pressure-treated lumber for the bottom plate.)

Measure the width of the plate stock and mark this dimension at each end of the subfloor. Snap a line between the two marks. To snap a line, extend a chalk line between the marked points, and then pull the line taut. Lift the line at its midpoint and quickly let it go. This "snap-ping" action transfers most of the chalk from the line to the subfloor. The result is a long straight line marked on the subfloor. The line represents the exact location of the bottom plate. Repeat the procedure for the remaining sides of the subfloor.

Step 2: Lay Out the Studs Starting with a long wall, measure the length of the subfloor and cut the bottom and top plates to the measured length. Temporarily tack the two plates to the subfloor to prevent them from shifting during the layout work.

Note: If you have a slab foundation, you'll first need to mark the anchor bolt centerpoint locations on the bottom plate, and then bore oversized holes at the marked points. See Illus. 4-13 for details on how to mark and bore these holes. After boring the holes, place the bottom plate onto the bolts. Locate the plate in its proper position on the slab, and then temporarily hand-tighten the bolts to secure the plate in place during the layout of the studs.

Begin the stud layout by marking for the two end studs. Use a try square to scribe a line 1½ inches from each end of the plates. Mark an X to show the end stud locations. **Note:** If you are using corner posts, see Step 7.

Next, scribe a line 23¼ inches from one end of the plates and mark an X to show on which side of the line the stud is located. Then, measuring from the marked line, scribe a line every 24 inches across the full length of the plates. Mark all the stud locations with an X after each line (Illus. 4-15). It is acceptable for the last stud to measure less than 24 inches from the end.

Step 3: Lay Out the Window If the wall has a window (or windows), you'll next need to lay out the window's rough opening. Your plans should indicate the rough opening dimensions. If the dimensions are not shown, the window manufacturer (or your supplier) can provide them.

Most plans indicate the window locations with a dimension from the end of the wall to the window centerline. Lay out and mark the window centerline on both of the plates.

Next, referring to the plans, determine the width of the rough opening. Then, on each side of the window centerline, mark a point that is equal to one-half of the rough opening. Also, mark two more points, 1½ inches apart. Scribe a line at the marked points. Mark a T between

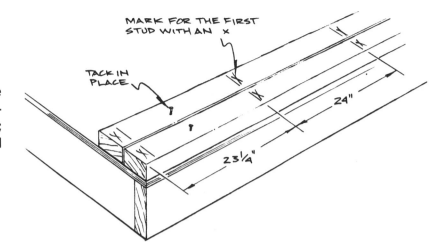

Illus. 4-15. When laying out the studs, mark all of their locations with an X after each line; this X indicates where the stud is located.

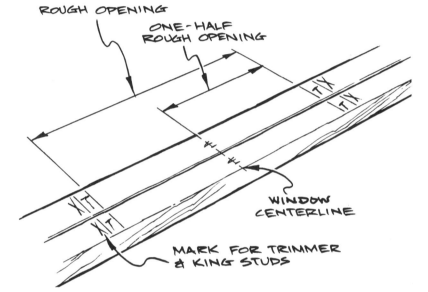

Illus. 4-16. Laying out the window.

the first two lines to indicate the location of the trimmer studs. Mark an X between the next two lines to indicate the king stud location (Illus. 4-16).

If any of the earlier marked studs (see Step 1) are located within the window's rough opening, replace the X mark with a C to indicate the location of a cripple.

Step 4: Lay Out the Door If the wall includes a door, the layout for the door's rough opening is next. As was the case with the window, plans normally show door locations with a dimension from the end of the wall to the door centerline. The rough openings for the door are generally found on the plans. If not, the door manufacturer (or your supplier) can provide them.

Lay out a door in the same way you lay out a window. That means you'll again follow the procedures shown in Step 3.

Step 5: Lay Out the Remaining Walls With the layout of the first wall complete, remove the

top plate and set it aside. Keep the bottom plate tacked to the subfloor, because the plate will help with the layout of the remaining walls. To keep the two parts together until it's time to assembly the walls, some carpenters nail the top plate to the bottom plate.

Working one at a time, lay out the remaining walls following the same procedure used for the first wall (see Steps 2 through 4). Keep in mind, however, that the measurements for the second stud are taken from the bottom plate of the adjoining wall (Illus. 4-17).

Step 6: Make the Headers Next, the headers are cut to size. Headers are an important framing component because they carry the weight of the roof across the openings for doors and windows.

Before starting, check the plans to determine the specific size and construction of each one. Header stock can range in size from 2×4 to 2×12. They are usually installed ''on edge'' to

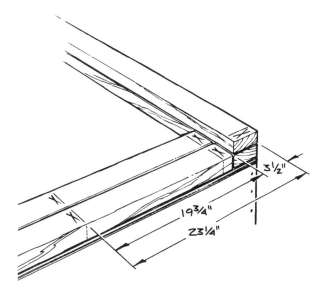

Illus. 4-17. Laying out the remaining walls.

provide maximum strength. The header length, which is equal to the rough opening dimension plus the thickness of two trimmer studs, can be taken directly from the layout on the bottom plates.

The double-header is probably the most common header design. It is made from a pair of "2 ×" members with ½-inch-thick plywood sandwiched in between. When the three members are assembled, they equal the 3½-inch wall thickness.

To construct a double-header, cut the two pieces of "2 ×" stock to length, making sure the ends are square. Next, cut a piece of ½-inch-thick plywood to equal the width and length of the "2 ×" stock. Then nail the three parts together with 16d nails spaced 12 inches apart (Illus. 4-18). Before driving the nails, check to see that all the edges are flush.

Step 7: Make the Corner Post (Optional) As discussed earlier, you need a corner post at the end of each wall only if you are planning to finish the inside of the walls with sheathing, Sheetrock, paneling, or other material. Corner posts are generally added to the ends of the long walls, while the short walls simply have an end stud. Square structures usually have the corner posts on the front and back walls.

There are several ways to make a corner post. One of the most common constructions, shown in Illus. 4-19, consists of an end stud, three filler blocks, and an inside stud. To make this type of corner post, cut the end and inside studs to final length and then cut three 2 × 4 filler blocks to lengths of about 16 inches. Using 10d nails, make a subassembly by attaching a filler block to the center and each end of one of the studs. Drive four nails into each block, making sure the blocks are flush to the ends and sides of the stud. Next, attach the remaining stud to the subassembly by nailing four 16d nails into each block. Space the 16d nails so they don't hit the 10d nails.

Step 8: Assemble the Full-Length Studs Referring to your plans, cut all the full-length

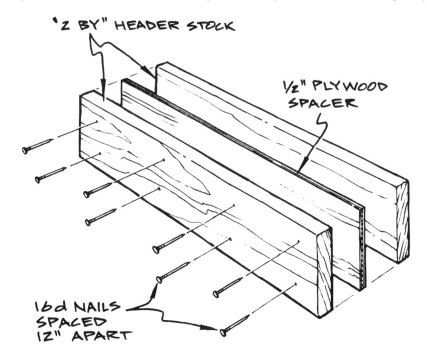

Illus. 4-18. To construct a double-header, cut two "2 ×" pieces for the headers, a piece of ½-inch-thick plywood as a spacer, and nail the pieces together.

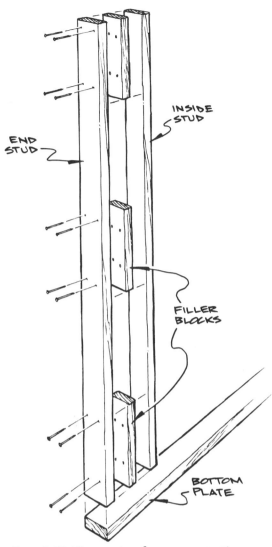

Illus. 4-19. The parts of a corner post.

subfloor. To do this, remove all the bottom plates that you previously tacked in place. Then, starting with the first wall, lay the bottom plate and its mating top plate on-edge on the subfloor. Space them far enough apart to allow the studs to fit between them with a foot or so clearance on each end. Position a stud for each X mark on the plates.

Now, join each of the full-length studs to the top and bottom plates with a pair of 16d common nails (Illus. 4-20). As shown, the nails are spaced about ¾ inch from the edge and driven through the plate and into the stud centerline. Before driving the nails, make sure all the edges are flush. Also make certain the stud is both square to the edges of the plate and properly located on the marked line.

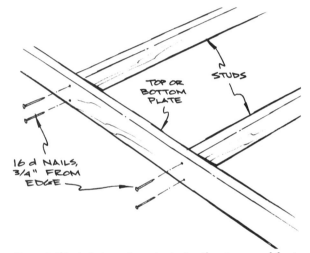

Illus. 4-20. Joining the studs to the top and bottom plates.

studs (the studs that extend from the bottom plate to the top plate) to required length. Studs are manufactured in standard lengths of 6 feet and longer in multiples of 1 foot, but chances are you won't find such a wide selection at your lumberyard. Studs are more likely to be available as either 8- or 10-foot lengths. Also, you can sometimes get studs that are precut to 7-foot, 8⅝-inch lengths. That might seem like an odd dimension, but it's popular with framing carpenters because it results in an 8-foot ceiling—the standard ceiling height used for residential home construction. To minimize waste, buy the studs in a length that most closely matches the length you need. By the way, before you buy studs, inspect them carefully and select only the straightest you can find.

Before assembling the studs, it will minimize confusion and save time if you place the plates and studs in approximate position on the

Step 9: Add Corner Posts (Optional) If the wall requires corner posts, join them to the end of the plates with 16d nails. Use five nails at each end of the posts—two into the end stud, one into the filler block, and two into the inside stud (Illus. 4-21).

Step 10: Constructing a Rough Frame for the Door Opening Referring to the plans, determine the length of the door trimmer studs and cut them to size. Assemble each trimmer stud to a mating king stud using a pair of 10d common nails every 16 inches or so. Drive the nails through the trimmers and into the king studs.

Next, position the double-header above the trimmer studs, making sure the edges of the headers and studs are flush. Drive four 16d common nails through the king stud and into each end of the header.

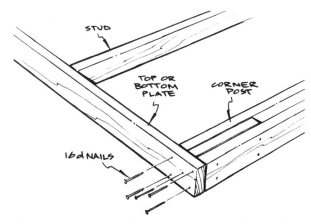

Illus. 4-21. Joining the corner post to the ends of the plates.

Refer to the layout marked on the top plate to determine the number of cripple studs (if any) above the header. Measure the distance between the top of the header and the underside of the top plate and cut the cripple studs to that length. Use a pair of 10d common nails to toenail one end of the cripple stud to the top of the double-header. To secure the other end, drive a pair of 16d nails through the top plate and into the end of the cripple stud (Illus. 4-22).

Step 11: Construct a Rough Frame for the Window Opening Referring to the plans, determine the location of the rough sill and mark its location on each of the king studs. Measure

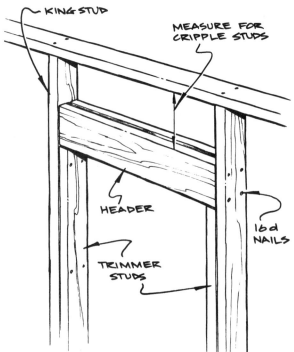

Illus. 4-22. The parts of the rough framing for the door opening.

the distance between the underside of the rough sill location and the top of the bottom plate; then cut the lower cripple studs (if any) and the two lower trimmer studs to their measured lengths. Join the two lower trimmer studs to the king studs with 10d nails.

Cut the rough sill to a length that equals the distance between the king studs, and then position it on the lower trimmer studs. Drive a pair of 16d common nails through the king studs and into the ends of the rough sill. Attach the lower cripple studs with 16d nails through the bottom plate and the rough sill.

Next, measure the distance from the top of the rough sill to the underside of the double-header. Cut the upper trimmer studs to that length, and then attach them to the king studs with a pair of 10d common nails every 16 inches or so. Then position the double-header above the upper trimmer studs, making sure the edges of the headers and studs are flush. Drive four 16d nails through the king stud and into each end of the header.

Next, refer to the layout marked on the top plate to determine the number of cripple studs (if any) above the header. Measure the distance between the top of the header and the underside of the top plate and cut the cripple studs to that length. Use a pair of 10d common nails to toenail one end of the cripple to the top of the double-header. To secure the other end, drive a pair of 16d nails through the top plate and into the end of the cripple.

Step 12: Add the Bracing Walls with plywood sheathing or siding generally do not require additional bracing. However, walls with vertical, diagonal, or horizontal board siding require bracing to add rigidity to the structure. *Let-in bracing*, made from 1 × 4 stock, is probably used most often. But short walls, especially if they have openings for doors or windows, may not offer enough space for adequate lengths of let-in bracing. In that case, *fill-in bracing* is sometimes used. (Illus. 4-14 shows both let-in and fill-in bracing.)

The wall must be squared before bracing can be added. To check for squareness, measure diagonally across the wall, from corner to corner. If the two measurements are the same, the wall is square. If not, temporarily secure the bottom plate, and then push or pull the top plate, as needed, to get equal diagonal measurements. At this point, don't spend too much time trying to get the measurements exactly equal—that's done after the wall is raised. For now, just get it reasonably close (say within ³⁄₁₆ of an inch or so).

Let-in braces usually extend from the end of the wall at the top plate to the middle of the wall at the bottom plate. When two braces are added to a wall, they form a V shape. Door and window openings must be avoided, so the bracing locations vary. Indeed, as shown in Illus. 4-14, the brace sometimes extends to the end joist.

To install let-in bracing, lay a length of 1 × 4 stock in position on the wall, allowing it to overhang at the top and bottom plates (or the end joists). Make sure there are no nails under the bracing that can interfere with the saw cut to be made. Scribe a line on each side of the 1 × 4 to mark its location on the plates and studs. Also, on each end of the 1 × 4 scribe a line to indicate the overhang.

Now, set your circular saw to make a cut about ⅛ inch deeper than the thickness of the bracing stock. Using the saw, make a pair of cuts at each marked line to establish the width of the cutout. Then, between these first two cuts, make a series of cuts spaced about ¼ inch apart. After making all the cuts, use a hammer to knock out the narrow strips of wood that remain. If necessary, use a chisel to clean up any rough spots.

Next, place the bracing in the notches and temporarily tack it in place with an 8d nail at each end. (The brace will be permanently secured after the wall is raised and final squared.) Trim each end flush with the top and bottom plates.

Fill-in bracing is usually installed after the walls are raised (Step 13) and the blocking is added (Step 15). To install fill-in bracing, measure the diagonal opening between the plates and the blocking and cut a 2 × 4 to that length. Place the 2 × 4 in position and scribe the angles to be cut on each end. Cut the angles with the circular saw and then install the bracing in the opening. The fit should be snug. Secure one end of each bracing with a pair of 16d nails driven through the plates. Square the wall (Step 14), and then nail all the remaining ends of the bracing.

Step 13: Raise the Wall

Before raising the wall, have couple of temporary braces ready to nail in place. Short walls (10 to 12 feet long) don't require a lot of braces; one on each end

will suffice. One end of the brace is nailed near the top of the end stud; the other end is nailed to a floor header or end joist.

You'll need at least one helper to raise the wall into position. Working together, lift the frame at the top plate, pivoting the wall on the bottom plate. Once the wall is vertical, locate the bottom plate in its approximate position on the subfloor chalk line (marked in Step 1), and then nail the two temporary braces in place.

Now, position the bottom plate in its exact position on the subfloor. Attach the bottom plate by driving 16d common nails through the plate and into the header or end joist. Drive two nails between each stud. However, don't add any nails in the section of bottom plate that's located under the door. Later in the construction, it will be cut out to allow for the door. (If you have a slab floor, place the wall on the anchor bolts, add the washers, and tighten the nuts firmly.)

Step 14: Plumb and Square the Wall

It's important for the walls to be perfectly vertical. A wall that is perfectly vertical is said to be *plumb*. A wall can be plumbed with a plumb bob, but, for small structures, a carpenter's level works just fine. Place the level against the end stud, and then relocate one end of the brace, as needed, to get a vertical reading on the level. Once the wall is plumb, secure the brace in its

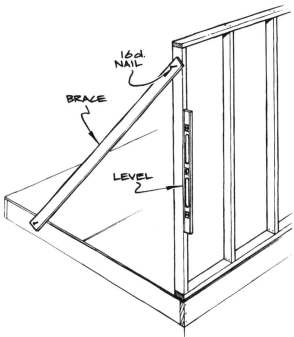

Illus. 4-23. Once the wall is plumb (perfectly vertical), position and secure the brace in its final location.

final position (Illus. 4-23). Repeat the procedure at the other end of the wall.

Next, the wall must be squared. Measure across the diagonals to check for squareness (a technique described in Step 12) and adjust the wall as necessary. Once square, secure the let-in bracing(s) by driving a pair of 8d nails through the bracing and into the stud or plate at each notch. If fill-in blocking is used, hold off squaring the wall until after adding the blocking.

Step 15: Add the Blocking Before starting, check your plans for the number of rows of blocks that are specified. The number of rows needed usually depends on the type of siding that is to be installed. Staggered blocking is easiest to install because the nails can be driven from the ends. It's a bit more difficult to install in-line blocking, because one end must be toenailed. Plywood panel siding and a few other types of siding require in-line blocking in order to provide a nailing surface along the entire edge of the panel.

Mark the elevation of each row at both ends of the wall, and then snap a line between the marks. Measure the distance between the studs and cut the blocking from 2 × 4 stock to the measured length. Stagger the blocking on each side of the line, securing it in place with a pair of 16d common nails driven through the studs and into the ends of the blocking (see Illus. 4-14). To install in-line blocking, attach one end as described for staggered blocking; then toenail the other end.

Step 16: Joining Additional Walls As each additional wall is raised, plumbed and squared, it is nailed to the adjoining wall. If both walls have end studs, drive 16d common nails spaced 6 inches apart to join the mating walls (Illus. 4-24). If one of the walls has a corner post, drive a pair of 16d nails spaced 12 inches apart through the face of the end stud and into the corner post.

Step 17: Add the Top Cap Now that all four walls are assembled, the top cap can be added. When cutting the top cap parts to length, keep in mind that the top cap should overlap the joints in the top plate (Illus. 4-25).

Before nailing the top cap, make sure it is flush with the edges of the top plate. To secure the top cap, use three 10d common nails at each end, and then add a pair of 10d nails every 16 inches along the entire length of the piece.

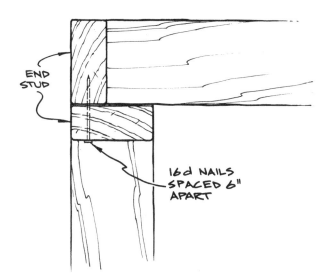

Illus. 4-24. Join the additional walls in a wall frame.

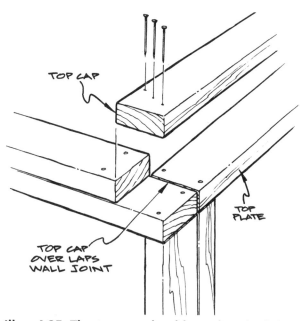

Illus. 4-25. The top cap should overlap the joints in the top plate.

ROOF FRAMING

The roof frame provides a rigid structure for attaching the roofing materials. Your backyard structure's roof must be strong enough to withstand high winds and, in many geographical areas, heavy snow loads. Local building codes and the structure's design are going to dictate the size and spacing of the rafters. Most roofs are framed with rafters spaced either every 16 or 24 inches on-center. The step-by-step instructions that follow are based on 24-inch rafter spacing.

Many small backyard structures are built using either a gable roof or a shed roof (Illus. 4-26). The look of a gable roof is often preferred, but, as a general rule, a shed roof requires less materials and is easier to build. The step-by-step instructions that follow show you how to make both gable and shed roofs.

A gable roof with an overhang on each end provides better weather protection for the structure. Such a roof is said to have a *gable overhang.* A gable roof without an overhang on its ends is called a *closed gable end.*

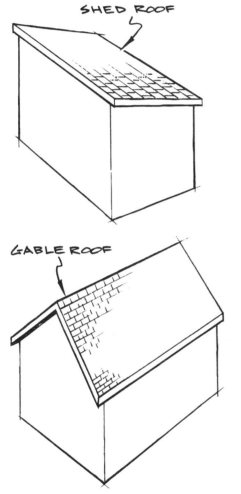

Illus. 4-26. Shed and gable roofs are the two types of roofs used most commonly on small outdoor structures.

FRAMING A GABLED ROOF

The typical components of a gable roof with a gable overhang are shown in Illus. 4-27. At the highest point on the roof is a long horizontal member called the *ridgeboard* or *ridge.* The *rafters* are the sloping frame members that span the distance from the ridgeboard to the top cap on

the framed wall. The rafters at the ends of a roof are sometimes called the *end rafters.* A triangular-shaped notch, called a *bird's-mouth,* is cut in each rafter. The flat area created by the bird's-mouth allows the rafter to rest firmly on the top cap. The lower ends of the rafters are covered by the *fascia board.* Some roof designs incorporate *collar beams* (also called *collar ties*) to help prevent the rafters from spreading apart. *Gable studs* are the vertical members added between the top cap and the end rafters.

Gable roofs with a gable overhang have *outriggers* that extend the roof on each end. The end rafter here is called a *fascia rafter, verge rafter,* or *barge rafter.*

GABLE ROOF TERMINOLOGY

As shown in Illus. 4-28, the *roof span* is the distance between the outside of the walls. The *rafter line* runs parallel to the edge of the rafter; it extends from the corner of the bird's-mouth to the centerline of the ridgeboard thickness. The *roof rise* is the distance from the top of the wall top cap to the end of the rafter line at the ridgeboard. The *roof run* is the distance from the outside of the walls to the center of the ridgeboard. (When the ridgeboard is centered on a roof, as it often is, the run is equal to one-half the span.)

The *roof pitch* is the ratio of the rise to the span. It is expressed as a fraction. Let's say, for example, that the shed shown in Illus. 4-28 has a 2-foot rise and an 8-foot span. The pitch, therefore, is ⅜. By reducing the fraction, the pitch becomes ¼.

The *roof slope* is a ratio of the rise to the run. It is expressed as the amount of rise (in inches) for every 12 inches of run. For example, a shed with a 2-foot rise and a 4-foot run has a slope of 6 in 12 (6 inches of rise for every 12 inches of run). Building plans include a triangular symbol to indicate the roof slope. The vertical leg of the triangle represents the rise, while the horizontal leg represents the run.

Following are the steps for constructing a roof:

Step 1: Determine the Overall Rafter Length
Before you can order lumber for the rafters, you need to determine the overall rafter length. Once the overall length is known, you can order lumber to the nearest standard length, allowing a little extra stock for damaged ends.

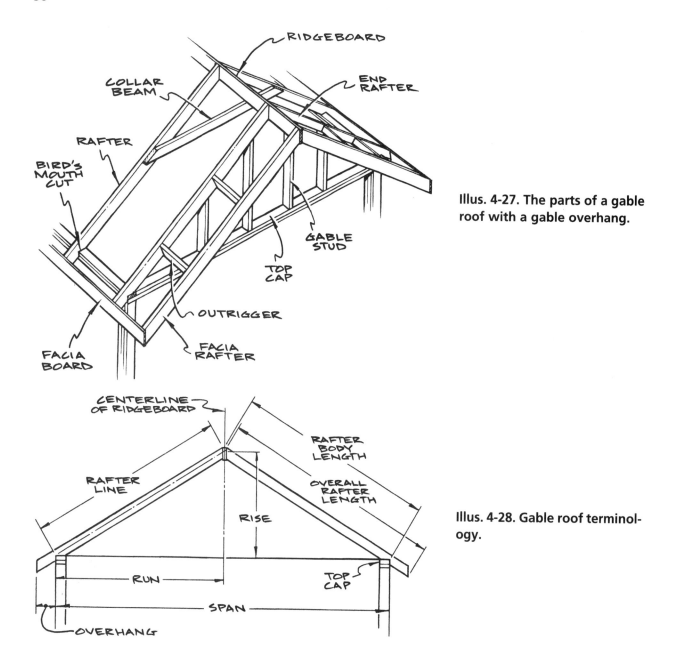

Illus. 4-27. The parts of a gable roof with a gable overhang.

Illus. 4-28. Gable roof terminology.

As shown in Illus. 4-28, the *rafter body length* extends from the centerline of the ridgeboard thickness to the corner of the bird's-mouth. To determine the overall rafter length, subtract one-half the ridgeboard thickness from the rafter body length, and then (if applicable) add the overhang dimension.

There are, in fact, several ways to determine the overall rafter length. Two quick and easy methods are discussed. One uses rafter tables found in carpentry books and the other uses dimensions taken from a framing square.

Rafter tables, which are found in some carpentry books, can be used to determine the rafter body length (Table 4-1). You need only

know the roof slope and the run (some tables use the span) to get the length. Most tables cover a wide range of roof slopes and runs. Referring to the tables shown, it can be seen that a shed roof with a 6-in-12 slope and a 4-foot run has a rafter body length of 4 feet, 5⅝ inches.

If the roof has an overhang, the rafter tables can also be used to determine the amount of additional rafter length needed for the overhang. Simply consider the overhang dimension as the run. Referring to the tables, a roof with a 6-in-12 slope and a 12-inch overhang requires an additional 1 foot, 1⅜ inches of rafter length.

Therefore, in the above example, the overall rafter length equals 4 feet, 5⅝ inches plus 1 foot,

RAFTER LENGTHS

6 in 12 Slope		8 in 12 Slope	
Run (feet)	**Rafter Body Length**	**Run** (feet)	**Rafter Body Length**
1	1 foot, 1⅜ inches	1	1 foot, 2⅜ inches
1½	1 foot, 8⅛ inches	1½	1 foot, 9⅝ inches
2	2 feet, 2⅞ inches	2	2 feet, 4⅞ inches
2½	2 feet, 9½ inches	2½	3 feet, 0 inches
3	3 feet, 4¼ inches	3	3 feet, 7¼ inches
3½	3 feet, 11 inches	3½	4 feet, 2½ inches
4	4 feet, 5⅝ inches	4	4 feet, 9¾ inches
4½	5 feet, ⅜ inches	4½	5 feet, 4⅞ inches
5	5 feet, 7⅛ inches	5	6 feet, ⅛ inches
5½	6 feet, 1¾ inches	5½	6 feet, 7⅜ inches
6	6 feet, 8½ inches	6	7 feet, 2½ inches

Table 4-1. You can use this table to determine rafter body length.

1⅜ inches minus ¾ inch (one-half the ridge-board thickness), for a total of 5 feet, 6¼ inches. A 12-foot length of stock, cut in half, yields a pair of rafters.

A carpenter's framing square can also be used to determine rafter lengths. The long leg of a framing square is called the *blade* (or *body*) and the short leg is called the *tongue.* You'll need a good-quality framing square, one that has rows and columns of numbers embossed along the blade. The uppermost row is the one used to figure the rafter lengths (Illus. 4-29). It represents the rafter length (in inches) per foot of run. The inch scale along the blade represents the rise per foot of run.

As an example, let's again consider a shed with a 6-in-12 slope and a 4-foot run. To determine the rafter length, find the 6-inch mark on the blade, which represents the rise per foot. Then, looking at the first column below the 6-inch mark, you'll find the number 13.42. This number is the rafter length per foot of run. To

Illus. 4-29. Use the uppermost row on a framing square to determine rafter lengths.

calculate the rafter body length, multiply 13.42 times the 4 foot run. The result is 53.68 inches, which rounds off to 53⅝ inches, or 4-feet, 5⅝ inches. If, as in the earlier example, the roof has a 1-foot overhang, add the 13.42 inches (the rafter length per foot of run) to the rafter body length. The overall rafter length equals 4 feet, 5⅝ inches plus 1 foot, 1⅜ inches (13.42 rounded to the nearest fraction) minus ¾ inch (one-half the ridgeboard thickness), for a total of 5 feet, 6¼ inches.

There is a third method that should be discussed here. Although you can lay out a rafter from the dimensions taken from book tables or framing squares, most carpenters find the step-off method easiest to use. You need only a framing square and a sharp pencil to "step off" a rafter.

It's important to select a length of straight stock for the first rafter. That's because the first rafter is used as a template for the remaining rafters.

The example shown in Illus. 4-30 is based on a gable roof with a 6-in-12 slope, a 4-foot run, and a 1-foot overhang. Begin the layout at the ridgeboard end of the rafter. Using the framing square, align the 6-inch mark (on the tongue leg) and the 12-inch mark (on the blade leg) with the top edge of the rafter; then use a pencil to scribe a line along the tongue. This line represents the location of the ridgeboard centerline. Also, mark the point where the blade meets the top edge of the rafter at the 12-inch mark.

Now, move the framing square 1 foot to the right and align the 6-inch mark (on the tongue leg) with the pencil mark you just made. Also, align the 12-inch mark (on the blade leg) with the top edge of the rafter and again mark this point. Continue this procedure until you have completed a "step-off" for each foot of run (four in our example).

The final pencil mark represents the location of the outside edge of the top cap. Scribe a line at this point. Now, turn over the framing square and scribe a horizontal line equal to the width of the top cap (about 3½ inches). As shown in Illus. 4-30, the intersection of the horizontal line and the vertical line creates the location of the bird's-mouth.

Next, use the framing square to lay out and mark the overhang. The overhang is usually cut plumb, although a square cut is sometimes used. Check your plans before making this cut. To complete the layout, the rafter must be short-

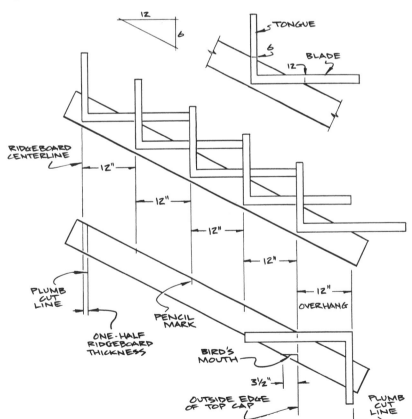

Illus. 4-30. The step-off method for laying out rafters on a gable roof.

ened at the ridgeboard end. From the ridgeboard centerline scribed earlier, measure a distance equal to one-half the ridgeboard thickness, and then use the framing square to scribe a line at this point. This new line represents the end of the rafter at the ridgeboard. To avoid confusion when cutting the rafter, it's a good idea to cross out or erase the line that represents the ridgeboard centerline.

Step 2: Cut the First Rafter The rafter can now be cut. Use care here, since the rafter is going to serve as a template. Four cuts complete the job—one at the ridgeboard end, one at the overhang end, and a pair at the bird's-mouth. Once all the cuts are complete, mark the word "template" on the rafter.

Step 3: Test-fit the Rafters Before using the template to cut all the remaining rafters, it's important to do a test to make sure everything is going to fit properly on the roof. There are several ways to do this when making an outdoor structure, but perhaps the easiest involves building a roof mock-up at ground level.

To build the mock-up, you must use the rafter template to make a second rafter. Also, you need a short spacer block made from stock that is the same thickness and width as the ridgeboard. And, finally, you need to cut a 2 × 4 to a length that equals the distance between the outside edges of the wall top caps (the span). This dimension is important to the accuracy of the mock-up, so measure it carefully.

Once all the parts are cut, temporarily tack the two rafters to the 2 × 4 and to the spacer block (Illus. 4-31). Now, check the mock-up to make sure the bird's-mouth fits properly on the 2 × 4 stock. Also, make certain that the top end of each rafter is parallel with the spacer block,

and that both rafter tops meet at the same elevation. If there is a problem with any part of the mock-up, recut the rafter template as needed to get a good fit.

Step 4: Cut the Remaining Rafters The mock-up can be disassembled once you are satisfied with the fit of the test rafters. Use the template to lay out all the remaining rafters and then cut each one. When marking the rafters, keep in mind that most lumber has a slightly bowed edge. It's best to lay out the rafter so the bowed edge faces upward. By doing so, the weight of the roofing material on the rafter is going to tend to straighten the bow.

Step 5: Mark the Rafter Locations on the Top Caps The rafter locations can now be marked on the top caps of both walls. First, mark for the end rafters. Use a try square to scribe a line 1½ inches from each end of the wall. Mark an X to show the end rafter locations.

Next, scribe a line 23¼ inches from the end of the wall and mark an X to show on which side of the line the stud is located. Then, measuring from the marked line, scribe a line every 24 inches across the full length of the plates. Mark all the rafter locations with an X after each line (Illus. 4-32). It's okay for the last stud to measure less than 24 inches from the end of the wall.

Step 6: Mark the Rafter Locations on the Ridgeboard Measure the length of the backyard structure (across the top caps) to determine the length of the ridgeboard. If the structure has a gable overhang, you'll need to add the overhang dimension to each end of the ridgeboard. Cut the ridgeboard to length and place it adjacent to the marked top cap. For a roof with a gable overhang, locate the ridgeboard so that it overhangs the correct amount

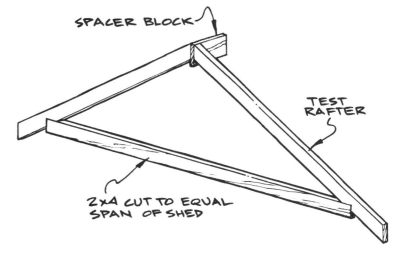

Illus. 4-31. Tacking the two test rafters to the 2 × 4 and to the spacer block.

SPACER BLOCK

TEST RAFTER

2×4 CUT TO EQUAL SPAN OF SHED

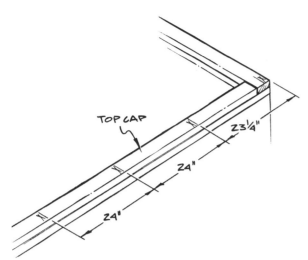

Illus. 4-32. Marking the rafter locations on the top caps.

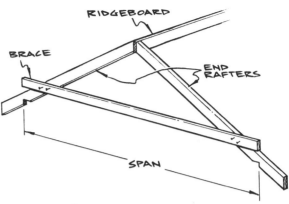

Illus. 4-33. The end rafter assembly.

on each end. It's helpful to add a couple of clamps to secure the ridgeboard in place.

Using a try square, transfer the rafter locations from the top caps to the ridgeboard. For a roof with a gable overhang, you'll also need to lay out and mark the location of the fascia rafters on the ends of the ridgeboard.

Step 7: Assemble the End Rafters The task of initially securing the end rafters to the ridgeboard and cap plates can present somewhat of a challenge. As a general rule, a backyard structure can best be started at ground level. You'll need a couple of helpers.

Secure the first end rafter by driving three 16d common nails through the face of the ridgeboard and into the end grain of the rafter. Then, toenail the rafter on the opposite side using 10d common nails. Use two nails on each side of the rafter. Make sure that the top edge of each rafter is flush with the top edge of the ridgeboard.

Next, using the 2 × 4 that was cut in Step 2, establish the distance between the outside edges of the wall top caps. Once you have the correct distance, tack a temporary brace between the rafters, and then remove the 2 × 4 (Illus. 4-33).

Step 8: Raise the End Rafters and Ridgeboard On one end of the structure, temporarily tack a ridgeboard support to the inside of the double plate. The support will serve as a means to secure one end of the ridgeboard while the first few rafters are attached on the other end. In order to provide adequate elevation, the support must be long enough to equal the rise of the roof. Position the support so that, when the

ridgeboard is attached to it, the ridgeboard is going to be centered between the walls.

Next, with the aid of your helpers, lift the ridgeboard/end rafter assembly into position on the wall top caps. Toenail the rafters to the top cap using three 16d common nails (two nails on one side, one on the other side). Then, level the ridgeboard and temporarily tack it to the support (Illus. 4-34).

Step 9: Add the Remaining Rafters The remaining rafters can now be assembled. As the rafters are added, make an occasional check to ensure that the ridgeboard remains level. Remove the ridgeboard support before adding the last pair of rafters. Also, remove the brace. Finally, check to be sure that the rafter assembly is plumb.

Step 10: Install the Fascia Board Check your plans to determine the size of the fascia board. Usually, the fascia board is made from "1 ×" stock that is at least one size wider than the width of the rafter stock. (For example, use 1 × 8 stock for a 1 × 6 rafter.)

Measure the distance between the outside edges of the end rafters and cut the fascia board to that length. If more than one board is required, cut them so that the ends are centered on the rafter. For structures with a gable overhang, you'll need to add the overhang dimension to each end of the fascia board.

Once the fascia board is cut to length, attach it by driving a pair of 8d common nails through the face of the fascia board and into the end of each rafter (Illus. 4-35). To prevent the fascia board from interfering with the roof sheathing later on in the construction, you'll need to bevel the top edge of the fascia board or allow clearance by locating it slightly below the top edge of the rafters.

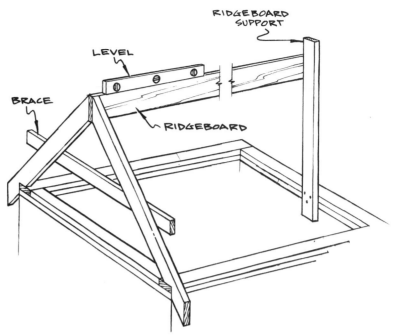

Illus. 4-34. Once you have leveled the ridgeboard, temporarily tack it to the support.

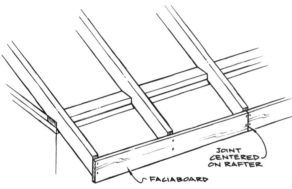

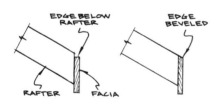

Illus. 4-35. To install the fascia board, nail a pair of 8d common nails through its face and into the end of each rafter.

Step 11: Add the Collar Beams Collar beams serve to keep the rafters from spreading apart (Illus. 4-27). They can be especially important on roofs with a low pitch (the lower the pitch, the flatter the roof), as such roofs have a greater tendency to push out the walls.

If your structure plan calls for collar beams, they should be added at this time. As a general rule, collar beams used on small structures are made from 1 × 6 or 2 × 4 stock, and they are added to every third pair of rafters. Locate each collar beam about one-third down the length of the rafter.

Step 12: Frame the Gable Overhang (Optional) Structures with a gable overhang require two additional pairs of rafters to be used as fascia-board rafters. Lay out the fascia rafters using the rafter template, but don't include a bird's-mouth. Next, cut the outriggers to length, and then lay out and mark the location of the outriggers on the fascia rafter and the end rafter. Outriggers are usually spaced 16 or 24 inches on-center. Check your plans for details.

The overhang can be partially assembled on the ground. Drive 16d common nails through the face of the fascia rafter and into the ends of the outriggers. Now, with the aid of a couple of helpers, raise the fascia rafter/outrigger assembly into position. The top end of the fascia rafter is attached to the ridgeboard, and the bottom end is attached to the fascia board. Secure the ends of the outriggers by driving 16d nails through the face of the end rafter. Repeat the procedure for the three remaining fascia rafters.

Step 13: Add the Gable Studs Refer to your plans to determine the layout of the gable studs. The top ends of the studs are beveled to match the roof slope. Both ends of each gable stud are toenailed in place with a pair of 10d common nails.

FRAMING A SHED ROOF

A shed roof has only one slope, so it's considerably easier to frame than a gable roof. Shed roofs can be built in a variety of ways. Illus. 4-36 shows a common construction that is both sturdy and uncomplicated. Note that the rafters on a shed roof require a bird's-mouth at each end.

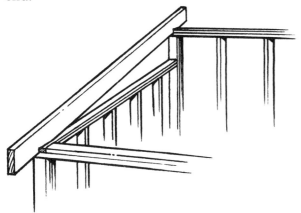

Illus. 4-36. A common type of shed roof.

SHED ROOF CONSTRUCTION

The construction of a shed roof differs somewhat from that of a gable roof. As shown in Illus. 4-37, the *roof rise* of a shed roof is equal to the difference in elevation between the front wall top cap and the back wall top cap. The *roof span* is the distance between the outside of the front wall and the outside of the back wall. The *roof run* is equal to the span minus the thickness of one wall. Note that on the upper end of the roof the overhang run is measured from the inside of the wall, while on the lower end of the roof the overhang run is measured from the outside of the wall. For this reason, if you want the same

overhang on both the front and back of the finished shed, you need to subtract the width of the wall top cap from the back overhang run dimension when laying out the rafter.

Following are the steps for framing a shed roof:

Step 1: Determine the Rafter Length   Before you buy lumber for the shed rafters, you need to know the overall rafter length. The procedure for determining the overall length of a rafter is found earlier in this chapter (see Framing a Gabled Roof, Step 1). However, unlike a gable roof, the rafter body length on a shed roof extends from the corner of the lower bird's-mouth to the corner of the upper bird's-mouth. Also, a shed roof doesn't have a ridgeboard, so it isn't necessary to factor the ridgeboard thickness into the arithmetic.

A rafter for a shed roof is stepped off in much the same way as a rafter for a gable roof. Before starting, it is helpful to read about the step-off method for gable roof layout described in Step 1 under framing a Gabled Roof. The example shown in Illus. 4-38 is based on a shed with a 3-in-12-inch slope, an 8-foot span, a 7-foot, 8½-inch run, and a 1-foot overhang for each end.

The first rafter serves as a template for the remaining rafters, so select straight stock and use care laying it out. Begin at the upper end of the rafter. Place the framing square on the stock and align the 3-inch mark (on the tongue leg) and 12-inch mark (on the blade leg) along the top edge of the rafter. Then use a pencil to scribe a line along the tongue of the square. This line represents the top end of the rafter.

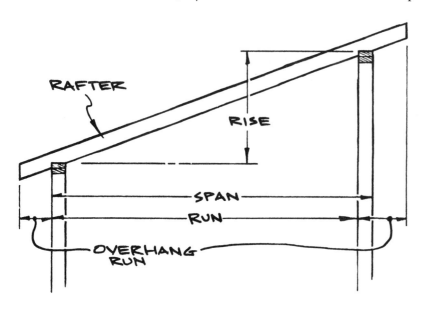

Illus. 4-37. A shed roof differs somewhat in construction from a gable roof.

Also, mark the point where the blade meets the edge of the rafter at the 12-inch mark.

Next, move the framing square 1 foot to the right and align the 3-inch mark (on the tongue leg) with the pencil mark just made. Also, align the 12-inch mark (on the blade leg) with the top edge of the rafter. Measure and mark a point 3½ inches from the outside corner of the rafter square. From the marked point, extend a vertical line to the bottom edge of the rafter. This line represents the inside edge of the wall top cap.

Next, move the framing square 12 inches to the right and once again align the 3- and 12-inch marks on the square with the top edge of the rafter. Mark the point where the blade meets the rafter at the 12-inch point. Continue this procedure until you have completed a "step-off" for each foot of run. After marking the final foot of run, scribe a line to the bottom edge of the rafter. This line represents the outside edge of the wall top cap.

Now, make one final step-off to mark the 12-inch overhang. Scribe a line at this point to establish the bottom end of the rafter. Finally, turn over the framing square and scribe a horizontal line equal to the width of the cap plate (about 3½ inches). The intersection of the horizontal line and the vertical cap plate line creates the location of the bird's-mouth. Do the same at the top of the rafter to lay out the upper bird's-mouth.

Step 2: Cut the First Rafter Carefully cut the rafter at the marked lines. Six cuts are needed, one at each end and a pair at each bird's-mouth. Mark the rafter with the word "template."

Step 3: Test-fit the Rafter Before cutting the remaining rafters, test the template rafter to make certain it fits well on the front and back wall top caps. Check to make sure each bird's-mouth fits properly and also that the front and back overhangs are correct. Make adjustments as required and, if necessary, cut a new template.

Step 4: Cut the Remaining Rafters Use the template to lay out all the remaining rafters and cut out each one. When laying out the rafters, make sure that their bowed edges face upward. The weight of the roofing materials, which are added later, will tend to straighten the bow.

Step 5: Mark Rafter Locations on the Cap Plates Refer to Step 4 (and Illus. 4-32) in Framing a Gabled Roof for details on how to

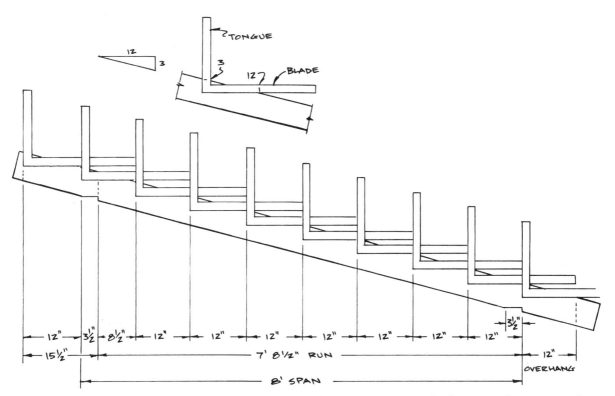

Illus. 4-38. The step-off method used on a shed roof with a 3-in-12-inch slope, a 7-foot, 8½-inch run, and a 1-foot overhang for each end.

mark the rafter locations on the front and back wall cap plates.

Step 6: Assemble the Rafters   Starting at one end of the structure, toenail the rafters in place at the bird's-mouth. Use three 16d common nails, two on one side of the rafter and one on the other side.

Step 7: Install the Fascia Board and Gable Studs   Refer to steps 10 and 13 (and Illus. 4-35) in Framing a Gabled Roof for details on how to add the fascia board and gable studs.

ADDING THE ROOF SHEATHING

The roof sheathing increases the strength and rigidity of the roof frame and provides a surface for attaching the roofing materials that follow. Various types of sheathing are available, but our discussion here is limited to two common types: plywood sheathing and spaced wood sheathing. Although the step-by-step procedures that follow are based on gable roofs, the same basic procedure applies to shed roofs.

Plywood Sheathing

Plywood is an excellent material to use for roof sheathing. It is sold in various thicknesses in 4 × 8-foot panels. See Chapter 1 for more information about plywood.

Plywood installs quickly, holds nails effectively, and adds considerable rigidity to the roof. Also, because of its cross-grain construction, plywood changes little in length and width as the relative humidity changes.

Select plywood that is sold specifically for use as roof sheathing. Check your plans to determine the specified thickness. The proper thickness depends upon the rafter spacing and the type of roofing material to be used. As a general rule, ½-inch-thick sheathing is acceptable for a 16- or 24-inch rafter spacing when asphalt or wood shingles are used. The grain of the plywood should run perpendicular to the rafters.

Following are the steps for installing plywood sheathing on a roof:

Step 1: Install the First Panel   Starting at a lower corner of the roof, position a 4 × 8 sheet of plywood so that one end is flush with the face of the outside rafter and the other end is centered on an intermediate rafter (Illus. 4-39). If the roof has a gable overhang, the plywood must be cut shorter, as needed, so that the end is centered on a rafter. The lower edge of the plywood

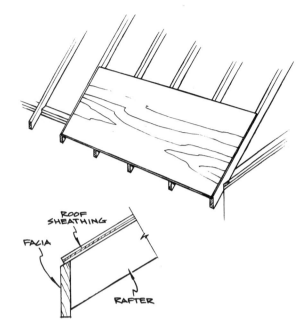

Illus. 4-39. When installing panels on a roof, position a 4×8-inch sheet of plywood so that one end is flush with the face of the outside rafter and its other end is centered on an intermediate rafter.

should be flush with the front face of the fascia board.

Attach the plywood with 8d common nails. Space the nails 6 inches apart along all edges and 12 inches apart along the intermediate rafters. Before driving the nails, make sure the panel is square.

It's a good idea to scribe lines across the width of the plywood, spacing the lines 24 inches on-center (some sheathing comes with the lines already marked). The lines make it considerably easier to locate the center of the intermediate rafters as you drive the nails.

Step 2: Add the First Course   The first course of plywood panels (also called the first row) is next. Continue adding plywood panels across the roof, allowing a space of ⅛ inch between the ends unless otherwise specified by the plywood manufacturer. Make sure that the plywood ends are centered on an intermediate rafter. Trim the last panel flush with the outside rafter.

Step 3: Add the Second Course   To provide maximum strength, the joints should be staggered, so you have to start the second course with a half sheet (4 × 4 feet) of plywood. Allow ⅛ inch between the edges unless otherwise specified by the manufacturer.

Small outdoor structures usually require only

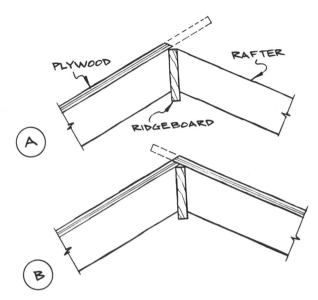

Illus. 4-40. A: Adding the second course of plywood sheathing. B: Completing the second side of the roof.

two courses on each side of the roof. Secure the second course, allowing it to overhang the ridgeboard. Snap a chalk line, and then use the circular saw to trim the plywood flush with the opposite-side rafters (Illus. 4-40A). If you plan on using a ridge vent, trim the plywood 1 to 2 inches short of the ridgeboard (Illus. 4-41).

Step 4: Complete the Remaining Side Repeat steps 1 through 3 to finish the second side of the roof. Note that the plywood is trimmed flush with the sheathing that was applied to the first side (Illus. 4-40B).

Spaced Wood Sheathing

Spaced wood sheathing is commonly used in conjunction with wood shingles and shakes. It's used because the spacings between the wood allow the shingles to dry more quickly. Also, spaced wood sheathing is often more economi-

cal than other sheathing materials (Illus. 4-42).

Both 1 × 4 and 1 × 6 boards can be used for spaced wood sheathing. The board size, and also the spacing between each board, is determined by the type of wood roofing material (shingle or shake) and the required exposure. Check your project plans for the specifics. The step-by-step information that follows is based on using 1 × 4 sheathing stock for 18-inch-long wood shingles spaced 5½ inches to the weather.

Step 1: Add the First Course Starting at a lower corner of the roof, position a 1 × 4 board so that one end is flush with the face of the outside rafter and the other end is centered on an intermediate rafter. If necessary, cut the board shorter in order for the end to be centered on a rafter. The lower edge of the board should be flush with the front face of the fascia board (see Illus. 4-39). Secure the board by driving in a pair of 8d common nails at each rafter.

Continue adding boards along this first course, trimming the last board flush with the outside rafter. Depending upon the length of your stock, a small project might only require one or two boards to complete the first course.

Step 2: Edge-Butt Several Courses The first few courses must butt edge-to-edge in order to cover both the overhang and the first 12 to 18 inches inside the wall line. Add these courses, as needed, to provide the necessary coverage. Stagger the boards across the roof to avoid having any end joints that meet on adjacent boards.

Step 3: Add the Spaced Sheathing The first spaced sheathing board must be positioned to ensure that the roof shingle nails are going to be driven along its centerline when the shingles are attached. (Chapter 5 discusses nail spacing for wood shingles.) The remaining courses are spaced 5½ inches apart to match the exposure of the wood shingles in our example (Illus. 4-

Illus. 4-41. If you want to use a ridge vent, trim the plywood 1 or 2 inches short of the ridgeboard.

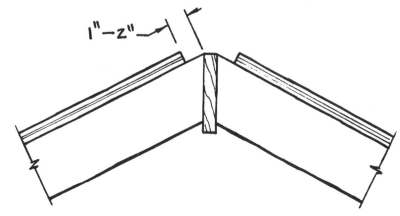

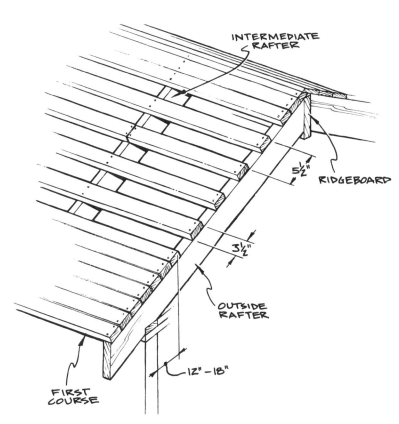

Illus. 4-42. Installing spaced wood sheathing on a roof.

42). Keep in mind that the recommended exposure can vary depending upon the pitch of the roof, the length of the shingles, and the shingle grade. It's a good idea to snap chalk lines across the roof to help keep the courses of spaced sheathing properly aligned.

Step 4: Edge-Butt the Top Courses The top two or three courses are butted together. Allow the final course to overhang the ridgeboard.

Snap a chalk line, and then use the circular saw to trim the final course flush with the opposite-side rafters.

Step 5: Complete the Remaining Side Repeat steps 1 through 4 to finish the second side of the roof. Referring to Illus. 4-42, note that the final course is trimmed flush with the sheathing applied earlier to the first side.

Chapter 5. Roofing

A well-constructed roof made from good-quality materials can protect your backyard project and its contents for years to come. Various kinds of roofing materials are used on backyard structures. They include asphalt shingle, asphalt roll roofing, wood shingle, wood shake, and tin. This chapter shows you how to apply two of the most common types: three-tab asphalt shingles and wood shingles.

Almost everyone agrees that a wood-shingled roof looks better than one with asphalt shingles. It's not that asphalt shingles are unsightly, it's just that the warmth and character of a natural material like wood can't be matched by a man-made product like asphalt. Aesthetics, however, come at a price. Wood shingles are more costly than those made of asphalt—and they take longer to install. If you want your project to have a special look to it, then wood shingles are the way to go. But if you only want the roof to protect the contents of your shed, save your money and install asphalt shingles.

Because wood shingles offer less resistance to fire, some building codes prohibit their use. You can purchase wood shingles impregnated with special fire-retardants, but that's no guarantee that the shingles are going to meet code. Before buying wood shingles, make sure they are permitted in your area.

To prevent falls, always use great care when working on a roof. A fall—even from the roof of a small project—can be very dangerous. Sturdy scaffolding makes the job safer and easier. Unsecured roofing felt can easily slip from under your feet, so don't walk on the felt until it has been firmly stapled to the sheathing. When using a ladder, don't try to reach farther than the length of your arm. If the pitch of the roof is too steep to allow you to walk comfortably, add roof brackets (sometimes called jacks) and wood planks as needed. Most tool rental stores have roof brackets available.

Roofing shingles are sold by the *square*. A square contains the amount of roofing shingles needed to cover 100 square feet of roof. To find out how many squares are required for your project, determine the total roof area and divide by 100; then add 10 percent to allow for cutting waste and starter courses.

The term *exposure* is used throughout this chapter, so we should define it before going on. The exposure is simply the distance between adjacent courses of shingles (Illus. 5-1). To put it another way, it's the amount of shingle that's exposed to the weather. The proper exposure varies depending upon the type of roofing material and the slope of the roof. As a general rule, flatter roofs require less exposure.

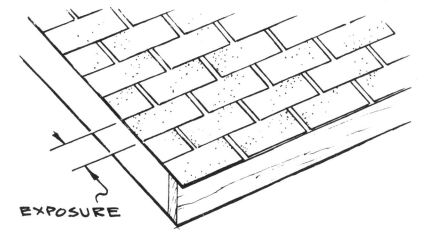

Illus. 5-1. Exposure is the distance between adjacent courses of shingles.

EXPOSURE

APPLYING ASPHALT SHINGLES

Asphalt shingles are available in many styles, colors, sizes, and weights. Most are made from wood and rag-fiber felt impregnated with asphalt and coated with fine granules. Of the various options, a three-tab shingle is a good choice for most small projects. Your local lumberyard or building supply center can suggest a suitable one to use.

The typical three-tab asphalt shingle (sometimes called a *strip*) measures 12 inches wide and 36 inches long (Illus. 5-2), although there might be some slight variation in both width and length. A pair of 5-inch-deep slots (sometimes called *keys*) divide the strip into three 12-inch-square sections called *tabs*.

Most three-tab asphalt shingle strips are self-sealing, which means they have long dabs of adhesive located above the ends of their slots. When the shingles are installed, the sun's heat softens the adhesive and bonds the overlapping shingles. Once bonded, the shingles are less likely to be lifted and damaged by strong winds, or to curl from exposure to the hot sun.

Three-tab shingles can be applied in different patterns. Each pattern gives a somewhat different look to the roof. The *centered pattern* is the most common, and the easiest to apply. The step-by-step instructions that follow are based on using the centered pattern.

It's important to use the correct nail when installing asphalt shingles, so be sure to follow the manufacturer's instructions. Most manufacturers suggest an 11- or 12-gauge galvanized steel nail with a ⅜- or ⁷⁄₁₆-inch-diameter head and a barbed shank. The nail should be long enough to penetrate almost completely through the sheathing. For most asphalt roofs, a 1¼- or 1½-inch-long nail will do the job.

When nailing, be sure to drive each nail straight into the shingle. The head of an angled nail could cut through the shingle, creating an area for water to penetrate. Also, for the same reason, avoid driving the nail below the surface of the shingle. Instead, drive the nail until it is just flush with the shingle surface.

Asphalt shingles can be cut with a sharp utility knife. Generally, it isn't necessary to cut all the way through the shingle. Instead, make a couple of passes to create a shallow cut, and then flex the shingle to break it off at the cut. Tin snips can also do the job effectively.

A layer of underlayment provides additional protection to the roof sheathing should wind-driven rain or snow find its way under the shingles. Also, underlayment protects the exposed sheathing from moisture while you are applying the shingles—something that can be important if you get started and then find yourself unavoidably delayed for several days, or longer. However, the underlayment is not a substitute for a roofing material, so try to get the shingles installed promptly.

Generally, 15-pound roofer's felt (also called *roofing paper* or *tar paper*) is used as an underlayment, but other acceptable products might be available in your area. You'll find that 15-pound roofer's felt comes in 36-inch-wide rolls. A roll covers about four squares, more than enough to take care of a small project. A sharp utility knife does a good job of cutting roofing felt.

Step 1: Add the First Run of Underlayment Trim away the folded end of the roll and then place the roll on a lower corner of the roof. Allow the end of the felt to overhang the end of the roof by an inch or two. The lower edge of the felt should overhang the eaves by ⅜ inch.

Using a heavy-duty staple gun equipped with

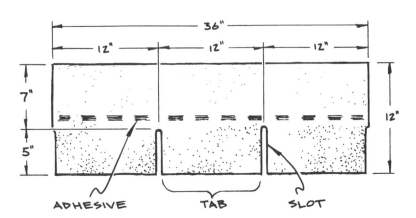

Illus. 5-2. A typical three-tab asphalt shingle.

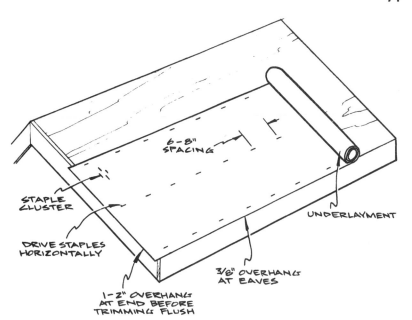

Illus. 5-3. Adding the first run of underlayment.

⅜- or ½-inch staples, drive four or five staples in a small cluster at the upper corner of the felt. Unroll 8 to 10 feet of felt; then pull the felt tightly to smooth out any wrinkles, and adjust it as needed to maintain the ⅜-inch overhang at the eaves. You'll find that the cluster of staples acts as a pivot point, making the adjustment easier.

Once everything looks okay, staple across the top, center, and bottom of the felt, spacing the nails 6 to 8 inches apart. For maximum strength, drive the staples horizontally. Never walk on felt unless it has been adequately stapled, because the felt can easily slip from under your feet. After the entire piece has been stapled, trim the ends of the felt flush with each end of the roof. When trimming the ends, keep in mind that you probably are going to have to allow extra material for any sheathing, siding, or trim that will be added later (Illus. 5-3).

Step 2: Add the Remaining Underlayment
Add the remaining runs of felt using the procedure explained in Step 1 (Illus. 5-4). Each new run must overlap the previous run by at least 2 inches. Any short lengths of felt require at least a 4-inch overlap. If the shed has a gable roof, trim the last run of felt so that it overhangs the ridge by 6 inches, and then staple the overhang to the other side of the roof.

Once the first side of a gable roof is completed, repeat steps 1 and 2 to complete the other side. If you have a shed roof, trim the last run so that it overhangs the edge of the sheathing by ⅜ of an inch.

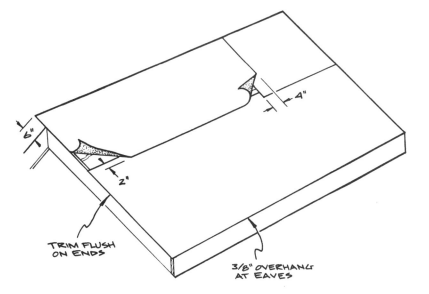

Illus. 5-4. Adding the remaining runs of felt on the roof.

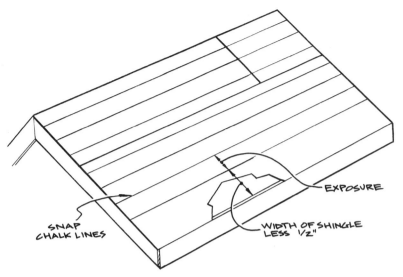

Illus. 5-5. Parallel, horizontal chalk lines can be used to ensure that the shingles remain properly aligned during installation.

Step 3: Snap Horizontal Chalk Lines A series of parallel horizontal lines can help ensure that the shingles remain properly aligned during the installation (Illus. 5-5). To locate the first line, measure the shingle width and then subtract ½ inch (the ½-inch dimension represents the shingle overhang at the eaves). Now, measuring from the eaves, mark this dimension at each end of the roof and snap a line.

Next, from the marked line measure the exposure (as recommended by the shingle manufacturer) and snap another line. Continue snapping additional exposure lines until you reach the ridge.

Before adding too many lines, it's a good idea to measure from the ridge to one of the exposure lines. Take the measurement at each end of the roof. The dimensions should be equal. If they are unequal, a bit of adjustment is required. As you snap each new line, reduce the space on the short side of the roof, as needed, to get the top exposure line parallel to the ridge.

Step 4: Install the Starter Course The starter course serves as a base for the first course of shingles. Also, the starter course covers the roof sheathing that would otherwise be exposed under each of the slots in the first course.

You can buy special shingles to use for the starter course, but most carpenters simply invert three-tab shingles so that their slots face up rather than down (Illus. 5-6). You'll need to trim about four inches from the first starter shingle in order to offset the ends of the starter course shingles from the ends of the first course shingles. Align this shortened shingle with the first horizontal line to establish the ½-inch overhang at the eaves. Then, position the shingle so that it overhangs the end of the roof by ½ inch, plus the thickness of any sheathing, siding, or trim that is to be added later.

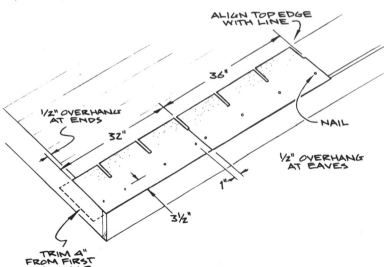

Illus. 5-6. Installing the starter course. The starter course serves as a base for the first course of shingles. Three-tab shingles can be used for the starter course.

Text Continues on Page 81

With almost 200 square feet of floor space, this handsome pole barn has plenty of storage capacity. See Chapter 9 for information on how to build the pole barn.

Below: A side view of the pole barn.

Right: A pair of wide doors provides easy access for a lawn tractor, a snowmobile, or even a small boat.

Left: Looking up at the vent along the eaves.

To keep out small animals and provide ventilation, hardware cloth is extended from the bottom of the pole barn to below the ground.

The wall framing provides a convenient place to store yard tools.

A look at the metal hangers used to fasten the roof joists to the top plate of the wall.

An inside view of the roof framing.

The woodshed accepts 16-to-18-inch lengths of firewood. When filled, it holds about one-third of a cord of wood. See Chapter 10 for information on how to build this woodshed.

With a frame made from 2x4 and 4x4 pressure-treated lumber, the shed can be expected to provide many years of service.

The woodshed's open sides provide plenty of air circulation and exposure to sunshine.

Cedar shingles add to the rustic appearance of the shed.

Firewood can be stacked from both sides.

Latticework adds an interesting look to the garbage house. It also allows for ventilation, while making it easy to wash down the shed with a garden hose. See Chapter 11 for information on building the garbage house.

The front doors and lid allow easy access to the shed from both the front and the top.

A side view of the project.

The interior end can be finished all in one color with a lot less work.

The doors when viewed from the inside have the same appearance.

The floor before hardware cloth is added to the interior.

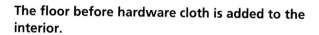

This pool or patio shed has a tiled countertop and backsplash, a feature that can be put to good use during outdoor parties. See Chapter 12 for information on how to build the pool or patio shed.

The shed is perfect for storing all sorts of pool and patio items.

Use four nails to secure the shingle in place, locating them about 3½ inches from the lower edge as shown. You don't want these nails to be exposed, so avoid locating them in the area that will be under the shingle slots when the first course is added.

The remaining starter course shingles are used full-size—no trimming required—until you reach the end of the roof. Butt the second starter shingle to the first one, aligning the top edge of the shingle to the horizontal line. Secure the shingle with four nails as shown. Repeat this procedure across the roof. Trim the last starter shingle so that it has the same overhang as the first starter shingle.

Step 5: Install the First Course The first shingle should be flush with the bottom and end edges of the starter course. Use four nails to secure the shingle in place, locating the nails as shown unless recommended otherwise by the shingle manufacturer (Illus. 5-7). Continue working across the roof, butting each new shin-

gle to the previous one and nailing the new shingle in place. Trim the last one so it is flush with the end of the starter course shingle.

Step 6: Add the Remaining Courses As mentioned earlier, the instructions in this section are based on installing the shingles with a centered pattern layout, the most common roofing pattern (Illus. 5-8). A centered-pattern roof can be easily recognized because the slots are centered on the tabs.

To create a centered-pattern roof, trim the first shingle in the second course by 6 inches (one-half of a tab). This shortened shingle is installed so that it is flush with the end of the first course and aligned with the horizontal exposure line. The remainder of the course is completed with full-length shingles. Trim the last shingle in the second course flush with the last shingle in the first course.

Each new course is applied in the same way; trim the first shingle in the course. The trimming pattern for a center-pattern roof is:

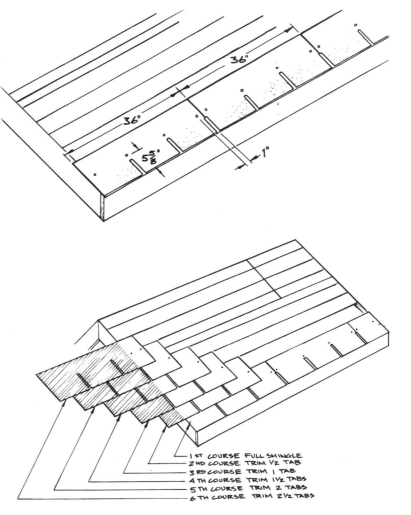

Illus. 5-7. When installing the first course, use four nails to secure each shingle in place.

36"

36"

$5\frac{5}{8}$"

1"

Illus. 5-8. A centered-pattern layout.

1ST COURSE FULL SHINGLE
2ND COURSE TRIM ½ TAB
3RD COURSE TRIM 1 TAB
4TH COURSE TRIM 1½ TABS
5TH COURSE TRIM 2 TABS
6TH COURSE TRIM 2½ TABS

82

Course	Amount Trimmed from First Shingle
First	No trim (full shingle)
Second	6 inches (one-half tab)
Third	12 inches (one tab)
Fourth	18 inches (one and one-half tabs)
Fifth	24 inches (two tabs)
Sixth	30 inches (two and one-half tabs)
Seventh	No trim (full shingle)
Eighth	6 inches (one-half tab)
Ninth	12 inches (one tab)
Tenth	18 inches (one and one-half tabs)

Note that the pattern repeats itself after six courses. Continue following this trimming pattern, adding courses until you reach the ridge. As you work along, check to make sure that the shingle slots are aligning vertically from the bottom of the roof to the top. Keep them aligned by adjusting the spacing between the shingles. The top course is trimmed flush with the ridge.

Step 7: Add the Ridge Cap You can buy shingles specially made to be used as ridge caps, but for a small project it generally makes more sense to make them yourself. Cutting the shingles as shown in Illus. 5-9 produces three 9 × 12-inch ridge caps. Tapering the cuts hides the edges when the ridge-cap shingles are installed.

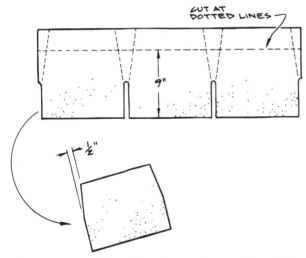

Illus. 5-9. Cutting shingles to be used as ridge caps.

Bend the first ridge-cap shingle at its center and secure each side of the bend with a single nail (Illus. 5-10). It should overhang the end of the roof the same amount as the other shingles. If the weather is cold, warm the shingle a bit before making the bend; otherwise, it's likely to crack. Add the succeeding shingles as shown in Illus. 5-10, overlapping them to create a 5-inch

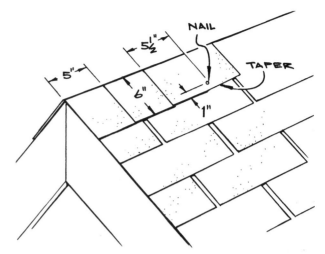

Illus. 5-10. To install a ridge-cap shingle, bend it at its center and secure each side of the bend with a single nail.

exposure. To help keep the shingles aligned, snap a line 6 inches from the ridge on each side of the roof.

APPLYING WOOD SHINGLES

Most wood shingles are made from either cedar or redwood. Both these woods provide an attractive appearance and offer good resistance to decay. Several grades of wood shingle are available.

Wood shingles are sold in standard lengths of 16, 18, and 24 inches. Their widths are random. The shingles taper in thickness. At their thickest end (called the *butt end*), they measure about ½ inch.

Each shingle is secured to the roof sheathing with a pair of galvanized nails. For 16- and 18-inch-long shingles, use 3d nails; for 24-inch-long shingles, use 4d nails. The nails should be driven flush with the surface of the shingle. Avoid driving the nails below the surface, as that could damage the wood or cause the shingle to crack. The nail spacing is detailed in the step-by step instructions that follow.

The correct exposure for wooden shingles depends upon the grade of the shingle, the shingle length, and the pitch of the roof. The recommended exposures for No. 1, No. 2, and No. 3 grade cedar shingles is shown in Table 5-1.

Wood shingles are usually applied over spaced wood sheathing. Before starting, make sure the sheathing has been properly installed and spaced as discussed in Chapter 4.

MAXIMUM RECOMMENDED EXPOSURE FOR CEDAR SHINGLE ROOFS

Roof Slope	Length								
	No. 1 Grade			No. 2 Grade			No. 3 Grade		
	16″	18″	24″	16″	18″	24″	16″	18″	24″
3 in 12 to 4 in 12	3¾	4¼	5¾	3½	4	5½	3	3½	5
4 in 12 & steeper	5	5½	7½	4	4½	6½	3½	4	5½

Table 5-1. The maximum recommended exposure for cedar shingle roofs.

Following are the steps for applying wood shingles:

Step 1: Install the Starter Course Wood shingles require a double course of shingles at the eaves. The double course consists of the starter course on the bottom, followed by the first course directly on top.

Position the first shingle of the starter course so that it overhangs the roof ends by 1 inch, plus the thickness of any sheathing, siding, or trim that is to be added later. Also, the first shingle should overhang the roof eaves by 1½ inches. Secure the shingle in place by driving two nails about 4 inches from the butt end of the shingle. To account for the overhang at the roof end, the first nail is located where it can penetrate into the roof sheathing from the shingle edge. All other nails are located ¾ to 1 inch from the edges of the shingles (Illus. 5-11).

Now, nail the second shingle next to the first one, allowing ¼ to ⅜ inch of space between them. This space, called a *shingle joint*, is important because it allows room for the shingles to expand when they get wet. Continue adding shingles across the roof until you reach the other end. Trim the last shingle so that the overhang equals that of the first shingle.

Step 2: Install the First Course The first shingle of the first course is located flush with the butt end and the outside edge of the first starter course. The width of the shingle should be such that it overlaps the starter-course joint by at least 1½ inches. For this course, and all remaining courses, the nails are located from the butt end an amount equal to the recommended shingle exposure plus 1 to 2 inches (Illus. 5-12). Continue adding shingles until the first course is complete, always making sure the shingle edges overlap the joints in the previous course by a minimum of 1½ inches.

Step 3: Add the Remaining Courses Snap a line to establish the exposure line of the next course. Each new course is added in the same way as the first. As you work along, be sure to remember the following: use two nails per shingle, not more; space all shingle joints between ¼ and ⅜ inch; and always allow joints of adjacent courses to overlap a minimum of 1½ inches. Also, the joints on alternate courses should not be aligned (Illus. 5-13).

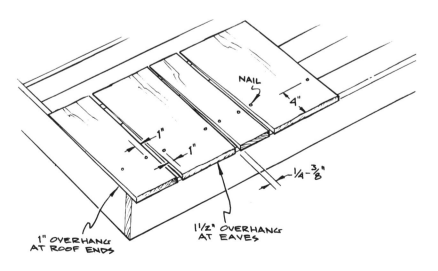

Illus. 5-11. Installing the starter course of wood shingles.

To make sure the courses remain parallel to the ridge, it's a good idea to occasionally measure from the ridge to an exposure line. To do this, take the measurement at each end of the roof. The dimensions should be equal. Unequal measurements means the ridge isn't parallel to the eaves, so a bit of adjustment is required. As you snap each new line, reduce the space on the short side of the roof slightly. After making several small adjustments at each course, you should be able to end up with the final course exactly parallel to the ridge.

As the shingle courses near the top of the roof, the addition of a couple of layers of roofing felt will serve to minimize the possibility of leaks at the ridge line (Illus. 5-14). After adding the last course of full-length shingles, lay a length of 24-inch-wide roofing underlayment across the length of the ridge. (For more information on underlayment, see Applying Asphalt Shingles.) Fold the underlayment down the middle so that 12 inches lie on each side of the roof. Trim the underlayment flush with the end of the roof on each end.

Now, add the next course of shingles and then trim the overhang flush with the ridge using a handsaw or electric saber saw. Lay a length of 12-inch-wide underlayment across the length of the ridge, folding the felt so that 6 inches hangs down on each side of the roof. Next, apply the final course of shingles, again trimming them flush at the ridge.

Step 4: Add the Ridge Cap Shingles are often used to make the ridge cap when a roof is added to a house, but it can be a time-consuming job. For a small project, it's faster and easier to simply use a couple of lengths of 1 × 4 cedar stock (Illus. 5-15). A hand plane or table saw can be used to bevel the stock's edges to match the slope of the roof. To create the cap, join the two lengths of stock with galvanized finishing nails.

Attach each leg of the cap to the roof with

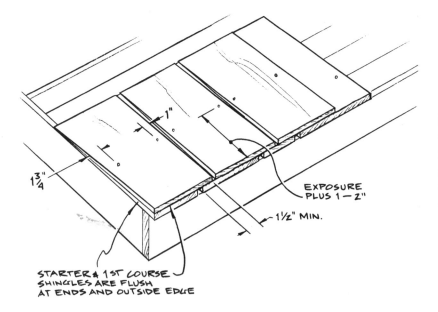

Illus. 5-12. When installing the first and all remaining courses, locate the nails from the butt end an amount equal to the recommended exposure plus 1 to 2 inches.

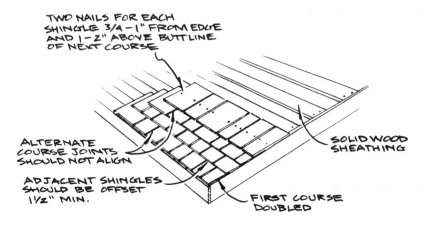

Illus. 5-13. Guidelines for adding the remaining roof shingle courses.

countersunk galvanized nails spaced 10 to 12 inches apart. The nails should be long enough to penetrate at least ⅝ inch into the roof sheathing. If you need two lengths of cap to span the roof, butt the ends tightly together before nailing. To complete the roof, fill the countersunk nail holes, and any butt joints, with a caulking that's compatible with cedar.

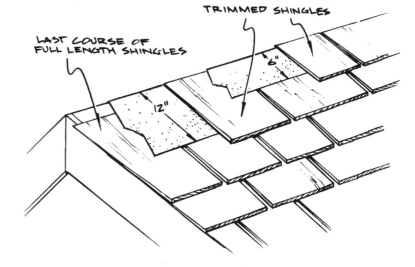

Illus. 5-14. Adding a few layers of roofing felt near the top of the roof while adding shingle courses will minimize leaks at the ridge line.

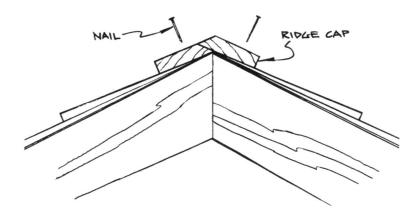

Illus. 5-15. Two lengths of 1 × 4 cedar stock can be used to make the ridge cap on a roof.

Chapter 6. Siding

Siding provides a durable, weatherproof surface for the outside of your project. In addition, siding has considerable impact on its appearance. Indeed, the color and style of the siding you choose is likely to affect the look of your project more than any other component.

This chapter presents some of the many types of siding that are available. Because siding options are so wide and varied, we can't provide installation information for each one of them. Your lumberyard or siding manufacturer can help you with those details. However, we do include installation instructions for two types of siding that are often used on sheds: tongue-and-groove solid-wood siding and plywood siding.

Some types of siding can be applied directly over studs, but for other types you must first install wall sheathing. Plywood is probably the most common sheathing material, but chipboard, particleboard, and spaced wood sheathing are also used.

If sheathing is required, the doors and windows (see Chapter 7) are usually added after the sheathing, but before the siding is installed. When sheathing isn't required, doors and windows are sometimes added after the siding is applied. Often, the options depend upon the type of door, window, and siding that you choose. Before starting to apply the siding, be sure to check with the door, window, and siding manufacturers, or your supplier, for the proper installation procedure.

Vertical, horizontal, and diagonal siding installations are possible, depending upon the type of siding you choose. Diagonal installations, however, tend to direct water towards trim, window casings, door jambs, etc. Before applying diagonal siding, make sure the trim, casings, and jambs are designed to handle the added water.

SIDING OPTIONS

A wide variety of siding options are available. They include solid wood, plywood panels, wood shingles, wood shakes, hardboard, aluminum, and vinyl. Each is described below. When properly applied, all of them offer excellent weather protection, so the best choice is often dictated by appearance and how much money you want to spend.

SOLID-WOOD SIDING

Solid-wood siding is available in a wide range of sizes and styles. Some of the popular options are shown in Illus. 6-1. Various wood species are used to make siding. They include cedar, cypress, redwood, pine, poplar, hemlock, and spruce, among others. Also, you have a choice of three siding surfaces: smooth, rough, or saw-textured.

PLYWOOD SIDING

Plywood siding, available in 4 × 8-foot, 4 × 9-foot, and 4 × 10-foot panels, produces a strong, rigid wall. Plywood lap siding is also an option. Several surface textures and patterns are available. A few of them are shown in Illus. 6-2. For more information on plywood siding, contact APA–the Engineered Wood Association, 7011 South 19th Street, P.O. Box 11700, Tacoma, Washington 98411-0700, or your local lumberyard.

WOOD SHINGLES AND SHAKES

Wood shingles and shakes, made from cedar or redwood, create an attractive siding. Shingles and shakes must be nailed to plywood or spaced wood sheathing. The sheathing is first covered

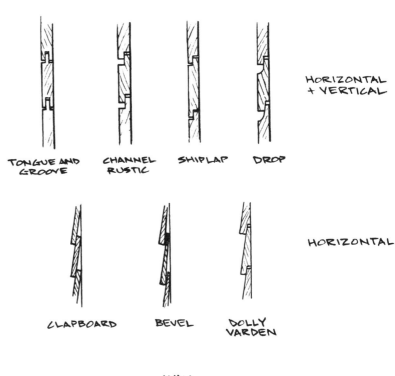

HORIZONTAL
+ VERTICAL

TONGUE AND GROOVE   CHANNEL RUSTIC   SHIPLAP   DROP

Illus. 6-1. A look at the many types of available wood siding.

HORIZONTAL

CLAPBOARD   BEVEL   DOLLY VARDEN

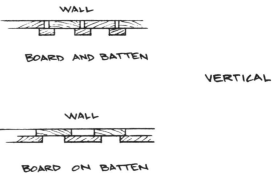

WALL

BOARD AND BATTEN

VERTICAL

WALL

BOARD ON BATTEN

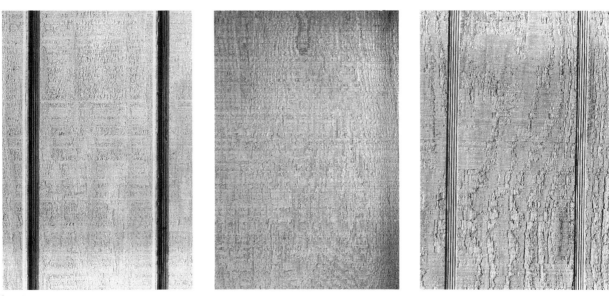

Illus. 6-2. Plywood siding is available in a wide variety of surface textures and patterns. Three examples are shown here. From left to right, they are: texture-, rough-sawn, and channel-groove plywood siding. (Photos courtesy of APA-the Engineered Wood Association.)

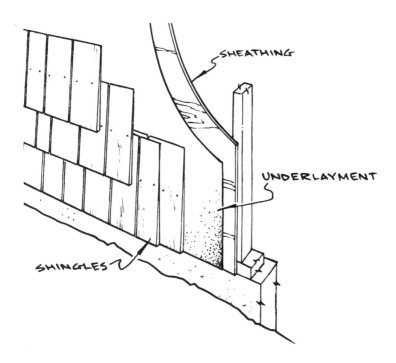

Illus. 6-3. Wood shingles and shakes are an option for siding. They must be nailed to plywood or spaced wood sheathing.

with an underlayment (Illus. 6-3). Cedar shingles are also available in 4 × 8-foot panels. For more information, write to the Cedar Shake and Shingle Bureau, 515 116th Avenue N.E., Suite 275, Bellevue, Washington 98004-5294, or contact your local lumberyard.

HARDBOARD SIDING

Hardboard siding has a hard, durable surface that resists denting and splitting. It is available in 4 × 8-, 4 × 9-, and 4 × 10-foot panels, and also as lap siding. You can choose from a number of surface patterns, most of them manufactured to look like solid-wood siding. Hardboard siding must be applied over sheathing, and the sheathing must be covered with an underlayment.

ALUMINUM AND VINYL SIDING

Aluminum and vinyl siding share many similarities, although they are two different products. Both offer low maintenance costs. Sheathing is required before adding either aluminum or vinyl siding. Installation instructions can vary a bit from one manufacturer to another, so study them carefully before starting.

APPLYING PLYWOOD SIDING

As a general rule, plywood siding should be at least ⅜ inch thick for 16-inch stud spacing, and at least ⅝ inch thick for 24-inch stud spacing. To provide adequate nailing surfaces, all edges of the plywood panel must backed by framing or blocking. There's no need to install wall sheathing when plywood siding is used—an advantage that saves considerable time and expense.

Plywood panels can be installed either vertically or horizontally. If you use a grooved plywood siding, and it is installed horizontally, an underlayment (usually 15-pound roofing felt) is required. When plywood siding (of any type) is installed vertically, an underlayment is not needed if the plywood joints are either caulked or covered with battens.

When shopping, be sure to purchase plywood that has been manufactured for use as exterior siding. Plywood made to use as siding is bonded with waterproof glue that can withstand moisture, and that's important for exterior applications.

The edges of the panel should be sealed before installation. Use primer if the panels are to be painted. For panels that are to be stained, apply a water-repellent preservative that is compatible with the finish.

Plywood panels are somewhat heavy and awkward to handle, so it's important to have a helper. You'll find that the extra pair of hands (and shoulders) make the job considerably safer and easier.

Most plywood panels are installed vertically, so the step-by-step instructions that follow are based on that configuration. In the procedures described, the door and window have not yet been installed. They are added after the siding has been applied.

Here are the procedures for applying plywood siding:

Step 1: Apply the First Panel Starting at a corner of the shed, place the first panel in position (Illus. 6-4). The bottom end of the panel should be an inch or so below the floor framing and at least 3 inches above ground level. (Plywood siding manufacturers usually specify that the bottom edge should be a minimum of 6 inches aboveground. However, that can be difficult to achieve when a project such as a shed must be low to the ground in order to facilitate easy access for a lawn mower, lawn tractor, or other such equipment.)

Depending on the wall height, and your project design, you might first have to trim the top edge of the panel so that it fits flush with the wall top cap or butts against a soffit. Also, it might be necessary to notch the panel to fit around the roof rafters.

As shown, the leading vertical edge of the plywood must be centered on a stud, and it also must be plumb. Check the panel edge with a level and adjust it as needed. Don't worry if the panel isn't perfectly flush at the corner of the wall, because the final trim, added later, will cover any unevenness. Keep in mind that if the first panel isn't plumb, the problem is going to get increasingly worse as additional panels are installed.

You don't want the nails to rust and stain the siding, so use galvanized or stainless steel nails. Use 6d nails for siding that's ½ inch thick or less. For thicker siding, use 8d nails. Space the nails 6 inches apart along all the edges and 12 inches apart along the intermediate studs.

Step 2: Add the Remaining Panels Position the second panel next to the first, with their bottom edges flush. Again, check the vertical edge to ensure the panel is plumb. Before nailing, allow a space of ⅛ inch between the panels, unless otherwise specified by the manufacturer.

Repeat this procedure for all the remaining panels. At the wall corners, cut the panel so that all the panels' edges overlap (Illus. 6-5).

Step 3: Cut Around the Door and Window Openings There's no need to make a lot of precise cuts to fit the panels around rough openings for doors and windows. Instead, install the panels across the openings, nailing the panel to

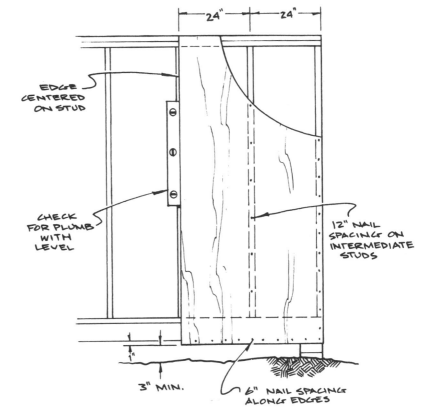

Illus. 6-4. Applying the first panel. Place this panel in position at the corner of the outdoor structure.

EDGE CENTERED ON STUD

CHECK FOR PLUMB WITH LEVEL

24"   24"

12" NAIL SPACING ON INTERMEDIATE STUDS

3" MIN.

6" NAIL SPACING ALONG EDGES

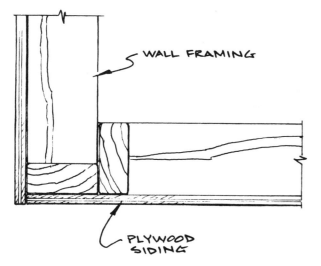

Illus. 6-5. Cut the panel at the wall corners so that all the panel's edges overlap.

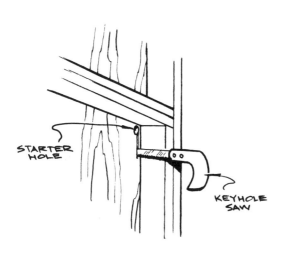

Illus. 6-6. As shown at the top, use a keyhole saw to start the saw cut, and then (as shown on the bottom) finish the cut with a panel saw.

the framing. Then, working from the inside of the project, bore a ¾- to 1-inch-diameter starter hole at one of the corners. Use a keyhole saw to start a saw cut, and then finish the cut with a panel saw. If necessary, use a hand plane to trim the edge flush with the rough opening (Illus. 6-6).

Step 4: Install the Upper Panels (If Required) Sometimes, on tall projects, an upper panel must be added in order to extend the siding to the ridge. In such cases add a strip of Z-flashing (sometimes called *Z-bar*) between the upper and lower panels (Illus. 6-7).

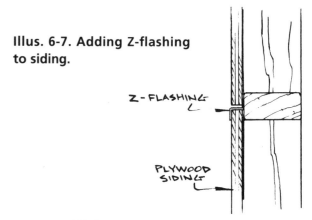

Illus. 6-7. Adding Z-flashing to siding.

Step 5: Add the Battens Battens help prevent water from penetrating the vertical joint between each panel. Battens are usually made from 1 × 2 stock. Secure them with 8d galvanized casing nails, spaced 12 inches on-center. Stagger the nails to minimize chances of splitting the stock (Illus. 6-8).

Step 6: Add the Corner Trim The trim at each corner of the structure is commonly made using 1 × 4 stock. Attach the trim with 8d galvanized casing nails, spacing the nails 12 inches apart (Illus. 6-9).

Also, if the shed has upper panels (see Step 4), install 1 × 4 stock to cover the horizontal joint and the Z-flashing.

APPLYING VERTICAL TONGUE-AND-GROOVE SOLID-WOOD SIDING

Vertical tongue-and-groove boards make an especially attractive outdoor project siding. The siding is made in a variety of patterns, and most lumberyards carry at least a few of them. Several standard widths are available.

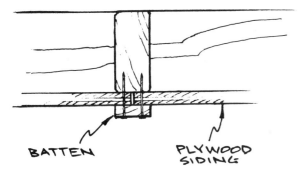

Illus. 6-8. The battens, which prevent water from penetrating the vertical joint between each panel, are secured to the siding with casing nails.

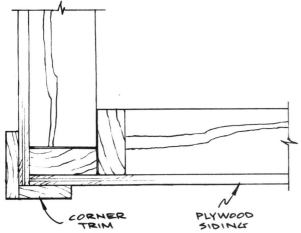

Illus. 6-9. The trim is added to the corner of the structure with casing nails.

When vertical siding is installed without sheathing, add horizontal blocking and space it

a maximum of 24 inches on-center. Also, the ends of the siding must also be fully supported by blocking.

It's a good idea to prefinish tongue-and-groove siding, especially if you plan to paint or stain the siding. Should the boards shrink in width after stain or paint is applied, you are likely to see a narrow line of unfinished wood along each partially exposed tongue. Prefinishing allows you to thoroughly cover all surfaces of the siding—including the tongues.

Galvanized nails offer good rust resistance and are commonly used to attach wood siding. Sometimes, however, when a clear finish is used on red cedar, a stain occurs around galvanized nails. If you prefer to avoid the risk of stain, pay the extra money and use stainless steel nails.

Tongue-and-groove siding that has a nominal width of 6 inches or less is attached by blind-nailing (Illus. 6-10A). When the siding has a nominal width of 8 inches or more it is face-nailed, with the nails spaced 3 to 4 inches apart (Illus. 6-10B). Use finishing or casing nails when blind-nailing, and siding or box nails when face-nailing. To maximize the nails' holding power, use ring-shank or spiral-threaded nails. The nails should penetrate 1½ inches into studs and blocking (1¼ inches for ring-shank nails).

Here are the procedures for applying vertical tongue-and-groove solid-wood siding:

Step 1: Apply the First Board You can begin at any corner of the shed (Illus. 6-11). The first

Illus. 6-10. As shown in A, tongue-and-groove siding with a nominal width of 6 inches or less is blind-nailed to the project. As shown in B, siding with a nominal width of 8 inches or more is face-nailed.

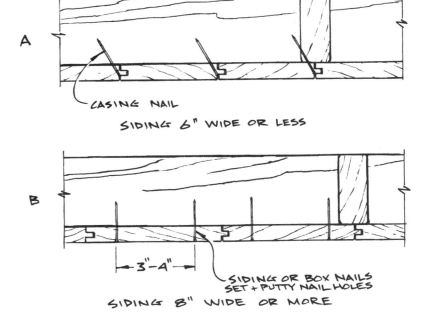

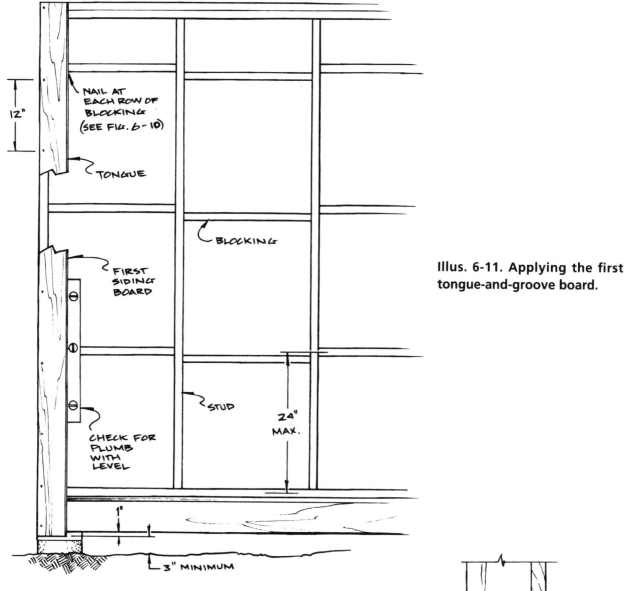

NAIL AT
EACH ROW OF
BLOCKING
(SEE FIG. 6-10)

12"

TONGUE

BLOCKING

FIRST
SIDING
BOARD

STUD

24"
MAX.

CHECK FOR
PLUMB
WITH
LEVEL

1"

3" MINIMUM

Illus. 6-11. Applying the first tongue-and-groove board.

board must have a square edge, so use the table saw or a portable circular saw to trim away the groove.

Position the board so that its bottom edge is an inch or so below the floor frame and at least 3 inches above ground level. Depending on the wall height and your project design, it might be necessary to cut the top edge of the board so that it fits flush with the wall top cap or butts against a soffit. Also, you might have to notch the board to fit around a rafter.

The tongue edge of the board should be plumb, so check it with a level and adjust the board as needed. Don't worry if the board isn't perfectly flush at the corner. The corners are going to be covered later on when the final trim is added.

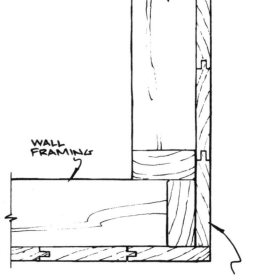

WALL
FRAMING

TONGUE-AND-GROOVE
SIDING

Illus. 6-12. Adding the remaining boards to the tongue-and-groove siding.

Next, secure the edge of the board to the end joist with siding or box nails spaced about 12 inches apart. Then, depending upon the width of the board, complete the attachment by either blind- or face-nailing it to the frame as shown in Illus. 6-10.

Step 2: Add the Remaining Boards
Position the next board, sliding its groove into the tongue on the first board. Make sure the bottom edges of each board are flush. Nail the board in place at the frame members.

Use this same procedure to install all remaining boards. Occasionally check for plumb to make sure the siding remains vertical. When you reach the wall corners, the edges of the boards should overlap (Illus. 6-12).

Step 3: Cut Around the Doors and Windows
Trim and notch the boards as needed to fit around the doors and windows. A saber saw is handy for making notching cuts (Illus. 6-13).

Step 4: Add the Corner Trim
Corner trim can be made from several sizes of stock, but 1 × 4 is a common size. Attach the trim with 8d finishing or casing nails spaced 12 inches apart (Illus. 6-14).

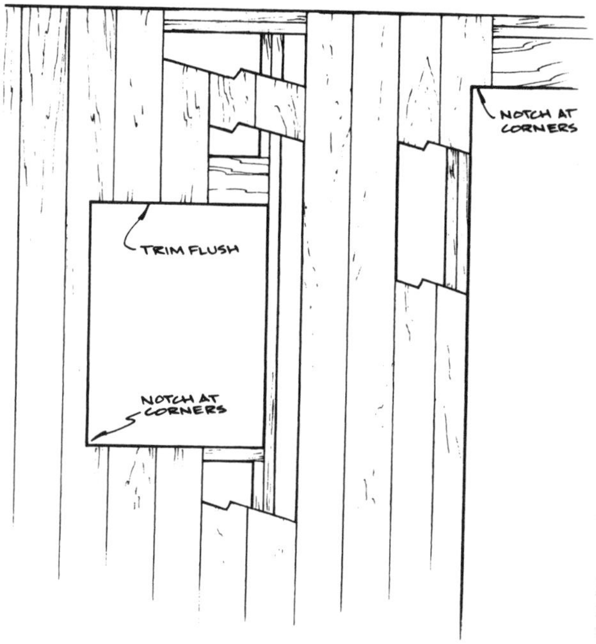

Illus. 6-13. Trim and notch the boards so they fit around the doors and windows.

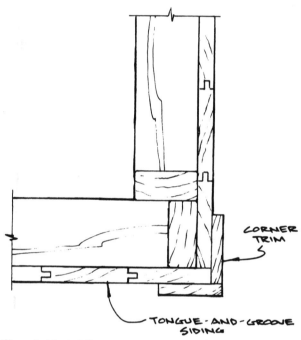

Illus. 6-14. Adding corner trim to the tongue-and-groove siding.

Chapter 7.
Doors and Windows

In this chapter, we explain how to install a prehung door and a basic window. (A prehung door is made up of a door frame with the door already installed.) Any number of commercial door and window options can be used in conjunction with outdoor structures. A visit to your lumberyard and or building supply center can give you a good idea of the many choices that are available. However, should you prefer to make your own, we show you how to build a sturdy board-and-batten door and a simple fixed-pane window.

The rough opening dimensions are based on the size of the door or window you plan to install. That means you must select the door and window sizes before you do the wall framing (see the Wall Framing section in Chapter 4).

When considering door and window sizes, keep in mind how you plan to use the outdoor structure. If it is a shed that is going to house a good-sized lawn tractor, make sure you choose a door wide enough to allow easy access. If you plan to use the structure for potting, woodworking, or other activities, you'll want to think about having several large windows that can provide plenty of natural light.

As mentioned in Chapter 6, when siding is attached directly to the wall framing, the doors and windows are sometimes added after the siding. When the siding is attached to the wall sheathing, the doors and windows are usually added after the sheathing, but before the siding. Before you start to add the siding, it's a good idea to check with the door, window, and siding manufacturers, or your supplier, for the proper installation sequence.

DOORS

Commercial exterior doors are made from wood or metal. A variety of styles are available, many of them appropriate for outdoor struc-

tures. Most exterior doors measure 6 feet, 8 inches high, although other door heights are also sold. You can choose from several door widths.

Exterior doors usually swing in, rather than out. You can order doors with left- or right-hand swings. The swing of the door is determined by viewing the door from the outside. If, when viewed from the outside, the door is hinged on the right side, it has a right-handed swing. Conversely, if it is hinged on the left side, the door has a left-handed swing.

INSTALLING A PREHUNG DOOR

A prehung door is the easiest to install. A typical prehung door assembly consists of head, hinge, and strike jambs (the three parts are collectively called the *jamb*), a *sill*, a *threshold*, and the door, doorstop, and hinges (Illus. 7-1). Sometimes the trim, doorknob, and lock are included.

The step-by-step instructions that follow provide a basic procedure for installing a prehung exterior door. However, depending upon the manufacturer, prehung door installations can vary somewhat. Most manufacturers provide detailed installation instructions, so be sure to read and follow them carefully.

Step 1: Remove the Bottom Plate   Before the door can be added, the bottom plate must be removed at the doorway (Illus. 7-2). Using a panel saw, cut the bottom plate flush with the trimmer studs.

Step 2: Position the Door Assembly   Some prehung doors have protective jamb extensions. If your door has these extensions, trim them off, and then place the door assembly into the door opening.

If your siding is attached directly to the wall framing, the front edge of the jamb should be flush with the siding (Illus. 7-3). If the siding is attached to wall sheathing, the front edge of the

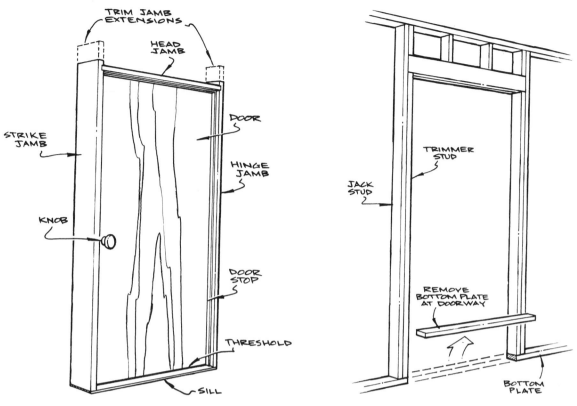

Illus. 7-1. The parts of a prehung door.

Illus. 7-2. The bottom plate must be removed at the doorway.

Illus. 7-3. If you are attaching siding directly to the wall framing, make sure the front edge of the jamb is flush with the siding.

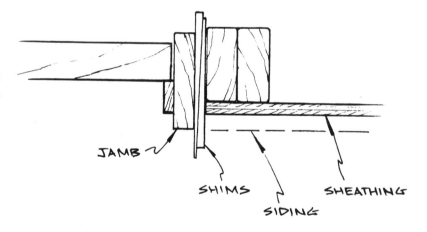

Illus. 7-4. If you are attaching the siding to wall sheathing, the front edge of the jamb should be flush with the face of the siding.

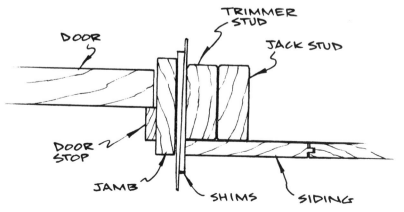

jamb should extend past the sheathing an amount equal to the thickness of the siding. Later, when the siding is added, the front edge of the jamb will be flush with the face of the siding (Illus. 7-4).

Position the door so that it is approximately centered between the two trimmer studs. Remove any shipping bracing, and then check the space between the door and the head jamb. The spacing should be about the same along the entire length. If it isn't, shim under the sill as needed to correct the spacing.

Step 3: Secure the Hinge Jamb Use a carpenter's level to plumb the hinge jamb. Once it is plumb, add shims between the hinge jamb and the trimmer stud at four points (Illus. 7-5). You can purchase shim stock at most lumberyards, or simply use cedar shingles.

Use 10d galvanized finishing or casing nails to secure the jamb, driving the nails at each shim location. At this point, it's best not to drive the

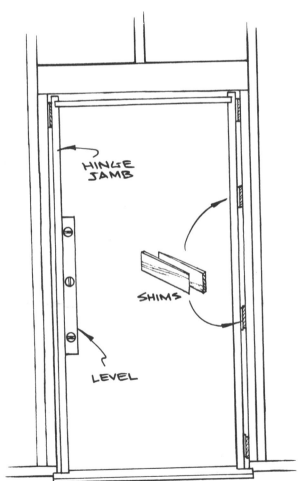

Illus. 7-5. Securing the hinge jamb. Add shims between the hinge jamb and the trimmer stud at four points.

nails all the way home. Instead, allow the nail heads to be slightly exposed so that the nails can be removed if any adjustment needs to be done later on. If the door stops have not been added, or they are removable, nail the jamb in place under the stops. Later, when the door stops are added, they will cover the nails. If you can't nail under the door stops, the exposed nail holes must be puttied.

Once again, check for an even space between the head jamb and the door. If necessary, shim under the sill as needed to correct.

Step 4: Secure the Strike Jamb Plumb the strike jamb with the carpenter's level. Add shims between the strike jamb and the trimmer stud at four points, as you did with the hinge jamb in Step 3. Again, partially drive 10d nails at the four shims.

Step 5: Secure the Head Jamb Add shims at a couple of points along the head jamb. Secure the jamb by driving nails at the shim locations.

Step 6: Attach the Sill It's best to use screws, rather than nails, to attach the sill to the subfloor. If the sill needs to be replaced at some point in the future, screws make it easier to remove.

Step 7: Test the Door Check the door to make sure it opens and closes to your satisfaction. If you find a problem, remove nails as necessary and refit it. Once all looks okay, countersink the nails and fill the holes with wood putty. Use a handsaw to trim the shims flush.

Step 8: Add the Trim Install the door trim (also called the *casing*) using galvanized nails. Countersink each nail and fill the holes with wood putty. If the door does not include a preinstalled lockset and doorknob, you'll need to add them next. Refer to the manufacturer's instructions for installation information.

MAKING YOUR OWN DOOR

The board-and-batten door is a classic door design often used on outdoor structures. It's not difficult to make and usually costs less than a commercial door. The door shown in Illus. 7-6 has the same basic design as the one used on the utility shed in Chapter 8. We used 1 × 6 tongue-and-groove siding for that door and 1 × 4 stock for the battens. The battens are attached to the door with 1¼-inch-long number-10 galvanized wood screws.

Text Continues on Page 105

A gazebo can add both value and charm to your house. See Chapter 13 for information on how to build the gazebo.

An interior view of the upper railing.

The gazebo is a perfect place to spend a warm summer afternoon.

The center of the deck.

An interior view of the roof framing.

The perimeter seating provides an ideal place to sit and chat.

The railing provides decoration.

On the pool deck leading to the gazebo. This simple fence detail is easy to make with flat stock.

The cedar roof is installed over spaced wood sheathing.

The cedar seating follows the interior all the way around.

Each seat support is made up of a pair of 2x4's and a 4x4.

You can always find a shady spot to sit.

Landscaping adds an additional attractive feature to the gazebo.

The stairs leading to the gazebo give it a grand appearance.

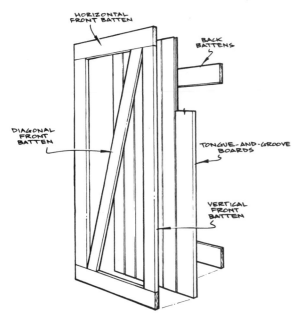

Illus. 7-6. The parts of a board-and-batten door.

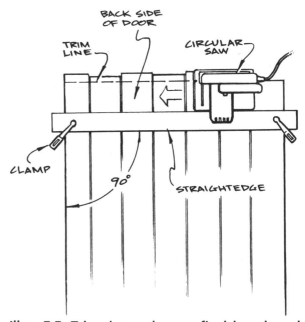

Illus. 7-7. Trimming a door to final length and width.

Following are instructions for making a board-and-batten door:

Step 1: Make the Door Frame Begin by cutting out the bottom plate at the doorway (see Installing a Prehung Door, Step 1). The door jambs, which frame the top and sides of the door, are made from 1 × 4 pine. Measure the length and width of the door's rough opening. Cut the hinge and strike jambs to extend the full height of the rough opening. The overall width of the door frame should be ½ inch less than the rough-opening width. The jamb is installed as detailed in the discussion of prehung doors. If the shed has double doors, each door is going to measure one-half of the door frame width.

Step 2: Cut and Assemble the Tongue-and-Groove Boards Cut the tongue-and-groove boards about 1 inch longer than the measured door-frame length. Then, assemble the boards, adding enough of them to provide more than the needed door width. Using a couple of pipe clamps, apply light clamp pressure to hold the tongue-and-groove boards together. There is no need to glue the tongue-and-groove joints.

Step 3: Add the Back Battens Cut the two back battens to a length that is equal to the width of the door frame opening minus 2 inches. Now, center the battens across the width of the door; then use screws to secure the battens in place. Drive the screws through the battens and into the back of the tongue-and-groove boards. Position the screws so that one is driven into the center of each tongue-and-groove board. When attached, the battens should be about 6 inches from the ends of the door. The pipe clamps can now be removed.

Step 4: Trim the Door Use a circular saw and a straightedge to trim the door to final length and width (Illus. 7-7). Make certain that the cuts are square to each other. When trimming the width, remove the same amount from each edge so that the back battens remain centered on the door.

Step 5: Add the Remaining Battens Cut the vertical and horizontal front battens to length, and then screw them in place. They should be flush with the edges of the door.

Next, cut the diagonal front batten slightly on its long side. Hold it in position on the door and mark the angle on its ends. Trim the ends with the circular saw and then attach the batten with several screws.

Step 6: Hang the Door Hang each door with 3 × 3-inch weather-resistant hinges. When you are satisfied that the doors close properly, the doorstops can be added. To complete the door, install the trim as described in the discussion of prehung doors.

WINDOWS

Outdoor project interiors can be dark and

gloomy unless windows are added to allow in natural daylight. You also enjoy the benefit of additional ventilation if you choose a window that can be opened and closed.

Almost any type of commercial window can be used in a shed. Double-hung, casement, hopper, and horizontal sliding windows are all good choices that are readily available at lumberyards and building supply centers. (A double-hung window is a window that has two sashes that slide up and down. Casement windows open to one side. Hopper windows hinge at the bottom. Horizontal sliding windows slide from side to side.) Commercial windows can be made of wood or metal, and they are sold in any number of sizes.

Most commercial windows are installed by nailing through either the attached casing or through a nailing flange. The following step-by-step instructions provide a basic explanation of how to install a flanged window. Windows usually come with complete installation instructions, so be sure to read and follow them carefully.

Step 1: Add the Side and Bottom Flashing Paper   Cut 15-pound roofers felt to strips about 6 inches wide. Staple one strip along the edge of the rough sill, and a pair of strips along each side (Illus. 7-8).

Step 2: Position the Window   Place the window in the rough opening. Check that it is level with a carpenter's level, adding shims if recommended to do so by the manufacturer (Illus. 7-9).

Illus. 7-9. If the window's manufacturer suggests so, add shims when placing the window in the rough opening.

Illus. 7-8. The first step in installing a flanged window is adding the side and bottom flashing paper. You can use 15-pound roofer's felt for the flashing paper.

Illus. 7-10. Nailing the window to the rough opening by driving common nails through the flange.

Step 3: Nail the Window Once the window is properly positioned, drive a couple of 8d galvanized common nails through the flange. Check to make sure the window opens and closes properly. If all looks okay, staple the top flashing paper over the outside of the flange. Add the remaining nails, spacing them 8 inches apart unless otherwise instructed by the manufacturer (Illus. 7-10).

MAKING A FIXED-PANE WINDOW

Following are step-by-step instructions for making a fixed-pane window:

Step 1: Cut the Frame Parts A simple fixed-pane window is easy and inexpensive to make. The window frame is made up of two side jambs, a head jamb, and a sill (Illus. 7-11). Cut the parts to size, keeping in mind that the assembled frame should fit in the rough opening with about ¼ inch space all around. (The space allows room for squaring and plumbing the frame when it is installed.) Use a hand plane or a table saw to cut the bevel along the front edge of the sill.

Step 2: Assemble the Frame Parts Use flathead wood screws to assemble the four frame parts. The screws are driven through the head jamb and sill into the ends of the side jambs.

Next, rip the stock for the front and back retainers, which are shown in Illus. 7-11. Use brass brads or small galvanized finishing nails to attach the back retainer to the inside of the frame.

Step 3: Install the Frame Place the window in the rough opening. Use a carpenter's level to make sure the window is level and plumb, and add shims if needed. Use 8d galvanized finishing or casing nails to secure the frame in place, driving the nails at the shim locations.

Step 4: Cut the Glass Measure the length and

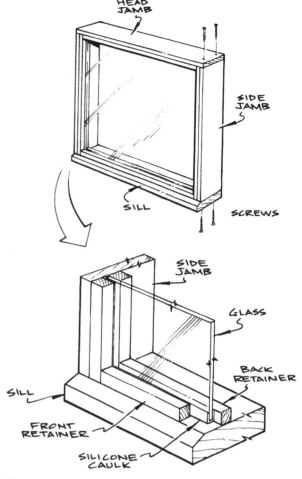

Illus. 7-11. The parts of a fixed-pane window.

width of the inside of the frame. You'll need a piece of ⅛-inch-thick glass that's cut ⅛ inch less than the measured dimensions. If you don't have a glass-cutting tool, your local glass shop can cut the glass to size for you.

Step 5: Install the Glass Add a bead of silicone caulking to the inside of the back retainer. Place the glass in position, and then use finishing nails to attach the front retainer all around the frame.

Chapter 8. Utility Shed

The handsome yard shed shown in Illus. 8-1 and described in this chapter is larger than the average storage shed. This allows for plenty of storage space, and offers the opportunity for additional use. Indeed, a potting shed or small workshop can fit nicely in this structure.

The shed, which measures 8 feet wide and 12 feet long, has tongue-and-groove vertical siding and a cedar shingle roof (Illus. 8-2–8-4). The gable overhang extends over the roof by a foot on each end. The distance from the roof ridge cap to the ground is about 10 feet. If you like the shed's look, but have something smaller in mind, scale it down in size to suit your requirements.

Determine the shed location and then remove all the soil under the shed to a depth of 4 inches. Fill the area with compacted gravel and level it off. With the site prepared, the work on the shed can begin. The steps for building the shed are listed as follows and described in later sections:

1. Install the skid foundation.
2. Assemble the floor framing.
3. Assemble and raise the walls.
4. Secure the walls.
5. Install the roof framing.
6. Shingle the roof.
7. Add the siding.
8. Install the door and windows.
9. Add the soffits and trim.
10. Make the ramp and shutters (optional).
11. Install the hardware.
12. Apply the finish.

Step 1: Prepare the Skid Foundation A wooden skid foundation was used so that the shed could be moved to a different site should the need arise. Also, a skid foundation costs less and is easier to construct than other types of foundations. The two skids are made from 6 × 6 pressure-treated stock that is suitable for ground contact (0.40 pcf as described in Chapter 1). Of course, the shed could also be permanently installed on a perimeter foundation or concrete posts (piers). Refer to Chapter 3 for complete instructions on how to install a skid foundation.

The floor frame measures 8 feet wide and 12 feet long. Therefore, the skids are going to be cut 12 feet long and set 8 feet apart from outer

Illus. 8-1. A quiet, out-of-the-way spot in our backyard was chosen for this large shed. Pages 33–40 show the shed in full color.

UTILITY SHED MATERIALS LIST (All Dimensions Actual)

Part	Size	Material	Quantity
Soffit	¼ in. × 4 ft. × 8 ft.	Exterior Plywood	2
Doorstop	½ in. × 2½ in. × 6 ft.	Pine	1
Trim	¾ in. × 2½ in. × 6 ft.	Pine	1
Trim	¾ in. × 2½ in. × 8 ft.	Pine	3
Subfloor	¾ in. × 4 ft. × 8 ft.	Plywood	3
Jamb	¾ in. × 3½ in. × 6 ft.	Pine	3
Door Batten	¾ in. × 3½ in. × 6 ft.	Pine	2
Door Batten	¾ in. × 3½ in. × 8 ft.	Pine	8
Spaced Sheathing	¾ in. × 3½ in. × 14 ft.	Pine	24
Ridge Cap	¾ in. × 3½ in. × 14 ft.	Cedar	2
Ridgeboard	¾ in. × 4¼ in. × 14 ft.	Pine	1
Siding	¾ in. × 5½ in.	Pine	as required
Fascia	¾ in. × 5½ in. × 6 ft.	Pine	2
Fascia	¾ in. × 5½ in. × 8 ft.	Pine	2
Fascia	¾ in. × 5½ in. × 14 ft.	Pine	2
Front Rafter	1½ in. × 3½ in. × 6 ft.	Pine	9
Back Rafter	1½ in. × 3½ in. × 8 ft.	Pine	9
General Framing	1½ in. × 3½ in. × 8 ft.	Fir	57
General Framing	1½ in. × 3½ in. × 12 ft.	Fir	6
Joist	1½ in. × 5½ in. × 8 ft.	Fir	7
Window Header	1½ in. × 5½ in. × 10 ft.	Fir	1
Joist Header	1½ in. × 5½ in. × 12 ft.	Fir	2
Door Header	1½ in. × 9¼ in. × 8 ft.	Fir	2
Skid	5½ in. × 5½ in. × 8 ft.	Pressure-Treated Wood	2
Shingles	18 in.	Cedar	7 bundles*

*25 square feet of coverage per bundle

MISCELLANEOUS MATERIALS

The following materials are also needed to build the utility shed: 3d and 8d galvanized finishing nails; 3d galvanized roofing nails; 6d, 8d, 10d, and 16d common nails; 8d flooring nails; triangle vent; windows; wood waterproofer; semi-transparent stain; flat white latex paint; flat blue latex paint; butt hinges; and a handle, a hasp, and a padlock.

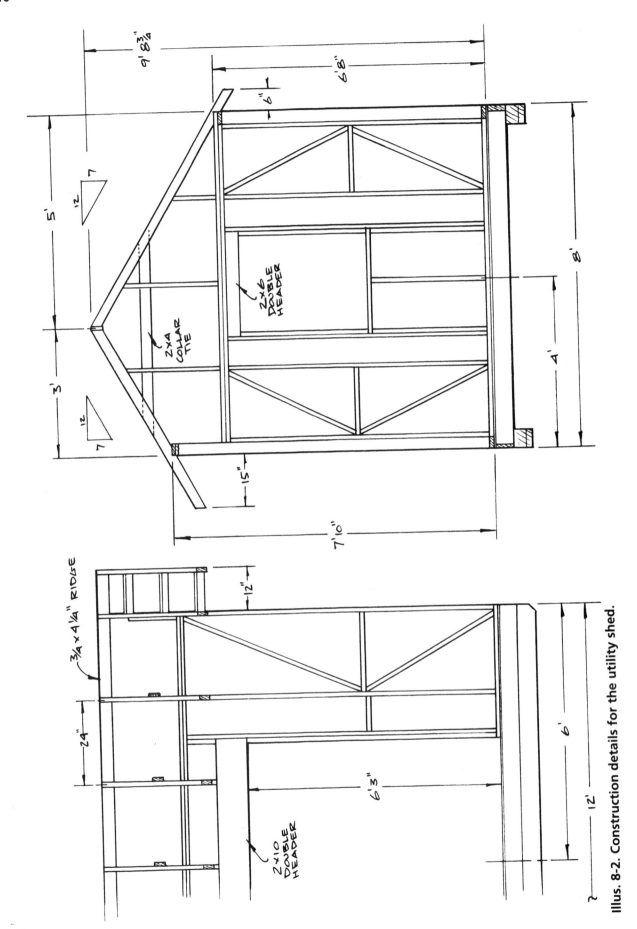

Illus. 8-2. Construction details for the utility shed.

Illus. 8-3. A look at the board-and-batten doors on the utility shed.

Illus. 8-4. A look at the windows on the utility shed.

Illus. 8-5. The skids must be level and square to each other.

edge to outer edge. Make sure the skids are level and square to each other. If they aren't, all the succeeding steps are affected (Illus. 8-5).

Step 2: Assemble the Floor Framing Once the skids are leveled, begin work on the floor frame. Refer to Chapter 4 for detailed instructions. The floor joists and header joists are made from 2 × 6 stock spaced 24 inches on-center (Illus. 8-6).

When the frame is assembled, measure across it diagonally. If its diagonal measurements are the same, the frame is square. If not, rack the frame until the diagonals are equal (Illus. 8-7).

Toenail the frame assembly to the skids. Attach the ¾-inch-thick plywood flooring to the frame with 8d flooring nails, 8d common nails, or 1¾-inch-long drywall screws (Illus. 8-8).

Step 3: Assemble and Raise the Walls Refer to Chapter 4 (the Wall Framing section) for instructions on making and raising the wall frame. The 2 × 4 studs are installed 24 inches on-

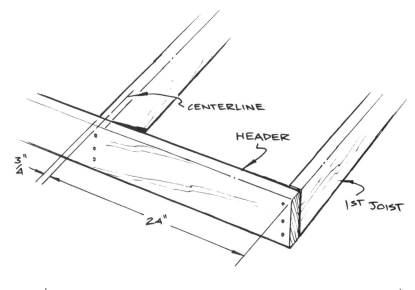

Illus. 8-6. The floor and header joists for the utility shed.

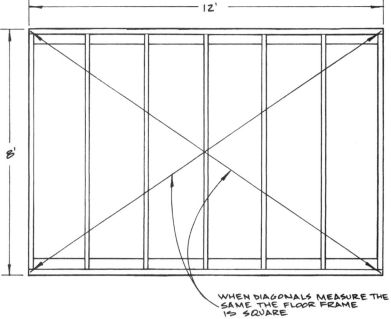

Illus. 8-7. When the frame's diagonal measurements are the same, the frame is square.

Illus. 8-8. Secure the plywood floor in place with 8d nails.

center. The door double-header is made from 2 × 10 stock, while the window double-header is made from 2 × 6.

Two people are needed when working on the walls. One person can hold a raised wall in position while the second person nails support braces in place. Larger sheds might require more than two people to safely raise the walls.

Step 4: Secure the Walls   Once the back-wall frame is assembled, raise it into position and nail it to the floor (Illus. 8-9). The nails should go through the plywood and into the floor frame. Add diagonal braces to temporarily hold the wall in place. **Note:** When adding temporary braces, don't drive the nails all the way into the wall frame. When the nails are not fully driven, it's easier to remove the braces.

The wall must be plumb. Use a level to check the wall and adjust the braces if necessary (Illus. 8-10). Three braces are needed: two to plumb the wall and one to hold it square. To check for square, use the level along the end of the wall. Push or pull the wall, as needed, to plumb it, and then fasten the diagonal brace with nails.

Next, assemble the end wall, and then raise and secure it to the floor (Illus. 8-11). Keep the end wall tight against the back wall. Align the end wall with the edge of the back wall and fasten them together with 16d common nails. The brace at this end can be removed and used as a diagonal brace. Check the edge of the end wall with the level. Push or pull it into plumb and nail a diagonal brace to the outside of the studs.

Now, assemble and install the second end wall and the front wall in the same fashion. As each wall is fastened in place, it is important to check

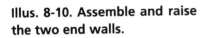

Illus. 8-9. Assemble all the parts, and then raise the back wall into position.

Illus. 8-10. Assemble and raise the two end walls.

Illus. 8-11. Position the end wall and secure it in place.

it for plumb. If small differences are apparent after erecting the walls, you can still rack the walls into plumb and secure them with a temporary brace.

Once all the walls are up, install the fill-in bracing and horizontal blocking (Illus. 8-12). Fill-in bracing won't be needed if you are using plywood sheathing or siding.

Blocking is needed for this shed because the exterior siding is vertical tongue-and-groove boards. Without blocking, many of the boards would be fastened only at the top and bottom. The blocking provides an intermediate surface to nail the siding.

Step 5: Install the Roof Framing With the walls completed, it's time to frame the roof. Refer to Chapter 4 (the Roof Framing section) for specifics on roof construction. Start by tacking a 2 × 4 temporary support to each end of the shed, directly under the ridgeboard. The temporary supports should be cut to the same height as the top edge of the ridgeboard, which in this case is 9 feet, 8¾ inches. The ridgeboard, which measures ¾ inches thick × 4¼ inches wide, is then tacked in place flush with the top of the temporary supports (Illus. 8-13). Check to make sure that the ridgeboard is level and make adjustments if necessary. If you plan to include the gable overhang, be sure the ridgeboard is cut so that it overhangs the proper amount on each end of the shed.

The rafters are added next. Each rafter is cut to size with four cuts. Two cuts (one horizontal, one vertical) create the bird's-mouth, and two plumb (vertical) cuts establish the rafter length. The slope of the cut (7 in 12) is laid out on the stock with a framing square.

Cut a front rafter to size and hold it in place on the framing to make sure it is the right size. Adjust the cuts as needed, and then use the rafter as a template to cut the remaining front rafters. Follow the same procedure for the back rafters.

Lay out and mark the rafter locations on the wall top cap and the ridgeboard, and then nail all the rafters in place. The first rafter of each front and back pair can be nailed through the ridgeboard, and then toenailed at the bird's-mouth. The second rafter is toenailed at both the ridgeboard and the bird's-mouth. After all

Illus. 8-12. Add the fill-in bracing and horizontal blocking after the walls are secured. You don't have to add fill-in bracing if you are using plywood sheathing or siding.

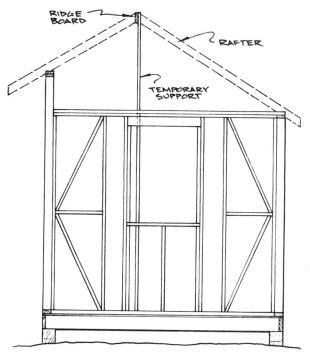

Illus. 8-13. When the roof framing is being installed, the ridgeboard is tacked in place flush with the top of the temporary supports.

the rafters are added, remove the two supports and check to make sure that the roof is plumb.

Next, cut and install the 2 × 4 collar beams. You'll need five of them, one for each of the five intermediate pairs of rafters. There is no need to add collar beams to the end rafters. Then add the gable studs, beveling the top ends to match

the slope of the roof. The location of the blocking that supports the vent is going to depend on the type of triangle vent you choose, so have the vents on hand before starting.

If you are including the gable overhang, add the outriggers and fascia rafters to create the overhang. The gable overhang can be preassembled on the ground and then nailed in place (Illus. 8-14).

Now, add the 1 × 6 fascia boards to the ends of the rafters. Also, miter and face-nail the end fascia boards to the end rafters.

Step 6: Shingle the Roof With all the rafters in place, you can begin work on the cedar shingle roof. See Chapter 5 for detailed information on this procedure.

Begin by adding 1 × 4 spaced wood sheathing across the rafters (Illus. 8-15). The spaced sheathing is placed 5½ inches on-center.

We constructed a temporary scaffold to make the roofing job safer and easier (Illus. 8-16). The scaffold is simply a pair of 2 × 4's bolted in place at each end of the shed. Long planks were then screwed to the top of the scaffold to create a platform.

The cedar shingles go on next. A wood waterproofer (such as Thompson's Water Seal) can help extend the life of the shingles. We put together a shallow "bathtub" (a cardboard box lined with a plastic trash bag) and dipped each shingle before installation. Allow an hour or two

Illus. 8-14. If you are including the gable overhang, add the outriggers and fascia rafter to create the overhang. Preassemble these parts on the ground and then nail the assembly in place.

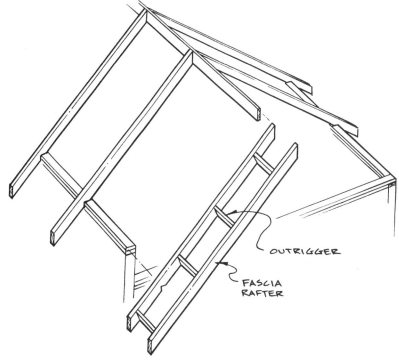

Illus. 8-15. The 1×4 spaced sheathing provides a nailing surface for the cedar shingles.

Illus. 8-16. Sturdy scaffolding makes the roofing job safer and easier.

for the shingles to dry a bit before starting to nail them in place. We found that dipping was much faster than brushing on the waterproofer (Illus. 8-17).

Illus. 8-17. A pair of good rubber gloves comes in handy for dipping the shingles in the wood waterproofer.

It takes a while to get into the rhythm of applying the shingles. However, once you get the hang of it, the process goes pretty quickly (Illus. 8-18).

Step 7: Add the Siding With the roofing complete, the scaffolding can be taken down and you can start applying the vertical siding. Chapter 6 provides more information on this procedure.

We used 1 × 6, pine V-groove tongue-and-groove boards for the siding. This is another operation that goes quickly, but it is a relief to be back on the ground when the job is completed.

As you progress across a wall with the siding, occasionally check to see if the remaining space at the top and the bottom of the boards is the same (Illus. 8-19). The siding has a tendency to creep out of alignment.

Step 8: Install the Door and Windows With the siding done, the door and windows can be installed. Chapter 7 details this step, including instructions on building the board-and-batten door. Most of the commercial windows can be used on this shed.

Begin by installing the door jamb made from 1 × 4 stock. It is important for the jamb to be

Illus. 8-18. Applying the shingles goes pretty quickly once you get a handle on the technique.

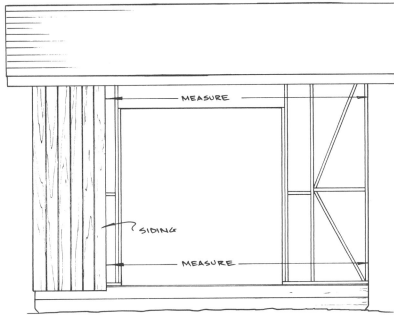

Illus. 8-19. As you add siding across a wall, occasionally make sure that the remaining space at the top and bottom of the boards is the same.

flush with the outside of the siding. If the jamb isn't flush, the trim won't fit properly. Screw the door jamb in place. Use shims as needed to adjust the jamb so that it is both plumb and level. Drive the fastening screws through the shims to hold the jamb in place.

Now, install the doorstop. It is simply a length of ½-inch-thick × 2½-inch-wide stock installed across the full length of the head (top) jamb. Use 3d galvanized finishing nails to secure the doorstop in place.

The two doors can be installed once the jamb is added. A pair of butt hinges is used to mount each of them.

Step 9: Add the Soffits and Trim   Use ¼-inch-

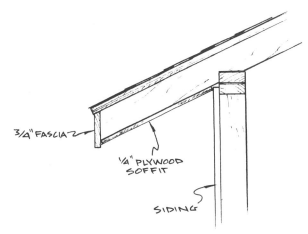

Illus. 8-20. The soffits can be made from ¼-inch-thick exterior plywood.

thick exterior plywood to make the soffits (Illus. 8-20). A couple of 4 × 8-foot sheets of plywood provides all the material you need.

Next, add the trim (casing) to complete the window and door installation. We used 1 × 3 stock for all the trim parts, securing them in place with 8d galvanized finishing nails. To dress up the trim just a bit, chamfer the edges.

Step 10: Make the Ramp and Shutters (Optional) A sturdy ramp can make it easier to use the shed, especially when you are storing a lawn tractor, lawnmower, bicycle, or just about anything else that rolls. The ramp should be made from pressure-treated wood suitable for ground contact (Illus. 8-21).

The shutters are made from 1 × 6 pine. Cut the stock to length and then join the parts with 1¼-inch-long zinc-plated wood screws driven through the back of the shutter stock and into the 1 × 3 battens. Secure the shutters in place by driving screws through the inside of the shed.

Step 11: Install the Hardware Any number of commercially made door handles can be used on the door. A hasp and padlock are a good idea if your shed is going to store valuable tools and equipment.

Step 12: Apply the Finish A semi-transparent stain was applied to the knotty-pine siding. The stain had a hint of blue, so it complemented the solid-blue, flat latex paint used on the door trim. The white latex paint, applied to the fascias and soffits, was used as a relief to the blue. All three colors worked well together, giving the shed a sharp look.

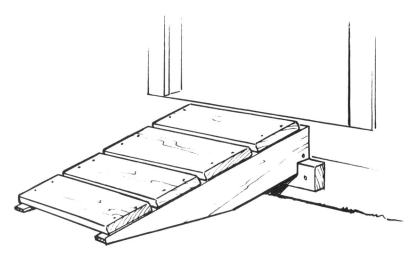

Illus. 8-21. A helpful option is a sturdy ramp that makes it easier to use the shed. Make sure you use pressure-treated wood suitable for ground contact.

Chapter 9. Pole Barn

When I first heard the expression "pole barn," I imagined a structure that looked something like an Indian teepee. However, the poles in this barn are not the round saplings I expected. Indeed, the poles are sturdy square posts, and the barn looks entirely conventional (Illus. 9-1 and 9-2).

A pole barn usually doesn't have a floor, at least not in the traditional sense. The ground serves as the floor. Now, before you instantly reject such a concept, consider that you won't have to invest the time and expense required to build a wood floor. Also, you won't need all the concrete or masonry work that goes along with building a slab or perimeter foundation—something that would likely be needed for a structure this size. Then, too, since the floor is at ground level, a ramp isn't needed to get into the barn. That means you can drive a lawn tractor in and out without having to take a roller-coaster ride.

The floor is created by adding a few inches of fine gravel or peastone. To keep out small critters, a layer of hardware cloth is extended from the bottom of the pole barn into the ground. This open area at the bottom, along with the roof vent, also helps provides ventilation for the barn.

This pole barn features a shed roof, tongue-and-groove vertical siding, asphalt shingles, and a generous-sized entry door. The door, which measures 5 feet wide × 6 feet, 10 inches high, allows room for a lawn tractor, small boat, snowmobile, or any other large item that needs to be stored. The barn doesn't have windows, but they could be added by doing a little extra framing work. The exterior of the pole barn is approximately 16 feet long and 12 feet wide. At the highest point of the roof, the barn measures about 10 feet (Illus. 9-3).

As discussed in Chapter 2, always check with your local building and zoning departments before starting. In some areas, a pole barn might not be permitted. Also, keep in mind that you are probably going to need a building permit for a structure this size.

Following are the steps for building the pole barn:

Step 1: Choose the Site Choosing a suitable site for a pole barn is more important than for the other structures in this book. Because the pole barn doesn't have a floor, the site is going to require some additional preparation. If water drains to the barn location, you'll end up with an indoor swimming pool. Make certain that water drains away from the barn.

If you choose your spot carefully, you can

Illus. 9-1. A side view of the pole barn. The pole barn has sturdy square posts, no floor, and a conventional appearance. Pages 73–75 show the pole barn in full color.

Illus. 9-2. (right) A close-up look at the door on the pole barn.

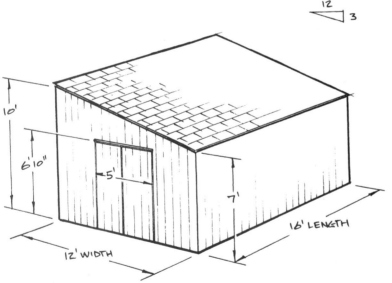

Illus. 9-3. The dimensions for the pole barn.

minimize the site work. The ideal spot would be relatively flat, but gently sloping, away from its center. The surrounding area should also be well drained. Look for another site if you see puddles of water after a heavy rain, or be prepared to move some earth.

Step 2: Lay Out the Posts Begin by driving two stakes into the ground about six feet farther apart than the width of the barn. Drive a nail

into the end of each stake and tie a string between the nails (Illus. 9-4).

Drive in two more stakes 16 feet (the length of the barn) from the first line. The lines must be parallel, so make sure the measurements are taken accurately (Illus. 9-5).

Next, drive in four more stakes to define the 12 foot width of the barn. The two parallel lines formed by these stakes should be at right (90-degree) angles to the first two strings. The in-

Text Continues on Page 129

Children are sure to enjoy this spacious, dry, airy, and well-lit playhouse. See Chapter 14 for information on how to build it.

The door is secured to the play-house with a pair of hinges.

Plenty of sunshine finds it way into the playhouse.

The inside of the entry door is framed with 2x3 stock.

Jordana heading for the play-house door.

Jordana checking out the new crib.

POLE BARN MATERIALS LIST (All Dimensions Actual)

Part	Size	Material	Quantity
Door Drip Cap	¾ in. × ¾ in. × 5 ft.	Pine	1
Siding	¾ in. × 6 in.	Pine	as required
Diagonal Bracing	¾ in. × 6 in. × 8 ft.	Pine	2
Diagonal Bracing	¾ in. × 6 in. × 10 ft.	Pine	4
Diagonal Bracing	¾ in. × 6 in. × 12 ft.	Pine	2
Rafter Spacer	2 in. × 4 in. × 8 ft.	Fir	2
Door Batten	2 in. × 4 in. × 8 ft.	Fir	6
Rafter Spacer	2 in. × 6 in. × 8 ft.	Fir	2
Door Batten	2 in. × 6 in. × 6 ft.	Fir	1
Filler Blocks	2 in. × 6 in.	Fir	as required
End Banding	2 in. × 6 in. × 12 ft.	Fir	5
Side Banding	2 in. × 6 in. × 16 ft.	Fir	7
Rafter	2 in. × 10 in. × 14 ft.	Fir	9
Banding	2 in. × 10 in. × 16 ft.	Fir	4
Door Sill	4 in. × 4 in. × 6 ft.	Pressure-Treated Wood	1
Door Header	4 in. × 4 in. × 6 ft.	Fir	1
Post	5 in. × 5 in.	Pressure-Treated Wood	9
Roof Sheathing	¾ in. × 4 ft. × 8 ft.	Plywood	7
Roofing	3-tab shingles	Asphalt	2 squares

MISCELLANEOUS MATERIALS

The following materials are also needed to build the pole barn: 12d and 16d galvanized common nails; hurricane ties; roofing underlayment; caulking; a drip cap; a vented drip cap; hardware cloth; cement; peastone; hinges; a door pull; and a hasp.

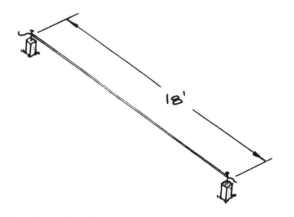

tersection of the strings marks the outside corners of the posts.

Check for right angles by using the 3:4:5 right-triangle method. To use this method, measure and mark a point 3 feet from an intersection of the strings. Then, from the same intersection,

Illus. 9-4. The first step in laying out the posts is to drive two stakes into the ground, drive a nail into the end of each stake, and tie a string between the nails.

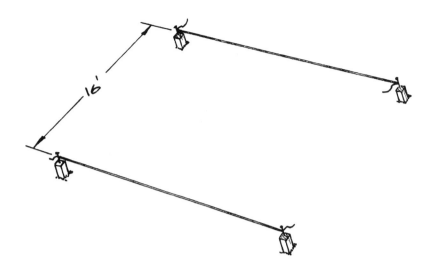

Illus. 9-5. When you drive in the second pair of stakes, make sure they are parallel to the first pair.

measure 4 feet on the adjacent string and again mark the point. Now measure the distance between the marked points. If the distance measures exactly 5 feet, the two strings form a right angle (Illus. 9-6).

When you have finished, double-check to see that the overall layout is accurate. Measure the diagonals of the rectangle formed by the strings. If the diagonals measure the same, the layout is square and true (Illus. 9-7).

Step 3: Install the Posts The nine posts are cut from 6 × 6 pressure-treated lumber. The pressure-treated posts must be rated for in-ground use (0.60 pcf), as discussed in Chapter 1.

Now, dig the holes for all the posts. Since the intersection of the strings represents the outside corners of the four corner posts, you'll need to locate the holes to ensure that the corner posts are correctly positioned. The intermediate posts

can be measured from the corners.

It's important for the holes to be deeper than the frost line for your region. In our area, Connecticut, the frost line is three feet. Dig about six inches deeper than the frost line to provide an area for drainage. The bottom of the hole should be undisturbed dirt. In regions where frost isn't a factor, check with your building department for the minimum required hole depth.

Pour in gravel for the first six inches to provide for the drainage. At this point in the construction, the posts should be cut longer than needed. They are trimmed to final length a bit later.

Next, place a post in a corner hole, and then add temporary braces to keep it vertical. Don't fully drive the nails when attaching the braces to the post. Instead, let the nail heads extend above the surface a bit. Doing so allows you to

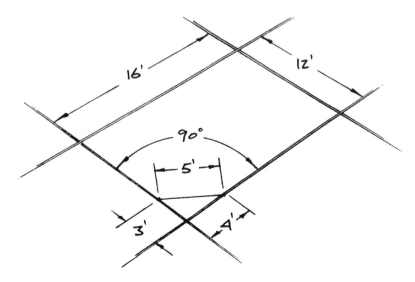

Illus. 9-6. To determine that the two strings form a right angle, mark one point 3 feet from an intersection of the strings, and another 4 feet from the same intersection on the adjacent string. If the distance between these two marks measures exactly 5 feet, the two strings form a right angle.

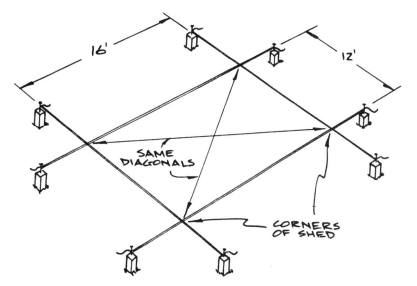

Illus. 9-7. If the diagonals of the rectangle formed by the strings measure the same, the post layout is square and true.

quickly remove the nails when you need to re-adjust the position of the post.

Continue in this fashion until all the posts are in place (Illus. 9-8). It is important for each of the posts to be plumb (vertical) when viewed from both the front and side. A plumb bob makes this job easy. Tack a stick (an ice-cream stick will do fine) near the top of the post. Notch the stick about 1 inch from the post (Illus. 9-9). Tie the plumb bob to the stick and lead the line

through the notch. The bob should hang down as far as possible without touching the ground.

Now, measure the distance between the pointed end of the plumb bob and the edge of the post. Also, measure the distance between the string and the post at the notched stick. If the measurements are the same, the post is plumb in one direction (Illus. 9-10). If it isn't plumb,

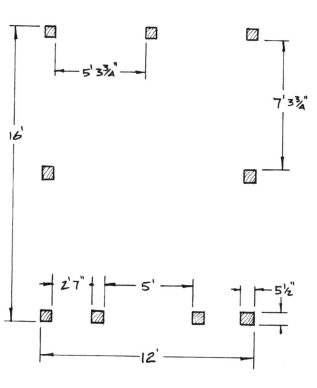

TOP VIEW

Illus. 9-8. A top view showing all the posts in place.

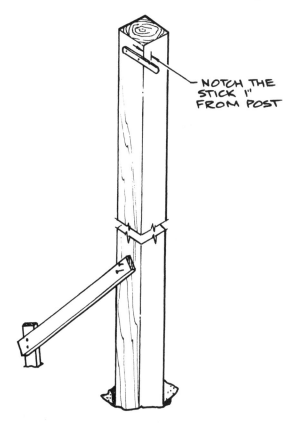

Illus. 9-9. To provide a means to hang a plumb bob, tack a stick to the post. Cut a notch in the stick about one inch from the post.

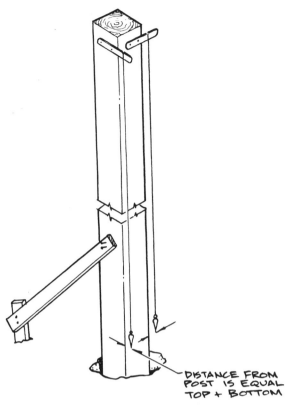

DISTANCE FROM
POST IS EQUAL
TOP + BOTTOM

Illus. 9-10. If the distances between the pointed end of the plumb bob and the edge of the post and between the string and the post at the notched stick are the same, the post is plumb in one direction.

remove the brace and adjust as needed to plumb the post. Once all looks okay, reattach the brace.

Since the post must be plumb when viewed from both the front and side, you now need to check for plumb along the adjacent side. Tack a new stick in place and again check for plumb. Once the adjacent side is adjusted for plumb, the post is then perfectly plumb. Set up all the other posts using the same procedure.

Next, measure 5 feet from the ground and mark the post at that point. Then, using a long straightedge and a carpenter's level, transfer the mark from the first post to all the other posts. This is an important reference mark, so work accurately.

Each of the nine posts can now be taken down and cut to final length. The final length is equal to the below-ground length plus the above-ground length. Notch the top end of the four corner posts and the two intermediate side posts (one on each side) to accept a 2 × 10. Also, the three intermediate end posts (two on one end, one on the other) are notched at 14 degrees to

accept the 2 × 10 end rafters. Once cut to length and notched, the posts can be re-erected for permanent installation (Illus. 9-11).

Next, place the posts into their holes, and then replumb and add braces to them. Check to make sure the 5-foot mark remains level on all nine posts. Adjust any posts that are not level by adding or removing gravel.

For a final check, place a 2 × 10 from corner to corner across the side posts. The 2 × 10 should fit properly in the notches and it must be level. Also, this is a good time to cut an end rafter and check the fit along the ends of the pole barn (see Step 6).

Once everything looks okay, mix a bag of concrete for each post and pour it into the hole. Wait two days, and then backfill over the concrete to level the earth. Tamp the loose fill firmly in place.

If you are doing this over a few weekends, it can save time if you install the corners first and then add the banding (see Step 4). With the banding in place, the intermediate posts only need to be plumbed in one direction. The posts also align with the banding, which saves the time that would be spent visually aligning them.

Step 4: Add the Banding The banding serves to strengthen the entire structure and to also provide a nailing surface for the vertical tongue-and-groove siding. Begin by measuring the overall length of the sides, and then cutting four 2 × 10's to the measured length. Place a 2 × 10 into the notched posts on each of the sides. Secure the 2 × 10's with 16d galvanized common nails. Now, nail the 2 × 10 banding to the face of the 2 × 10's that are notched in the posts (Illus. 9-12).

The 2 × 6 banding for the sides is cut to the same length as the 2 × 10 stock. It is face-nailed to the posts with 16d galvanized common nails. The banding along the ends is cut to fit between the posts and is toenailed in place with 12d galvanized common nails. Or, as an option, the banding along the ends can be notched into the posts. Locate all the lower banding 3 inches from the ground, and then space the remaining banding a maximum of 24 inches apart.

On both sides, between the banding, you'll need to nail 2 × 6 filler blocks to the posts. The filler blocks add strength and also provide additional nailing surfaces for the siding (Illus. 9-13).

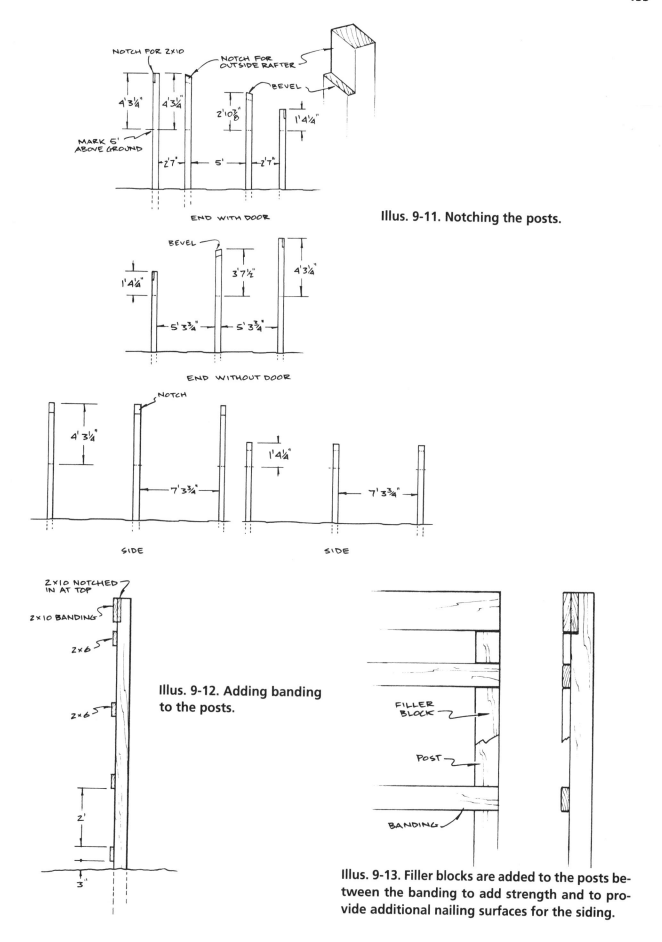

NOTCH FOR 2X10

NOTCH FOR
OUTSIDE RAFTER

BEVEL

4' 3½"

4' 3¼"

2' 10⅞"

1' 4¼"

MARK 5'
ABOVE GROUND

2' 7"

5'

2' 7"

END WITH DOOR

Illus. 9-11. Notching the posts.

BEVEL

1' 4¼"

3' 7½"

4' 3¼"

5' 3¾"

5' 3¾"

END WITHOUT DOOR

NOTCH

4' 3¼"

7' 3¾"

1' 4¼"

7' 3¾"

SIDE

SIDE

2X10 NOTCHED
IN AT TOP

2X10 BANDING

2X6

Illus. 9-12. Adding banding
to the posts.

2X6

2'

3"

FILLER
BLOCK

POST

BANDING

Illus. 9-13. Filler blocks are added to the posts between the banding to add strength and to provide additional nailing surfaces for the siding.

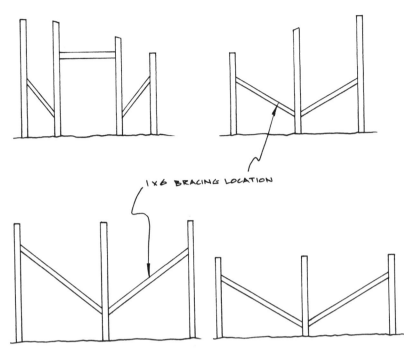

Illus. 9-14. Adding the diagonal bracing.

1×6 BRACING LOCATION

Another time-saving approach is to assemble the posts for each end and the banding while the parts lie flat on the ground. Pour a small amount of concrete into each hole, and then erect each end wall. Check to make sure the walls are at the correct elevations and that they are plumb. Once everything looks okay, dump the remaining concrete into each hole. Keep in mind that you'll need extra manpower to lift up these very heavy walls.

Also, add the diagonal bracing at this time. Use 1 × 6 stock, face-nailing the bracing to the inside of the posts (Illus. 9-14).

Step 5: Finish the Floor   The floor should be level. If it is not, make it level and add about 3 inches of peastone or other fine gravel to the entire floor. The peastone ensures that if any water gets in, the water must rise to a height of three inches before it begins to affect the interior of the barn. As a further precaution, it pays to dig a small trench around the perimeter of the floor. The trench can be directed to a drainpipe. Pitch the drainpipe down and away from the barn and into in a gravel-filled ditch. The ditch can be covered with soil and seeded so as not to be obtrusive.

Before backfilling the trench, tack hardware cloth around the entire perimeter of the barn (except at the door). Use 2-inch-long galvanized roofing tacks to secure the hardware cloth to the lower banding. Backfill the trench with gravel around the hardware cloth (Illus. 9-15).

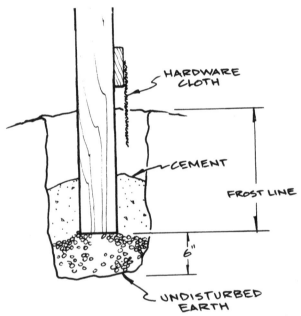

HARDWARE CLOTH

CEMENT

FROST LINE

6"

UNDISTURBED EARTH

Illus. 9-15. Tack hardware cloth around the entire perimeter of the barn (except at the door), to ward off small animals. Secure the cloth to the lower banding with roofing tacks.

At the door entry, bury a sill made from 4 × 4 pressure-treated stock (0.40 pcf, as discussed in Chapter 1) in the gravel trench. Level the sill and toenail it in place with galvanized nails. The sill is rabbeted to form a stop for the door (Illus. 9-16).

The door header is made from 4 × 4 stock. Toenail it in place at a point 6 feet, 8 inches from the top of the sill.

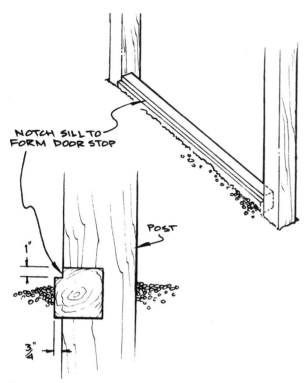

NOTCH SILL TO FORM DOOR STOP

POST

Illus. 9-16. The sill should be buried at the door entry, leveled, and toenailed in place with galvanized nails.

Step 6: Install the Roof Frame

The roof frame is next. Make an end rafter first. Cut the upper end of a 2 × 10 to 14 degrees. With the aid of a helper, hold the rafter in position along the outside of the end posts, mark the end of the rafter on the lower end, and then make a plumb cut (Illus. 9-17).

Next, cut a 1½ × 7-inch bird's-mouth on the upper end of the rafter (Illus. 9-18) and a 7-inch flat at the lower end (Illus. 9-19). Again using your helper, place the rafter on the posts and check for a good fit. If everything looks fine, use the rafter as a template to make the second end rafter and the middle rafter.

The top ends of the remaining six rafters do not align with a post. Instead, they rest entirely on the doubled-up 2 × 10 stock, so the bird's-mouth has a different cut. Cut the bird's-mouth to ¾ × 3 inches (Illus. 9-20). The lower end has the same flat as the end and middle rafters.

Lay nine rafters across the 2 × 10 bands, spacing them 24 inches on-center (Illus. 9-21). The two end rafters are toenailed in place with 12d galvanized common nails. Also, the lower end of the center rafter is toenailed. The ends of the remaining rafters are attached to the 2 × 10's with commercial hangers. Hangers of this style are often called *hurricane ties* (Illus. 9-22).

To finish off the roof framing, add 2 × 4 spacer/nailers at the upper end of the roof and 2 × 6 spacers at the lower end of the roof (see Illus. 9-18 and 9-19). Cut the spacers to a length that allows them to fit snugly between the rafters.

Step 7: Install the Roofing

Use ¾-inch-thick plywood to deck the roof. Be sure to select a plywood that's made to be used as roof sheathing. Use 15-pound roofing felt as an underlayment, and add three-tab asphalt shingles to com-

Illus. 9-17. When installing the roof frame, make an end rafter first, position it on the outside of the end post, and make a plumb cut.

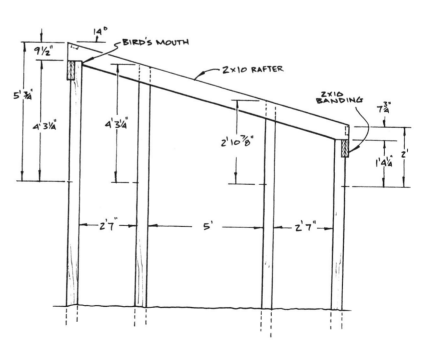

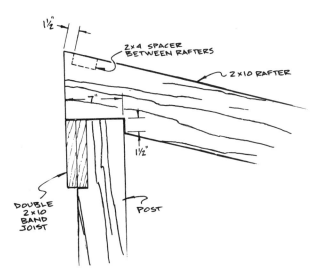

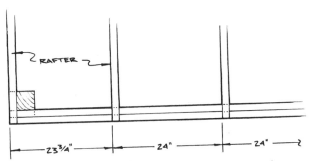

Illus. 9-21. Nine rafters should be laid across the 2 × 10 bands. Space them every 24 inches on-center.

Illus. 9-18. Cut a 1½ × 7-inch bird's-mouth on the upper end of the rafter.

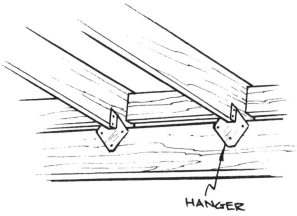

Illus. 9-22. Hurricane ties are used to attach the ends of the remaining rafters to the 2 × 10's.

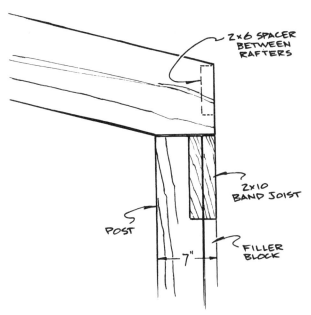

Illus. 9-19. Cut a 7-inch flat on the lower end of the rafter.

plete the job. For details about applying sheathing, underlayment, and three-tab asphalt shingles, refer to Chapters 4 and 5.

Also install a drip cap on the roof. At the eaves, one leg of the drip cap goes between the sheathing and the underlayment, and the other leg goes over the siding (Illus. 9-23). Along the shed ends, however, one leg of the drip cap goes between the underlayment and the shingles, and the other leg goes over the siding.

A vent provides ventilation at the ridgeboard (Illus. 9-23). You should have the vent on hand before applying the sheathing. That's because you have to trim the sheathing short of the ridge to provide for the vent. If you have the vent available, you can quickly determine the proper sheathing spacing.

Step 8: Add the Siding   Refer to Chapter 6 for information on how to install the 1 × 6 pine tongue-and-groove vertical siding. At the top of the door opening, trim the siding to create a 1-inch lip. The lip serves as a doorstop (Illus. 9-24).

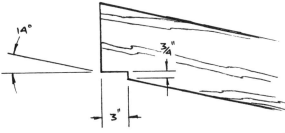

Illus. 9-20. The bird's-mouth should be ¾ × 3 inches.

Illus. 9-23. The drip cap and vent on the pole barn.

Also, cut a 60-inch length of 1 × 1 stock to use as a drip cap over the door. Secure the cap to the siding with galvanized finishing nails. To help keep out water, apply a bead of caulking along the top edge of the cap.

Step 9: Make and Hang the Doors Make the doors next. The door faces are made from 1 × 6 pine tongue-and-groove siding and are held together with battens (made from "2 ×" stock)

on the back (Illus. 9-25). Refer to Chapter 7 for information on making and hanging a board-and-batten door.

Step 10: Paint the Barn The entire outside surface of the tongue-and-groove siding, and also the doors, are finished with two coats of a flat, opaque stain.

Illus. 9-24. Cut the siding 1 inch short of the door opening to create a doorstop. A length of 1 × 1 stock over the door serves as a drip cap.

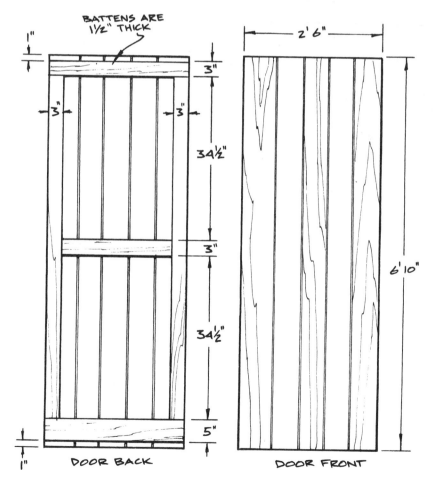

Illus. 9-25. The faces of the doors for the pole barn are made from 1 × 6 pine tongue-and-groove siding held together with battens.

Chapter 10. Woodshed

Perfect for storing firewood, this small, open-sided shed (Illus. 10-1 and 10-2) can be made in just a weekend or two. The construction is rock-solid, so you can expect it to stand up to plenty of hard use for years to come. Pressure-treated lumber and a red-cedar shingled roof add to the durability. The shed is sized to hold 16- to 18-inch lengths of firewood (Illus. 10-3), but it can be widened to accept longer logs. Although wind-driven rain can wet some of the firewood,

the open sides permit plenty of direct sunlight and ventilation, so the logs quickly dry. When filled, the shed holds about one-third of a cord of wood.

Pressure-treated lumber provides excellent long-term moisture protection for the various 2 × 4 and 4 × 4 frame parts. A naturally decay-resistant lumber such as cedar or redwood is also a good option. If you choose pressure-treated lumber, the stock used for the posts should be

Illus. 10-1. This small, durable shed can be easily and fairly quickly built. It is perfect for storing firewood. Pages 76 and 77 show the woodshed in full color.

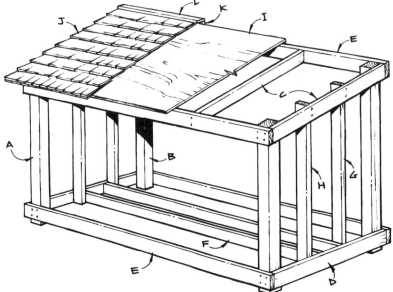

Illus. 10-2. The construction details for the woodshed.

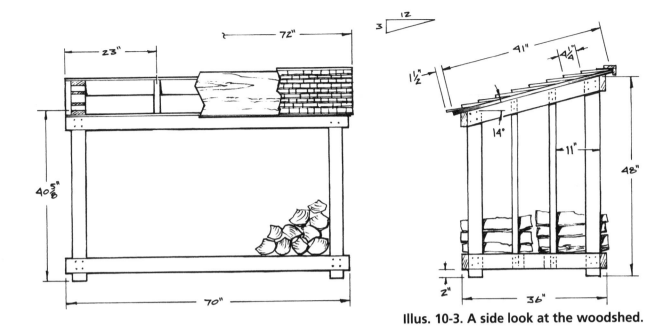

Illus. 10-3. A side look at the woodshed.

WOODSHED MATERIALS LIST (All Dimensions Actual)

Label / Part		Size	Material	Quantity
A	Front Post	3½ × 3½ × 40⅝ in.	Pressure-Treated Wood	2
B	Back Post	3½ × 3½ × 48 in.	Pressure-Treated Wood	2
C	Roof Support	1½ × 3½ × 34⅞ in.	Pressure-Treated Wood	4
D	Lower Side Support	1½ × 3½ × 33 in.	Pressure-Treated Wood	2
E	Stretcher	1½ × 3½ × 70 in.	Pressure-Treated Wood	4
F	Spacer	1½ × 3½ × 67 in.	Pressure-Treated Wood	2
G	Long Blocking	1½ × 3½ × 43 in.	Pressure-Treated Wood	2
H	Short Blocking	1½ × 3½ × 40⅞ in.	Pressure-Treated Wood	2
I	Roof Sheathing	½ × 41 × 71 in.	Exterior Plywood	1
J	Shingles	18 in.	Cedar	as required
K	Ridge Cap Back	¾ × 1½ × 72 in.	Cedar	1
L	Ridge Cap Top	¾ × 2¾ × 72 in.	Cedar	1

MISCELLANEOUS MATERIALS

The following materials are also needed to build the woodshed: 3d (for cedar shingles), 8d, and 16d galvanized common nails; 4d and 6d galvanized finishing or casing nails; and wood waterproofer.

rated for ground contact (minimum 0.40 pcf), as discussed in Chapter 1.

To maintain the rustic look of the shed, we used red-cedar shingles (number-1 grade) on the roof. However, if you are looking to keep costs to a minimum, consider substituting three-tab asphalt shingles. The recommended exposure for a wood-shingled roof with a 3-in-12 pitch is 4¼ inches.

Following are the steps for building a woodshed:

Step 1: Cut the Posts to Length The two front posts (A in Illus. 10-2) and the two back posts (B) are cut from a pair of 8-foot-long 4 × 4's. Working on one 4 × 4 at a time, lay out and mark the 40⅝-inch length of the front post and scribe a 14-degree angle at the mark (Illus. 10-4A). A protractor and sliding T-bevel can be used to measure and mark the angle.

The angled cut is made with a portable circular saw. However, the cut must be made in two passes because a circular saw can't cut through 3½-inch-thick stock in one pass. Set the blade for a 1⅞-inch depth of cut and make the first pass. Then, turn the stock over and make a second pass to complete the cut. The second pass must align exactly with the first one.

Now, lay out and mark the 48-inch length of the back post. Cut the bottom end square with the circular saw, again using two passes to complete the job (Illus. 10-4B).

Step 2: Cut the Roof Supports A pair of 8-foot-long 2 × 4's provides enough material for the four roof supports (C in Illus. 10-2). Working on one 2 × 4 at a time, scribe a line at a 14-degree angle, measure 34⅞ inches, and scribe a

second line at the same angle (Illus. 10-5A). Cut along both lines to produce the first support.

Next, measure and mark a point 34⅞ inches from the angled end of the 2 × 4 stock, and then scribe another angled line (Illus. 10-5B). Cutting along this line produces the second support. Using the same procedure, the third and fourth supports are cut from the remaining 2 × 4.

Step 3: Cut the Lower Side Supports and Stretchers From 2 × 4 stock, cut the two lower side supports (D in Illus. 10-2) to 33-inch lengths. Also, cut the four stretchers (E) to 70-inch lengths. The two upper stretchers have a 14-degree bevel along their top edges. The bevel can be cut with a table saw, portable circular saw, or by hand with a sharp plane.

Step 4: Assemble the Side Frames The two side frames can now be assembled (Illus. 10-6). Each side frame is made up of a front post, back post, lower side support, and roof support. The parts are assembled with 16d galvanized common nails.

As you assemble the parts, keep in mind that the two frames are mirror images of each other. That means that the supports on each frame must be attached to opposite sides of the posts. Attach the lower side support 2 inches from the bottom end of each post. Before nailing, make sure the lower side-support ends are flush with the edges of the posts. Also, check for squareness with a framing square. Use four nails at each joint, staggering the nails slightly to reduce the chance of splitting the stock.

Add the roof support, again using four staggered nails. The roof-support ends are flush

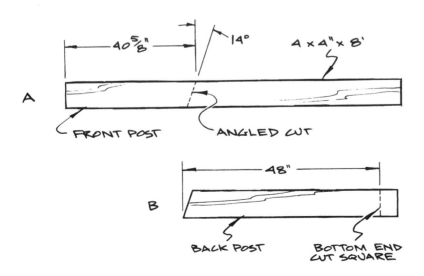

Illus. 10-4. A: When cutting posts to length, first lay out and mark the length of the front post, and then scribe a 14-degree angle at the mark. B: Then lay out and mark the length of the back post and cut its bottom end square with a circular saw.

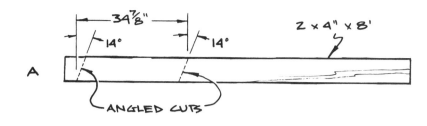

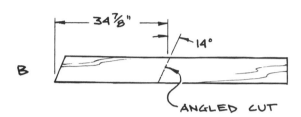

Illus. 10-5. A: The first step in cutting roof supports consists of scribing a line on 2 × 4's at a 14-degree angle, measuring 34⅞ inches, and then scribing a second line at the same angle. Then cut along both lines. B: Next, mark a point 34⅞ inches from the angled end of the stock and scribe another angled line. Cut along this line.

Illus. 10-6. Assemble the side frames with 16d galvanized common nails.

with the edges of the posts. Also, the top edge of the support is flush with the top ends of the posts.

Step 5: Add the Stretchers The stretchers are assembled to the side frames with 16d galvanized common nails. Add the two bottom stretchers first. Before nailing, make sure the bottom stretchers are square to the posts. Also, make certain that the stretcher ends are flush with the lower side supports.

After the bottom stretchers are assembled, it's helpful to level the shed. Check for level by placing a carpenter's level on the bottom stretchers and lower side supports. Add blocks under the posts, as needed, to level the structure (Illus. 10-7).

Once the woodshed is level, add the two upper stretchers. The top edges of the stretchers should be flush with the top end of the front and back posts.

Illus. 10-7. Level the posts after attaching the bottom stretchers.

Step 6: Assemble the Spacers Measure the distance between the inside faces of the lower side supports, and then cut the two spacers (F in Illus. 10-2) to their measured lengths. Secure them in place by driving a pair of 16d galvanized common nails through the lower side supports and into the ends of the spacers.

Step 7: Add the Remaining Roof Supports Lay out and mark the location of the two middle roof supports. Secure them in place by driving a pair of 16d galvanized common nails through the stretchers and into the roof-support ends. When installed, the top edge of the roof supports should be flush with the top edges of the stretchers (Illus. 10-8).

Illus. 10-8. Attach the two middle roof supports.

Step 8: Add the Long and Short Blocking Measure for the long blocking (G in Illus. 10-2) and short blocking (H) and cut the parts to length. Once they're cut to length, use a table saw or portable circular saw to bevel the top end to 14 degrees.

Next, secure the bottom end of the blocking by driving a pair of angled nails through the blocking and into the spacers. The top end of the blocking is toenailed to the roof supports. When toenailing, it's often a challenge to keep the stock from shifting out of position as the first nail is driven. To make the job easier, tack a block of wood in place to support the stock (Il-

lus. 10-9). After the first nail is driven, remove the block and add the remaining nails.

Illus. 10-9. Toenail the upper end of the blocking to the end roof support. To prevent the blocking from shifting while driving the nail, butt a piece of scrap wood against the blocking, and then tack the scrap wood to the roof support.

Step 9: Install the Roof Sheathing Just about any type of ½-inch-thick exterior plywood can be used for the roof sheathing (I in Illus. 10-2). Cut the plywood to overhang ½ inch on the ends, 1½ inches on the front, and 2½ inches on the back. Secure the roof sheathing with 8d nails spaced 6 inches apart at the edges and 12 inches apart along the middle roof supports.

Step 10: Add the Cedar Shingles See Chapter 5 for step-by-step procedures on how to install the cedar shingles (J in Illus. 10-2). For this project, the shingles overhang the sheathing by 1½ inches at the front and ½ inch at the sides.

Before applying the shingles, it's a good idea to apply a wood waterproofer (Thompson's Water Seal is a good one) to all surfaces. The wood waterproofer provides moisture protection that adds to the life of the shingles.

Step 11: Attach the Ridge Cap From a piece of 1 × 6 cedar stock, rip the ridge cap back (K in Illus. 10-2) to 1½ inches wide and the ridge cap top (L) to about 2¾ inches wide. Measure the length of the shed and cut the ridge cap parts to that dimension. Now join the two parts with 4d galvanized finishing or casing nails spaced 6 to 8 inches apart.

Attach the ridge cap assembly to the roof with 6d galvanized finishing or casing nails driven through the ridge cap back and into the back edge of the roof sheathing. Space the nails 6 to 8 inches apart.

Chapter 11.
Garbage House

If you live in the suburbs or the country, then, like many of us, you have the frustration of dealing with refuse. The garbage houses we use to store the garbage don't always work so efficiently. Three basic problems are at work here. The first is getting someone to actually remove the garbage. One common refrain in many houses is "Dad, it's not my turn to take out the garbage." Of course, no one, including Dad, wants to do the deed.

Second, the smelly and leaky plastic bags often make the garbage house smell and look filthy. This, in turn, attracts the third problem—mice, raccoons, and other assorted small, furry creatures. This is when the fun really begins, because the raccoons apparently work in cooperation with the garbage collectors.

It goes like this: First the garbage collectors slam the lid of the garbage house down, eventually bending or breaking the fastener. Once the fastener doesn't work, the raccoons get into the unlocked house and tear up every plastic bag, leaving garbage strewn all around the inside.

If all this happened far from the house, it wouldn't matter much. But, for most of us, this is not the case. The garbage house is usually situated directly in front of the main house, where every guest can see why the neighborhood raccoons are living fat and happy. What to do?

The typical garbage house is simply a box with a lid—a design that makes for a particularly nasty job when it comes time to clean out the house. Adding doors to the front of the house goes a long way towards solving the problem.

The garbage house described and illustrated in this chapter (Illus. 11-1 and 11-2) goes even further in an effort to deal with the problem. The front, bottom, and sides of the garbage house are open, allowing plenty of air circulation, which helps keep odors to a minimum. When the house becomes dirty, it can be hosed down inside and out. The water runs out the open bottom.

The house must be used in tandem with closed plastic garbage bins. Should a raccoon get inside, it won't be able to maneuver the top off the bins to get at the garbage. Also, as an option, the bottom, door backs, and end backs can be covered with galvanized hardware cloth. The hardware cloth helps keeps mice and other small animals from entering the garbage house.

By adding some color to the decorative lattice, the lowly garbage house almost looks classy. For those who don't want to spend the time making the lattice doors, they can be replaced with easier-to-make tongue-and-groove or board-and-batten wood siding. If you choose wood siding, be sure to add vents that allow plenty of air circulation.

Following are the steps for making the garbage house:

Step 1: Make the Door and End-Panel

Illus. 11-1. The front, bottom, and sides of this garbage house are open, allowing for plenty of air circulation. It also has front doors, which makes it easier to clean than other garbage houses. Pages 78 and 79 show the garbage house in full color.

143

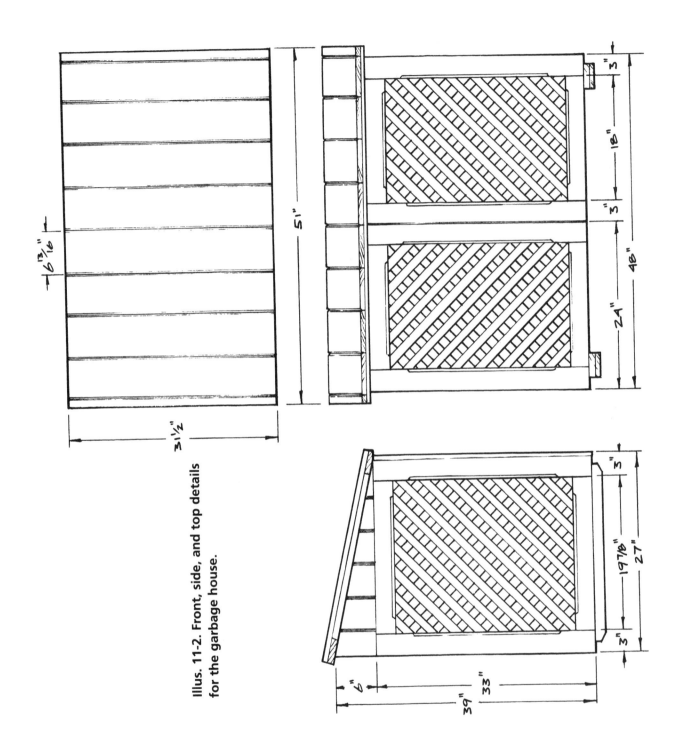

Illus. 11-2. Front, side, and top details for the garbage house.

GARBAGE HOUSE MATERIALS LIST (All Dimensions Actual)

Part	Size	Material	Quantity
Door Stile	$1\frac{1}{8} \times 3 \times 33$ in.	Pine	4
Door Rail	$1\frac{1}{8} \times 3 \times 18$ in.	Pine	4
End Stile	$1\frac{1}{8} \times 3 \times 33$ in.	Pine	4
End Rail	$1\frac{1}{8} \times 3 \times 19\frac{7}{8}$ in.	Pine	4
Lattice	$\frac{1}{4} \times 1\frac{1}{4}$ in.	Pine	as required
End Panel	$\frac{3}{4} \times 5\frac{1}{2}$ in.	Tongue-and-Groove Pine	8 ft.
End Backer	$\frac{3}{8} \times 8 \times 28$ in.*	CDX Plywood	2
Bottom Stile	$\frac{3}{4} \times 5\frac{1}{2} \times 45\frac{3}{4}$ in.	Pine	2
Bottom Rail	$\frac{3}{4} \times 5\frac{1}{2} \times 14\frac{1}{8}$ in.	Pine	4
Back	$\frac{3}{4} \times 7\frac{1}{4}$ in.	Tongue-and-Groove Pine	as required
Back Upper Batten	$\frac{3}{4} \times 3\frac{1}{2} \times 45\frac{3}{4}$ in.**	Pine	1
Back Lower Batten	$\frac{3}{4} \times 1\frac{1}{4} \times 45\frac{3}{4}$ in.	Pine	1
Lid	$\frac{3}{4} \times 7\frac{1}{4}$ in.	Tongue-and-Groove Pine	22 ft.
Lid Batten (Long)	$\frac{3}{4} \times 3 \times 51$ in.	Pine	2
Lid Batten (Short)	$\frac{3}{4} \times 3 \times 25\frac{1}{2}$ in.	Pine	2
Support Rail	$1\frac{1}{8} \times 3 \times 46\frac{1}{2}$ in.***	Pine	1
Support Stile	$1\frac{1}{8} \times 3 \times 31\frac{1}{8}$ in.	Pine	1
Cleat	$1\frac{1}{8} \times 1\frac{1}{8}$ in.	Pine	as required
Skid	$1\frac{1}{2} \times 3\frac{1}{2} \times 24$ in.	Pressure-Treated Pine	2
Butt Hinge	3 in. long $\times$ 2 in. wide (open)	Brass	4

*Length and width allow extra material for trimming.
**Width allows extra material for trimming.
***Length includes rabbets.

MISCELLANEOUS MATERIALS

The following additional materials are needed to build the garbage house: water-resistant or waterproof glue; $\frac{3}{8}$-inch-diameter $\times$ 2-inch-long dowel pins; $\frac{5}{8}$-inch-long brass brads; $1\frac{1}{4}$-inch-long drywall screws; 1-inch-long $\times$ No. 8 flathead wood screws; 2-inch-long $\times$ No. 10 flathead wood screws; 3-inch-long $\times$ No. 10 flathead wood screws; hinges; locking hardware; exterior stain; and waterproof sealer.

Frames Begin by building the frames for the doors and the end panels. The door and end panel construction is identical (except for overall size); however, the end panels have an upper portion added later on. Don't worry if you haven't made a frame before. By following the method we show you here you'll make a high-quality joint, even without any prior experience.

You'll need at least 36 feet of stock that is $1\frac{1}{8}$ inches thick and 4 inches wide for the frame parts. Rip the stock to 3 inches wide, and then cut all the frame pieces to length. Lay them out and check their dimensions to be sure they are correct.

Clamp one frame together. Be sure to use protective blocks to prevent marring of the soft wood. Set the clamp next to, but not on top of, the joint. Don't put too much pressure on the clamp or it can bend the wood. Check to see that the faces of the frame are flush and that everything is square.

Next, with a long ⅜-inch-drill bit (at least 4 inches of the bit must be exposed after it's chucked in the drill), bore two holes into the side of the frame at the joint. The holes should go in about 4 inches. Continue this procedure at each joint until the whole frame is drilled. Mark the parts carefully before removing the clamps (Illus. 11-3).

Using a waterproof or water-resistant glue, swab it into the holes of the two rails and tap in

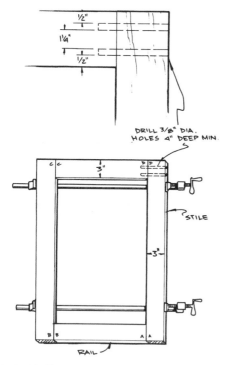

Illus. 11-3. Drill two holes into the side of the frame at the joint. The holes must be at least 4 inches deep and ⅜ inch in diameter.

2-inch-long grooved dowels. With the dowels fully seated, swab glue into the holes of the stiles. Also brush glue onto the ends of the rails.

Next, assemble the frame and clamp it up. Again, you need clamp blocks. This time you can clamp over the joint. Place a piece of plastic wrap between the clamp blocks and the stiles to prevent the blocks from adhering to the stiles. If you have any glue squeeze-out when clamping

up a frame, scrape it away while it is still wet. This improves joint strength and makes sanding easier.

After the glue is sufficiently dry, remove the clamps and set the frame aside to dry thoroughly. Continue until all the frames are done.

When all the frames are dry, sand the faces. Patience and a random orbital sander are

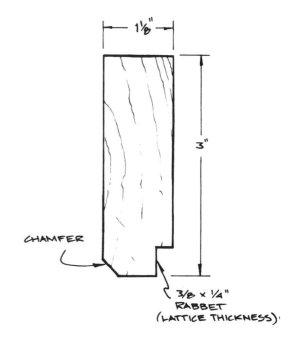

Illus. 11-4. A cross-section of the rail or stile used for the doors and sides.

Illus. 11-5. A stopped chamfer is applied to the front of the frame.

needed here. Start with 80-grit sandpaper and work your way up to 180 grit.

Now, rout the back of the frames to form a ledge for the lattice. Use a ⅜-inch bearing-guided rabbeting bit and cut the rabbet as deep as the lattice thickness—¼ inch in this case. On the face of the frame, make a stopped chamfer with a bearing-guided chamfer bit (Illus. 11-4). Stop the chamfers about 1½ inches short of the corners (Illus. 11-5).

Step 2: Add the Lattice The ¼-inch-thick × 1¼-inch-wide lattice strips are added in a two-step process. First, the back lattice strips are attached to the frame rabbet and then the front lattice strips are added (Illus. 11-6 and 11-7).

The back strips are cut on a 45-degree angle and start from the corner of the frame. Use the lattice itself to create the 1¼-inch space between strips. Glue and nail the lattice in place with waterproof or water-resistant glue and ⅝-inch-long brass brads. The lattice strips should be sanded before they are fastened in place.

When the back lattice is done, flip the frame over and begin work on the front lattice strips. The front lattice sits on top of the back lattice only. The strips are glued down and held in place with weights or brads. Again, sand each lattice piece before fastening it in place.

Step 3: Make the Bottom Frame The bottom frame can be made in much the same way as the door frames, except use 1 × 6 stock (Illus. 11-8). However, if boring through 5½-inch-wide stock is going to present a problem, you can cut the rails longer, lay them on top of the stiles,

and simply screw them together. If you use this alternate procedure, make sure the rails are on top when you assemble the house later on. Placing the rails on top allows the garbage cans to slide in place.

Step 4: Make the Back Next, make the back using 1 × 8 tongue-and-groove stock (Illus. 11-9). Cut the tongue-and-groove pieces to allow about ½ inch extra on the length of the back. Lay them out on a flat surface and insert the tongues into the grooves. Use a clamp if neces-

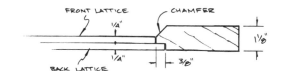

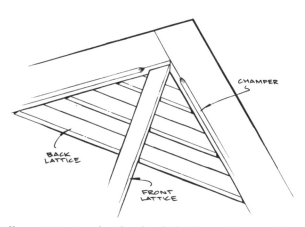

Illus. 11-6. Apply the back lattice strips to the frame rabbet first, and then the front lattice strips.

Illus. 11-7. Lattice applied to the doors and end panels adds an interesting look and allows plenty of ventilation.

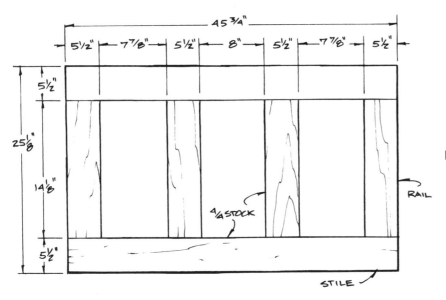

Illus. 11-8. The bottom frame.

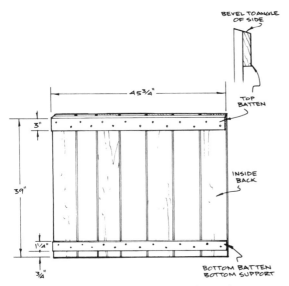

Illus. 11-9. The back for the garbage house.

sary to bring the pieces firmly together. Only light clamping is needed.

Check to ensure that the panel is square by measuring its diagonals. If the diagonals are the same, the panel is square. At this point, it's okay if some ends jut out and form a jagged line at the edge of the panel. We will come back shortly and trim them straight.

Now, place the two battens in position and attach them with 1¼-inch-long drywall screws. The screws do not have to be predrilled if you are using a softwood such as cedar, pine, or redwood. A cordless drill driver is a great advantage here. Position the screws so that they won't be hit by the saw blade when you trim the edge of the batten to a straight line. If you find a screw in a bad spot, remove and reposition it.

Once the back is fastened together, trim it to final size, making sure the edges are straight and square. The trimming can be done with a circular saw, a table saw, or a 1-inch bearing-guided trim bit in a router. See Squaring a Panel, below.

SQUARING A PANEL

Sometimes both ends of a panel are not straight or square to the edges. This problem typically occurs in my shop when I have to cut the end of a plywood panel with a jigsaw because the 4 × 8-foot sheet is too big for me to maneuver alone. However, it's easy to straighten and square the ends using either a router or a table saw.

In the router method, hold a straightedge under the rough edge. Using a try square, bring the straightedge square to the side, and then nail or clamp the straightedge in place. Don't worry about the nail holes in your stock; you'll fill the holes with putty after the ends are trimmed.

Place the panel on a table with the straightedge facing down. Using a router with a 1-inch bearing-guided trimmer bit, trim the offending rough edge straight by using the straightedge as a guide. Keep the trimmer-bit bearing firmly against the straightedge as you cut. (This procedure is very much like the method used to trim laminate.) With one end trimmed straight and square (Illus. 11-10), you can trim the opposite end in the same way—or you can use the table saw for this cut.

In the table saw method, a different approach

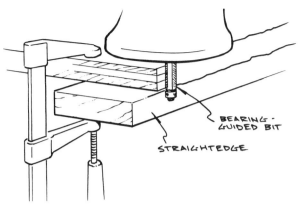

Illus. 11-10. The router method for squaring a panel.

is used to trim the panel ends. Place the panel on the saw with its rough edge against the rip fence. Using the try square, square one edge of the panel to the fence.

Next, take a straightedge, place it on top of the panel at the fence, and nail it down. Now you can trim the panel on its opposite end using the table saw. When the opposite end is trimmed, remove the straightedge and trim the

rough edge using the freshly sawn end as a guide (Illus. 11-11).

Step 5: Make the Lid The lid is constructed in the same manner as the back (Illus. 11-12). Note, however, that in addition to the long front and back battens, there is also a short batten applied at each end.

Step 6: Add the End Panel Tops The triangular-shaped portion that fits at the top of each end panel can now be made and applied. Glue up 1 × 6 tongue-and-groove siding to form a panel. You can cut the panel to shape on the table saw using a piece of ¾-inch-thick plywood or particleboard as a jig. Set the saw to just "kiss" the edge of the plywood jig (Illus. 11-13).

After the jig is trimmed, attach the tongue-and-groove panel to it with screws or nails. Position the panel so that the part to be removed hangs over the edge of the jig (Illus. 11-14) hanging section of the panel.

Once they have been shaped, the tops of the end panels can be installed. To do this, cut a rabbet into the top of each end panel with the

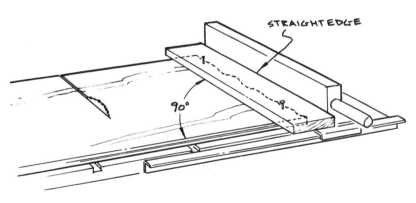

Illus. 11-11. The table-saw method for squaring a panel edge.

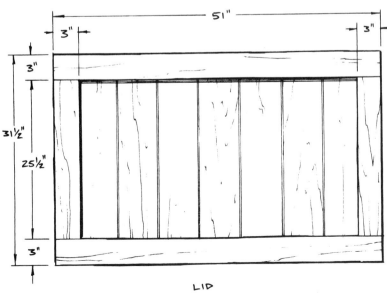

Illus. 11-12. The lid for the garbage house.

Illus. 11-13. Cutting the tongue-and-groove end panel is easier if you make this simple jig.

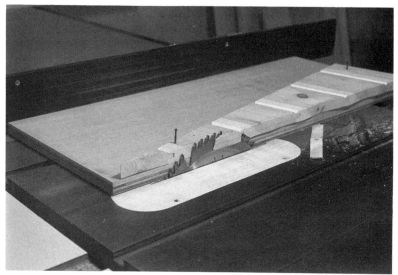

Illus. 11-14. Secure the panel to the jig, and then trim the panel edge with the table saw.

table saw. The depth of the rabbet should be 1⅛ inches, and it should be cut so that the remaining material is the same as the thickness of the tongue-and-groove panel (Illus. 11-15).

Make the two backer pieces from ⅜-inch-thick CDX plywood. CDX is a grade of plywood that can be found at most lumberyards. It is made with waterproof glue, and that's important for an outdoor project like this.

The plywood backers can be left square for the moment. Use glue and 1-inch-long × number-8 flathead wood screws to attach each backer to the rabbet cut in the end panels. Next, attach the tongue-and-groove panels to the backers by gluing and screwing from the back of the backers. Once the panels are in place, the plywood overhanging the top can be trimmed close with a handsaw or saber saw, and then trimmed flush

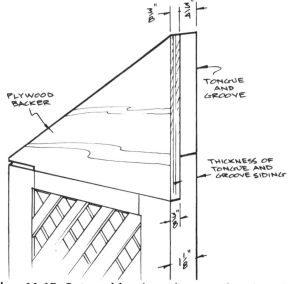

Illus. 11-15. Cut a rabbet into the top of each end panel.

Illus. 11-16. A router equipped with a flush-trimming bit is used to trim the panel overhanging the top of the plywood backer.

with a 1-inch bearing-guided flush-trimming bit in a router (Illus. 11-16).

Step 7: Assemble the End Panels, Bottom, and Back   With all the panels made, it's time to assemble the house using 1⅛ × 1⅛-inch wooden cleats. Use one long cleat if the backs of the panels are flat. If the backs are uneven, such as near the top of the ends, use several short cleats.

Screw the cleats in place, attaching them flush to the frame edges on each end, but setting them back ¾ inch from the frame's back edge. (The ¾-inch setback allows for the thickness of the lower back batten.) Then, holding the bottom against the back, fasten the bottom flush to the bottom edge of the back. The end panels

can now be fastened to both the bottom and the back. As you assemble each of the panels, check to make sure they are square and plumb.

Step 8: Add the Support Rail and Stile   The support rail and stile help to further strengthen the project. You'll need 1⅛-inch-thick stock cut to a width of 3 inches to make the two parts (Illus. 11-17).

Make the support rail first. Cut it to length and then use the table saw to cut a rabbet on each end. With a chisel, chop out a matching notch in the inside face of the end frames. Add glue to the mating surfaces and then assemble the rail to the frames. For added strength, and to provide clamping pressure, drive 3-inch-long × number-10 flathead wood screws through the

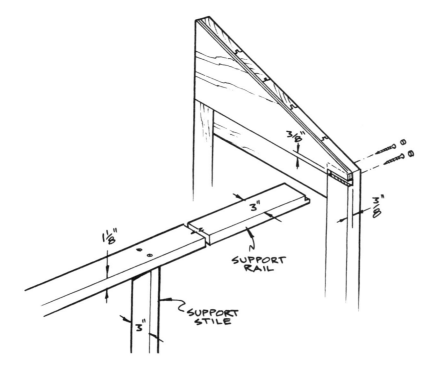

Illus. 11-17. The support rail and stile on the garbage house.

end-panel frames and into the ends of the horizontal support rail. Be sure to predrill and countersink for each of the screws. After driving the screws, glue wood plugs into each hole using a water-resistant or waterproof glue. When dry, sand the plugs flush to the surface.

Install the support stile next, locating it midpoint along the length of the support rail. Cut the stile to length so that it fits snugly between the bottom frame and the underside of the support rail. Secure the stile in place by driving 3-inch-long screws into the stile ends. Add wood plugs and sand them smooth.

Step 9: Final Details The two bottom skids (shown in Illus. 11-2) are made from 2 × 4 stock cut to a length of 24 inches. Pressure-treated wood is a good idea here; just be sure the wood is rated for ground contact. Cut a bevel on each end and then attach the parts by driving 2-inch-long × number-10 flathead wood screws through the bottom frame and into the skids.

Give the entire project a thorough final sanding in preparation for the final finish. Take particular care to round over any sharp edges on the lid or door frame. Then add the hinges to the doors and lid, and check to make certain everything opens and closes properly. Finally, install locking hardware of your choice.

Step 10: Apply the Finish To complete the garbage house, add a good-quality siding stain in accordance with the manufacturer's instructions. Applying three complementary colors, as we did, gives the project an especially interesting look.

Chapter 12.
Pool or Patio Shed

If it's difficult to keep things in neat order around your pool or patio, a storage shed like this one (Illus. 12-1) might just be the answer to your problem. Whether it's used at the pool or on the patio, this handsome shed can add order to all the paraphernalia that needs a place to call home. Also, the countertop surface makes a perfect server, something that comes in handy during outdoor parties. The tiled countertop and backsplash surfaces are another nice feature. The tile accepts hot food items right off the grill, plus it's easy to clean.

The shed is perfect for storing pool and patio chairs, and the many other odds and ends that collect out-of-doors. The overall dimensions of the shed are shown in Illus. 12-2 and 12-3. This

Illus. 12-1. This handsome storage shed has a tiled countertop and a backsplash, and will provide a perfect storage area for the items around the pool or patio. Page 80 shows this shed in full color.

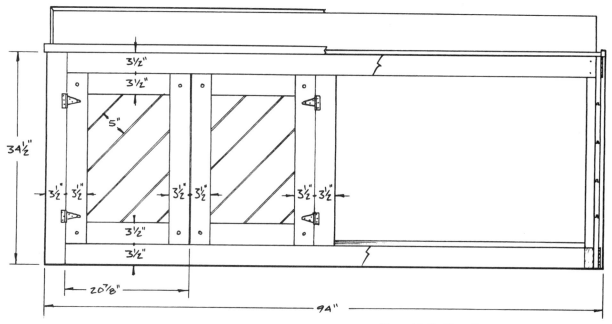

Illus. 12-2. The dimensions of the shed.

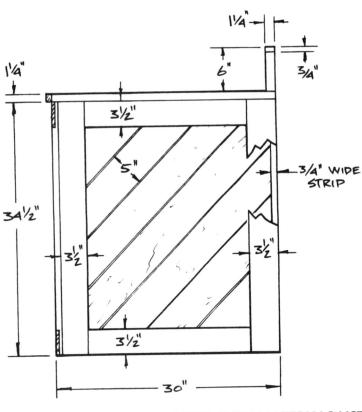

Illus. 12-3. A side view of the pool or patio shed.

POOL AND PATIO SHED MATERIALS LIST (All Dimensions Actual)

Part	Size	Material	Quantity
Shed Frame	1½ in. × 3½ in. × 8 ft.	Fir	9
End framing, face framing, door framing, strips, and edging	¾ in. × 3½ in. × 8 ft.	Cedar	14
Facing	¾ in. × 5½ in. × 8 ft.	Tongue-and-Groove Cedar	8
Subfloor, Top	¾ in. × 4 ft. × 8 ft.	CDX Plywood	2
Back	¾ in. × 4 ft. × 8 ft.	Exterior Plywood	1

MISCELLANEOUS MATERIALS

The following materials are also needed to build the pool and patio shed: 6d, 8d, 10d, and 16d common nails; 2d, 3d, 4d, and 6d finishing nails; 2½-inch-long × No. 12 flat-head wood screws; sixteen 1¼-inch-long ⅜-16 carriage bolts, nuts, and flat washers; ⅜-inch-thick tiles; 8 door hinges; 2 hasps; 4 door handles; and one gallon of wood waterproofer.

project accepts chairs less than 24 inches wide (when folded), but you can increase the shed size somewhat to accommodate larger chairs.

The countertop and backsplash are covered with ⅜-inch-thick slate flooring tile. However, tile materials and sizes can vary throughout the country, so it's a good idea to find out what's available in your area before starting the shed.

Following are the steps for building the pool and patio shed:

Step 1: Make the Floor Begin by making the floor frame (Illus. 12-4). Using 2 × 4 lumber, cut the stock to length, and then assemble the frame parts with a pair of 16d galvanized steel common nails at each joint. You can use ¾-inch-thick CDX plywood for the subfloor. (The subfloor is the panels that are attached to the top edge of the floor.) When cutting the plywood to length and width, work carefully to ensure that the four corners are square to each other.

Assemble the plywood subfloor to the frame, making sure that the edges of the subfloor are flush with the 2 × 4 frame. Use 8d galvanized steel common nails to secure the subfloor in place. Space the nails 6 inches apart along the edges and 12 inches apart along the center sup-port. At this point in the construction, it's helpful to level the shed. Using a carpenter's level, check for level around the entire perimeter of the subfloor. Add blocks and shims under each corner, as needed, to level the shed.

Step 2: Add the Uprights and the Top Frame Next, add the six vertical uprights and the top frame (Illus. 12-5). Using 2 × 4 stock, cut each upright to 27½ inches long. Toenail the uprights to the subfloor and frame with 10d galvanized steel common nails. (If you find it difficult to toenail, see Chapter 10, Illus. 10-9, for a tip that makes the job easier.) The horizontal members of the center frame can be nailed to the uprights before toenailing.

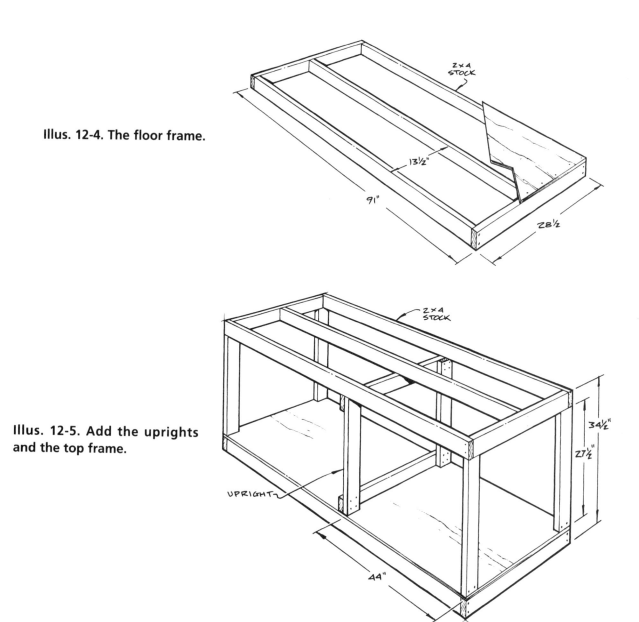

Illus. 12-4. The floor frame.

Illus. 12-5. Add the uprights and the top frame.

Make the top frame from 2 × 4 stock, then toenail it to the uprights. Once all the parts are assembled, check to make sure the entire frame is square and plumb.

Step 3: Make the Back The back, which is made from ¾-inch-thick plywood, extends above the top to create a backsplash (Illus. 12-6). Because the front surface of the back is going to be covered with tile, and the back of this shed faces a wall where it can't be seen, you can save money by using plywood with lower face-veneer grades, such as grade B-C or grade C-C plugged. Since much of the back is exposed to the weather, make certain the plywood is rated for exterior use.

To make the back, rip a 4 × 8 sheet of plywood to 41 inches wide, and then measure the length of the shed frame and crosscut the plywood to the measured length. Make sure that all

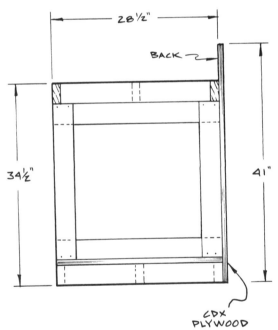

Illus. 12-6. The back of the pool or patio shed.

the plywood cuts are square. Assemble the back to the shed frame with 6d galvanized common nails, spacing the nails as you did for the subfloor. When the back is assembled, the shed frame should be square and plumb. Also, the ends of the plywood should be flush with the ends of the shed frame.

If your shed is to be located where its back can be easily viewed, you might want to make the back more attractive. Rather that using plywood, consider framing the back and adding tongue-and-groove facing, as detailed in Step 5.

Step 4: The Ends Each of the ends is made up of an end frame with a tongue-and-groove facing (Illus. 12-7). The end frames, made from 1 × 4 cedar stock, have a half-lap joint on each end (Illus. 12-8).

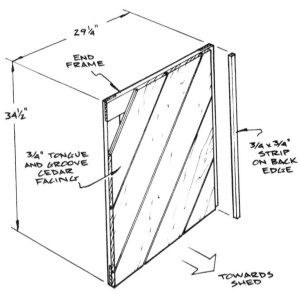

Illus. 12-7. The ends of the pool or patio shed are made of end frames with tongue-and-groove facings.

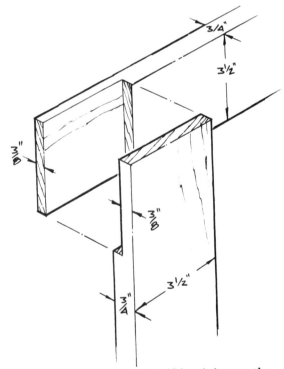

Illus. 12-8. A look at the half-lap joint on the end frames.

The half-laps can be cut on the table saw or radial arm saw. To make the joints, set the saw blade to cut slightly less than one-half the ¾-

inch thickness and then make repeated passes over the blade to create the 3½ × 3½-inch lap.

After cutting a pair of half-laps, assemble the parts and check to see how much additional material must be removed. Raise the blade slightly and repeat the procedure, keeping in mind that the final cut is going to be double the blade adjustment. Keep making small adjustments until the mated parts fit perfectly flush. Once the correct blade height is established, you can cut all the remaining half-laps.

Next, tack each of the end-frame half-lap joints together by driving a couple of ⅝-inch brass brads from the front of the frame. Use brass brads because they won't rust.

Now, check the end frames for squareness. Also, make sure they fit properly on the shed frame. The top of the end frame should be flush with the top edge of the shed frame. Also, the end frame should be flush with the front of the shed frame and the back face of the plywood back.

The inside facing is made from 1 × 6 tongue-and-groove cedar siding. As shown, the facing is installed diagonally, but it can also be applied horizontally or vertically. If installed diagonally or horizontally, it's best to have the grooves facing down (Illus. 12-9). Grooves that face up are likely to fill with rainwater, and the water might find its way inside the shed. In addition, moisture trapped in the grooves can shorten the life of the facing.

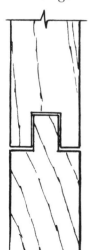

Illus. 12-9. The grooves on the face should face down if the facing is installed diagonally or horizontally.

Also, when the facing is installed diagonally or horizontally, you need to add a ¾ × ¾-inch strip at the back of the end frame. The strip prevents water from entering the shed through the exposed ends of the tongue-and-groove siding.

Cut the tongue-and-groove siding to fit flush with all four edges of the end frame (except for the diagonal and horizontal facing, which butt up to the strip at the back). Use 3d common nails to secure the facing to the end frame. A single nail at the center of each board will suffice. By the way, fasteners and hardware made from galvanized steel can sometimes stain red cedar when a clear finish is used. If you expect to apply a clear finish to this shed, any fasteners (nails, screws and bolts) that come in contact with red cedar should be made from stainless steel.

The end frames can now be installed on the shed frame. Attach them with 2½-inch-long × No. 12 flathead wood screws driven through the end frame and into the shed frame.

Step 5: Assemble the Face Frame The face frame, made from half-lapped 1 × 4 cedar stock, covers the front of the shed framing (see Illus. 12-2). Cut the half-laps by following the same procedure used to make the end frames. Once the half-laps are cut, the face frame is attached to the 2 × 4 shed frame with 6d finishing nails.

Step 6: Install the Top and the Filler Blocks The top can be made from ¾-inch-thick CDX plywood. When properly cut to size, the top should fit flush with the end and face frames, and it should butt against the plywood back. Secure the top to the shed frame with 1¼-inch-long drywall screws. Drive the screws slightly below the surface of the top.

Next, cut two cedar filler blocks for each end of the shed, one block measuring ¾ × ¾ × 1½ inches, the other block measuring ½ × 1¼ × ¾ inch. Join the blocks using a couple of 2d finishing nails (Illus. 12-10). Once joined, secure each filler-block assembly to the back corner of the plywood top with a couple of 4d finishing nails (Illus. 12-11).

Step 7: Add the Edging You'll need to cut about 22 feet of ¾-inch-thick × 1¼-inch-wide cedar edging to cover the exposed edges of the plywood top and the backsplash. The edging not only serves to cover the plywood edges, it also creates a "lip" for the ⅜-inch-thick tiled countertop that's added later. (If your tile has a different thickness, adjust the width of the edging as needed.)

Secure the edging with 6d finishing nails

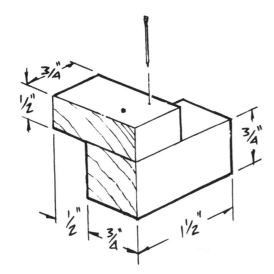

Illus. 12-10. Cut two cedar filler blocks for each end of the shed.

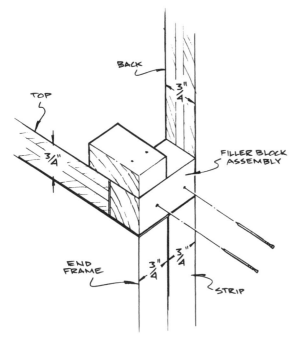

Illus. 12-11. Each filler-block assembly is attached to the back corner of the plywood top.

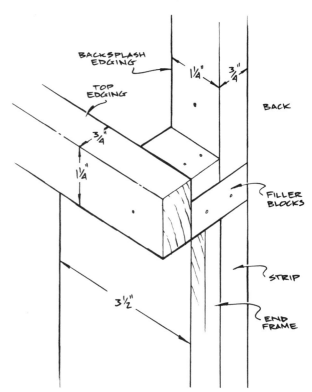

Illus. 12-12. The top edge is installed flush with the underside of the top. The backsplash edging is installed flush with the back surface of the back.

spaced 8 to 10 inches apart. Install the top edging flush with the underside of the top, and the backsplash edging flush with the back surface of the back. Miter the edging at each of the corners (Illus. 12-12).

Step 8: Make the Doors   The four doors are next (Illus. 12-13). Each door consists of a half-lapped frame with a facing made from 1 × 6 tongue-and-groove cedar siding. The frame is made from 1 × 4 cedar stock. Measure the openings in the shed face frame to determine the length and width of the door frames. Allow

a clearance space of about 1/16 of an inch between the doors and the face frames.

After the door frame parts are cut to length, make the half-lap joints on each end of the stock. Bore a 3/8-inch-diameter hole at the center of each joint, and then assemble the joints with 1 1/4-inch-long, 3/8-16 carriage bolts, along with matching nuts and washers. The bolts add both strength and an interesting decorative look. Check the door frames for squareness and make adjustments if necessary.

Next, cut and assemble the facing. As shown in Illus. 12-13, allow the tongue-and-groove siding to overlap the inside edge of the door frame by 1 inch all around, and then secure the tongue-and-groove side with 3d finishing nails. Use three nails at the end of each board. Then mount the hinges to the doors and face frame as shown in Illus. 12-2.

The addition of a hasp and padlock keeps the door secure. If you like, a doorknob or handle can also be installed.

Step 9: Install the Tile   Because this is an outdoor shed, you'll need tile and grout that can stand up to the weather. Some tiles are only acceptable for indoor use. A good tile supplier can help you choose from the many options. Also, since the installation procedure depends upon the type of tile, adhesive, and grout that is used, your supplier can provide you with plenty of helpful how-to information for your specific needs.

An accurate layout is important when installing tiles. Arrange the tiles on the shed, properly spaced, before setting them in adhesive. If tiles along the edges must be trimmed, make sure they are all the same size and measure more than one-half a tile in width. Most rental outfits have tile cutters available. For a small project like this, a snap cutter can do the job just fine. A snap cutter scores the tile at the cutting line, and then snaps the tile into two parts at the scored line.

For additional protection from the weather, apply a clear finish to the tiles. Be sure to choose a finish that's acceptable for outdoor use and compatible with the tile and grout you select. Again, your tile supplier can help you here.

Step 10: Apply the Shed Finish The natural look of cedar has a lot of appeal, so a clear finish makes good sense. A couple of coats of a wood weatherproofer (such as Thompson's Water Seal) provides good protection against the elements. To maintain the protection, you should plan on adding a coat or two of the waterproofer every couple of years.

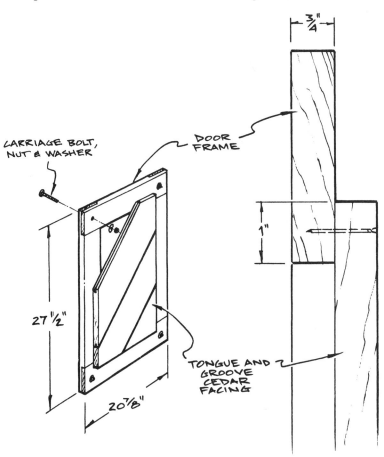

Illus. 12-13. Each of the four doors for the pool or patio shed has a frame made from 1 × 4 cedar stock and a facing made from 1 × 6 tongue-and-groove cedar siding.

Chapter 13. Gazebo

What could be more relaxing on a warm summer evening than to sit in your gazebo and watch the sun go down while sipping on a cool drink? A gazebo is also a delightful place to sit and chat with friends while the kids play in the sun. Useful during the warm months, and pleasant to look at all year round, this fascinating structure adds both value and charm to your home. While this project (Illus. 13-1) is more challenging than some of the other projects presented in this book, it will reward you with the pleasure of its use and the pride of a considerable accomplishment.

Following are the steps for building a gazebo:

Step 1: Choose a Location The gazebo is contained in a 10½-foot-diameter circle, so choose a spot that allows enough room for the structure. If the spot is fairly level, it is going to make

Illus. 13-1. This gazebo is a challenging project, but will prove to be a delightful place to relax in. Pages 97–104 show the gazebo in full color.

GAZEBO MATERIALS LIST (All Dimensions Actual)

Part	Size	Material	Quantity
Cupola Band	⅜ × 1½ in.	Cedar	As required
Cupola Trim	¾ in. × 2 in. × 8 ft.	Cedar	1
Rafter Support	¾ in. × 3½ in. × 8 ft.*	Cedar	6
Railing Support	¾ in. × 3½ in. × 10 ft.*	Cedar	4
Roof Sheathing	¾ × 3½ in.	Cedar	As required
Lower Railing Trim	¾ in. × 3½ in. × 6 ft.*	Cedar	14
Upper Railing Trim	¾ in. × 3½ in. × 6 ft.*	Cedar	14
Seat Edging	¾ in. × 3½ in. × 6 ft.	Cedar	7
Fascia	¾ in. × 5½ in. × 6 ft.	Cedar	8
Cupola Ends	¾ in. × 2 ft. × 4 ft.	Exterior Plywood	1
Lower Railing Rail	1½ in. × 1½ in. × 6 ft.	Cedar	21
Upper Railing Rail	1½ in. × 1½ in. × 6 ft.	Cedar	14
Lower Railing Baluster	1½ in. × 1½ in. × 8 ft.	Cedar	13
Upper Railing Baluster	1½ in. × 1½ in. × 8 ft.	Cedar	4
Cupola Post	1½ in. × 1½ in. × 8 ft.	Cedar	1
Cupola Upright	1½ × 1½ in.	Cedar	As required
Cap Rail	1½ in. × 3½ in. × 6 ft.	Cedar	7
Seat Support	1½ in. × 3½ in. × 8 ft.	Cedar	3
Entry Top Rail	1½ in. × 3½ in. × 6 ft.	Cedar	1
Deck Octagon	1½ in. × 5½ in. × 4 ft.	Cedar	1
Seat	1½ in. × 5½ in. × 6 ft.	Cedar	14
Band Joist	1½ in. × 5½ in. × 6 ft.	Cedar	8
Deck Frame	1½ in. × 5½ in. × 10 ft.	Cedar**	4
Joist Support	1½ in. × 5½ in. × 6 ft.	Cedar**	1
Deck	1½ × 5½ in.	Cedar	As required
Brace	1½ in. × 5½ in. × 8 ft.	Cedar	4
Post	3½ in. × 3½ in. × 8 ft.	Cedar	8
Roof Octagon	3½ in. × 3½ in. × 6 ft.	Cedar	1
Rafter	3½ in. × 3½ in. × 6 ft.	Cedar	8
Seat Brace	3½ in. × 3½ in. × 8 ft.	Cedar	2
Entry Step Support	3½ × 3½ in.	Cedar	As required
Roof Shingles	18 in.	Cedar	As required

*Width allows for extra stock.
**Pressure-treated lumber can be used.

MISCELLANEOUS MATERIALS

The following materials are also needed to build the gazebo: 8d, 10d, and 12d galvanized finishing nails; 10d, 12d, and 16d galvanized common nails; 12d galvanized deck nails; 9 cardboard tube forms that are 10 inches in diameter; wood waterproofer; and insect screening.

for less work later in the construction. When you have chosen a good location, drive a stake into the ground at the center of the circle.

Step 2: Mark for the Concrete Piers   The upright posts in the gazebo are supported by con-

crete piers. Marking the position of these piers is next. The marking is done in three steps. First, you make an outer row of stakes. Then you accurately adjust the position of the stakes. Finally, you make an inner row of stakes at the centerpoint of the pier positions. The outer row of stakes helps when you remove the inner row in order to dig the holes for the piers.

Drive a nail into the center stake and tie two strings to it. The strings should be about 9 feet long. Cut a stick to a length of 6 feet, 1⅜ inches. Drive a nail into each end of the stick. Holding the string taught, mark a point 8 feet from the center stake. Tie the string to one end of the stick. Do the same for the other string, tying it to the other end of the stick (Illus. 13-2).

Rotate the triangle formed by the two strings and the stick until the stick is in the same relative position where you want the entry to the gazebo. Drive in two more stakes, one at each end of the stick (Illus. 13-3).

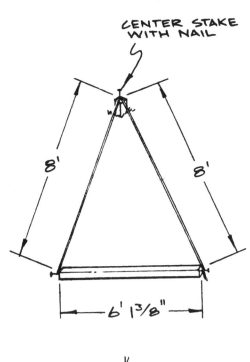

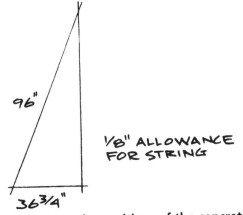

Illus. 13-2. Marking the positions of the concrete piers. The first step consists of marking a point 8 feet from the center stake.

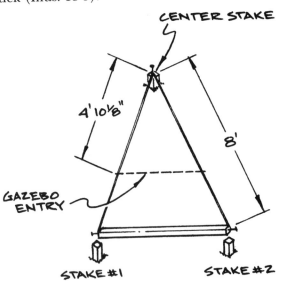

Illus. 13-3. Locate the entrance to the gazebo and then drive in two more stakes, one at each end of the stick.

Rotate the triangle again until one end of the stick lines up with stake number 2, and then drive in a new stake at the other end of the stick. Continue in this fashion until you have 8 stakes plus the center stake (Illus. 13-4).

Step 3: Adjust the Stakes for Accuracy   The stakes will have certain geometric relationships if they have been laid out accurately. One, the stakes opposite each other form a line that passes through the center stake. To check for this alignment, drive a nail into the end of each

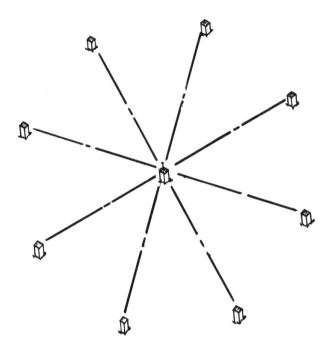

Illus. 13-4. With the 8 stakes and the center stake positioned, the concrete piers have been located.

stake. Tie a string to one of the stakes, and then stretch the string to the opposite stake. The string should pass over the centerpoint of the center stake. Repeat this step for each opposing pair of stakes (Illus. 13-5).

Second, a second line between the opposing stakes should be at 90 degrees to the first string (Illus. 13-6). To check for the 90-degree angle,

mark a point on the second line exactly 4 feet from the centerpoint of the center stake. On the first line, mark a point 3 feet from the stake centerpoint. Next, measure the distance between the two marks. If it measures 5 feet, the angle is exactly 90 degrees.

Third, there should be two more lines at 90 degrees to each other that are midway between the first two lines (Illus. 13-7).

Once the adjustments are made, you can mark for the centerpoint of the concrete piers. Measure along the string and mark a point 4 feet, 10⅛ inches from the centerpoint of the center stake. This point represents the centerpoint location of the pier. Drive stakes into each of these positions to mark them until the holes are dug for the piers.

Step 4: Make the Piers The holes for the piers must be deep enough to extend below the frost line for your region. The frost line in our area, Connecticut, is 3 feet below ground level. You'll need to dig 9 holes—one for the center pier and eight for the perimeter piers.

To allow for drainage, dig the holes a few inches below the frost line. We made the holes 3 feet, 6 inches deep, and then filled the first 6 inches with gravel to provide for drainage. Now, place 10-inch-diameter cardboard tube forms into each hole and level the tops of the tubes. The tops should be about 2 inches aboveground.

Illus. 13-5. If the stakes have been laid out accurately, the stakes opposite each other should form a line that passes through the center stake.

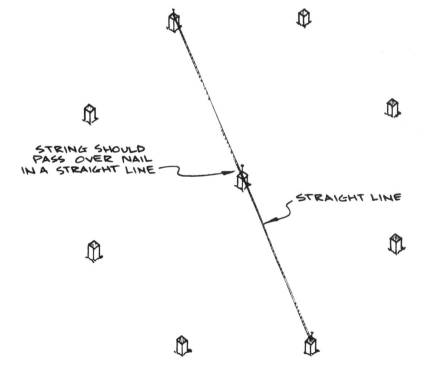

STRING SHOULD PASS OVER NAIL IN A STRAIGHT LINE

STRAIGHT LINE

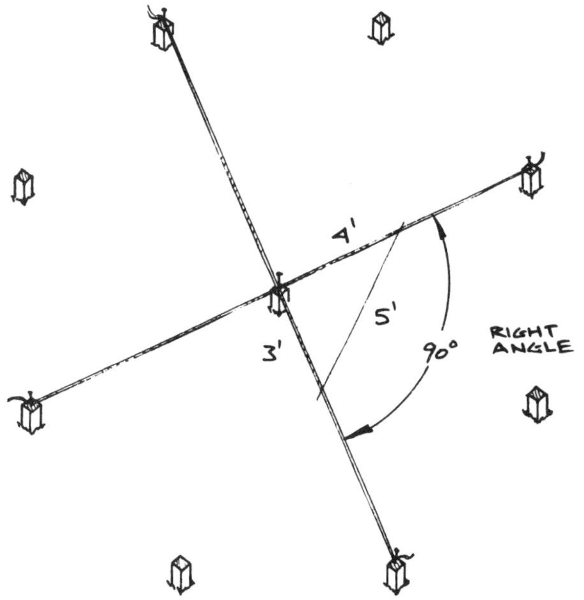

Illus. 13-6. A second line between the opposing stakes should be at 90 degrees to the first string.

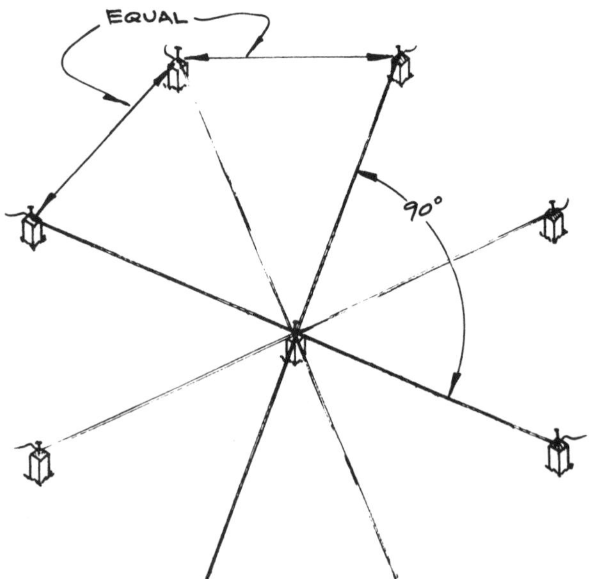

Illus. 13-7. Two lines midway between the first two lines should be at 90 degrees to each other.

It's important for all 9 of the tubes to be level with each other. You can use a line level to check that they are so, or you can use a flat, straight 2 × 4 as a straightedge. Place the straightedge on the tops of two cardboard tubes and check that they are level with a carpenter's level. Adjust one of the tubes, as needed, to get things level and then move the straightedge to the next tube. Repeat this procedure until all tubes are level with each other.

Next, add the concrete to the cardboard tube. Before the concrete sets, push a 4 × 4 post anchor into the wet concrete, making sure that the anchor is centered on the tube. Also, be sure that the open side of the post anchor (which is U-shaped) faces the center pier. When the open side faces the center pier, the joist hangers can be nailed to the bottom of the post later in the construction (see Step 8). Finally, check to see that the post anchors are equidistant and that the tops of the piers remain level.

Now, carefully fill in with soil around the tubes and let the concrete set for two days. Re-

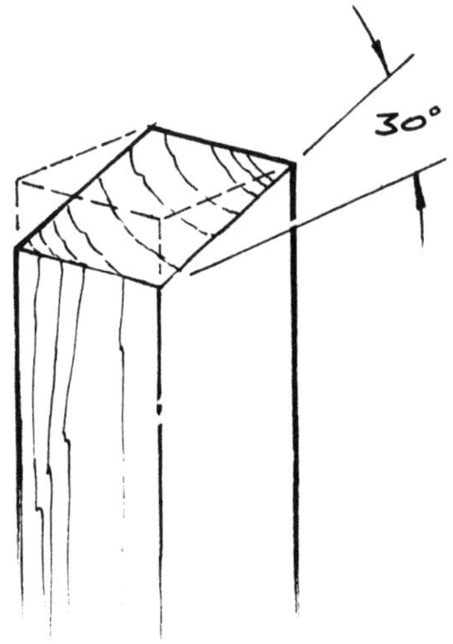

Illus. 13-8. Bevel the top of the post to 30 degrees.

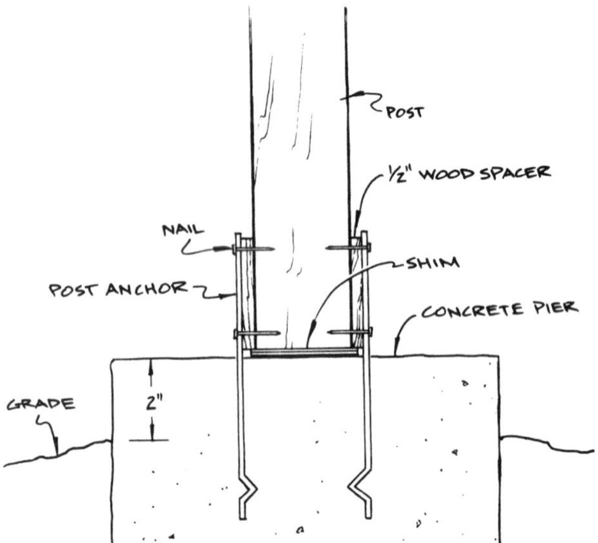

Illus. 13-9. Fasten the post to the post anchor with galvanized nails or bolts.

check that the tubes are level and the distances between the posts before continuing.

Step 5: Install the Posts   Cut a 4 × 4 cedar post to a length of 6 feet, 11 inches. Bevel the top of the post to 30 degrees (Illus. 13-8), and then fasten the post to the post anchor with galvanized nails or bolts (Illus. 13-9). Use a shim (made from pressure-treated lumber or cedar) between the bottom end of the post and the concrete. If necessary, add spaces between the post and the post anchor.

Next, mount the ¾ × 2¾ × 32-inch-long rafter supports. The rafter supports extend above the top of the posts and are beveled at the same angle (Illus. 13-10). To determine the exact position of the rafter supports, take a scrap piece of 4 × 4 and hold it on the top bevel of the post. The rafter supports should be cut flush with the top of the scrap piece. If you prefer, the rafter supports can be attached to the posts before the posts are erected.

Step 6: Make the Roof Frame   Start the roof frame by making the center octagon from 4 × 4 stock. After cutting the eight segments to size, join them by driving a pair of 16d galvanized common nails at the end of each piece. Stagger the nails to avoid having them hit each other (Illus. 13-11 and 13-12).

Next, make the first rafter. The rafter is cut 5 feet, 3¼ inches long from 4 × 4 stock. Bevel the upper (inner) end to a 60-degree angle (Illus. 13-13). Bevel the lower (outer) end 22½ degrees (Illus. 13-14).

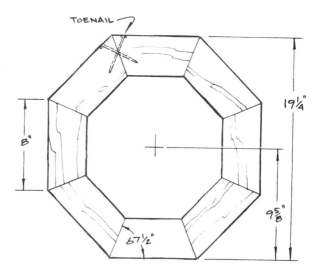

Illus. 13-11. Center octagon dimensions.

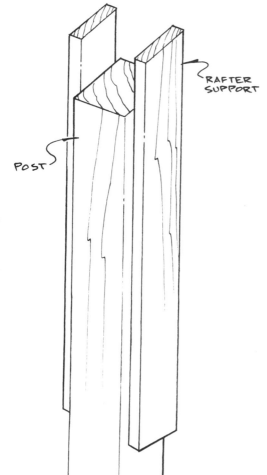

Illus. 13-10. Mount the rafter supports to the post.

Illus. 13-12. The center octagon for the roof is made from 4×4 stock. The ends are beveled to 22½ degrees.

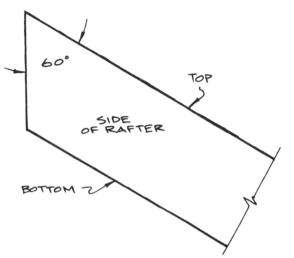

Illus. 13-13. Bevel the upper end of the rafter to a 60-degree angle.

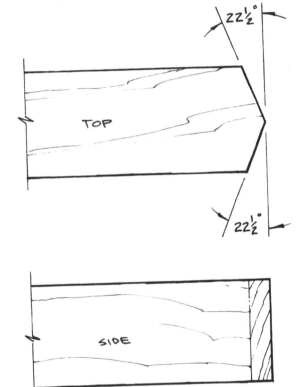

Illus. 13-14. Bevel the lower end of the rafter to 22½ degrees.

The upper end of each rafter attaches to the center octagon, while the lower end sits on top of the post. The lower end of the rafter should extend past the post by 3½ inches (Illus. 13-15). Check that the rafter fits properly, and then make all the rafters.

At the top end, toenail the rafters to the center octagon with 16d galvanized common nails. At the lower end, nail the rafters with 12d gal-

vanized common nails driven through the rafter supports.

Cover the lower ends of the rafters by applying fascia boards all around the perimeter of the roof frame. Make the fascia boards from 1×6 cedar stock, mitering the ends of the boards to 22½ degrees. Drive 10d galvanized common nails through the fascia boards and into the ends of the rafters. For a nice decorative effect, the bottom edge of each fascia board can be arched.

Step 7: Install the Roof Follow the procedure for installing a wood shingled roof as discussed in the Spaced Wood Sheathing section of Chapter 4 and the Applying Wood Shingles section of Chapter 5. Use 1×4 cedar for the spaced wood sheathing, and 18-inch-long, number-1-grade cedar shingles. The shingle exposure is 5½ inches. To cover the seams where the roof sections meet, add shingles cut to 3 inches wide and beveled to fit (Illus. 13-16).

The shingles can be applied right up to the peak, or you can leave an opening above the roof octagon for ventilation. If you leave an opening, it needs a covering of some sort. We added a decorative cupola. On a hot summer day, the cupola allows warm air under the roof to rise and start circulating the air around the perimeter of the gazebo.

If you want to include the cupola, make (see Step 14) and attach it before installing the shingles. To attach the cupola, place it on top of the roof octagon and then drive screws through the bottom plate of the cupola and into the roof octagon. To drive the screws, you'll need to work from inside the shed, reaching up and into the cupola from the underside.

With the cupola attached, the roof shingles can be added to the base of the cupola.

Step 8: Frame the Deck Make the deck frame from 2×6 cedar or pressure-treated stock. Use metal hangers to attach the joists in place. Start with one full-length joist between two opposing posts. Next, add the joist at right angles to this. This second joist is in two pieces. Each piece is hung between the post and the first joist (Illus. 13-17).

Next, nail the joist supports to create a box, and then add the remaining joists between the box and the posts. Finish the deck frame with a band joist made of 2×6 cedar on the outside of the posts. Nail these joists to the posts with

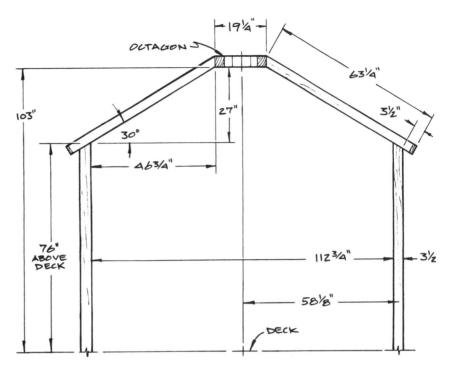

Illus. 13-15. The lower end of each rafter should extend 3½ inches past the post.

Illus. 13-16. Each of the eight roof ridges is covered with a ridge cap made from beveled cedar shingles.

12d galvanized common nails, keeping the posts level with the joists (Illus. 13-18).

Step 9: Make the Deck Begin by making the center octagon from 2 × 6 stock (Illus. 13-19). Nail the octagon together; then scribe a 3-inch-diameter center circle and cut it out with a saber saw. From "2 ×" stock, cut a disk to fill the center circle (Illus. 13-20). Place the octagon and the disk in the center of the deck frame and nail the parts in place with 12d galvanized deck nails.

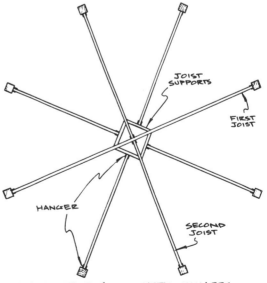

DECK FRAME 2×6 WITH METAL HANGERS

Illus. 13-17 (right). The deck frame for the gazebo.

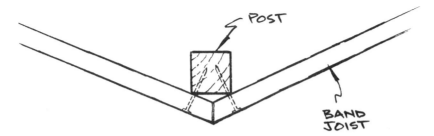

Illus. 13-18. Nail the band joists to the posts, keeping them level with the joists.

Illus. 13-19. The center octagon for the deck is made from 2×6 stock.

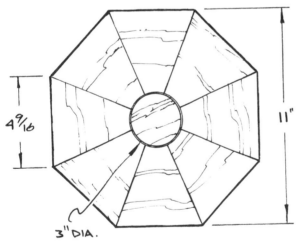

Illus. 13-20. A disk for the center octagon for the deck.

Continue adding decking outside the octagon (Illus. 13-21). Space the decking about no more than ¼ inch apart. Maintain the straight lines at the miters. The last row of the deck should overhang the band joist by ½ inch. Also, you'll need to notch the last row to fit around the posts.

Step 10: Make the Lower Railing Start work on the lower railing by nailing ¾ × 2¾ × 29-inch-long railing supports to the sides of the

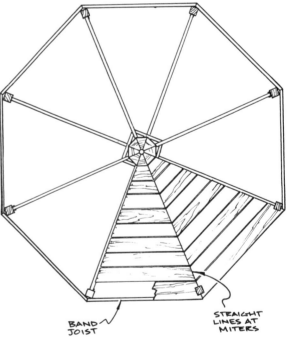

Illus. 13-21. Adding decking outside the octagon.

posts (Illus. 13-22). Next, from 2 × 2 cedar stock, cut three lengths of rails for each octagonal section except the entry (a total of 21 rails). Miter the ends of the rail stock to 22½ degrees. When measuring for the rail lengths, keep in

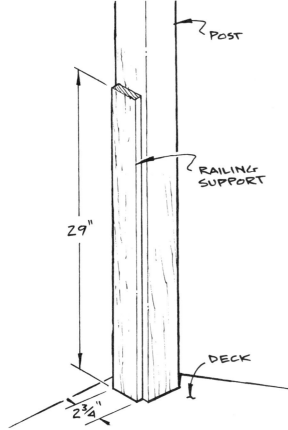

Illus. 13-22. Nail railing supports to the sides of the posts.

mind that the rails should fit between the railing supports about 1½ inches from the outside of the post.

Next, from 2 × 2 cedar stock, cut the balus-

ters to length, and then lay out and mark the baluster locations on the top, center, and bottom rails. Attach each baluster by driving a pair of 10d galvanized finishing nails through the rail stock and into each end of the baluster. Now, attach the baluster/rail subassembly to the railing supports with 10d galvanized finishing nails.

Cut the cap rail from 2 × 4 cedar stock. The cap rail fits between the posts, and rests on top of the railing supports. Attach the cap rail to the top end of the railing supports with a pair of 12d galvanized finishing nails. Further secure the parts by driving pairs of 8d galvanized finishing nails along the cap rail into the top rail, spacing the pairs of nails about 12 inches apart.

Once installed, the lower railing should start about 1 inch above the deck and measure 30½ inches high, including the 2 × 4 cap rail (Illus. 13-23 and 13-24). For a nice ornamental touch add the scalloped trim to the outside of the railing (Illus. 13-25 and 13-26).

Step 11: Make the Upper Railing   The upper railing construction is similar to the top section of the lower railing (Illus. 13-27 and 13-28). Note that the top rail is located 8 inches from the top of the rafter support.

The braces, which serve to stiffen the entire structure, are made from 2 × 6 cedar stock. As shown, a simple scallop detail is cut along one edge, and a 45-degree miter is cut on each end. Toenail the braces between the rafter supports and the underside of the upper railing assem-

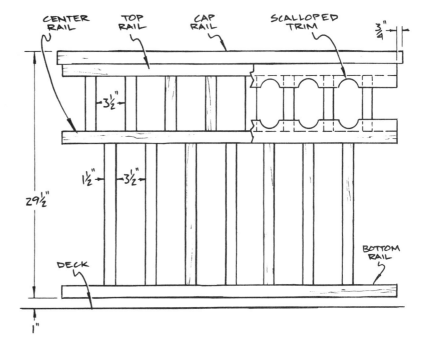

Illus. 13-23. The lower railing should measure about 30½ inches high.

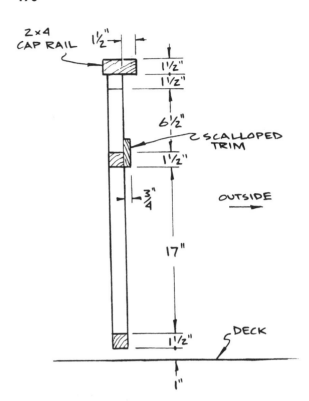

2×4 CAP RAIL

1½"

1½"

1½"

6½"

SCALLOPED TRIM

1½"

¾"

OUTSIDE →

17"

1½"

DECK

1"

Illus. 13-24. A side view of the cap rail.

Illus. 13-25. The scalloped trim provides an interesting detail to the railings.

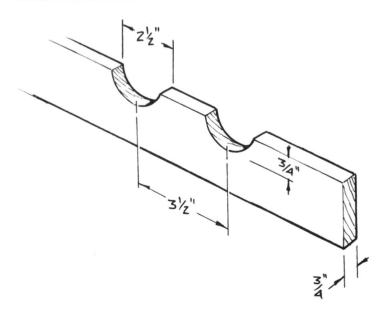

2½"

3½"

¾"

¾"

Illus. 13-26. The dimensions of the scalloped trim.

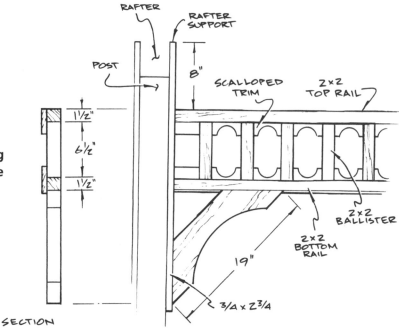

Illus. 13-27. The upper railing construction as seen from the inside.

Illus. 13-28. The upper railing is constructed in much the same way as the lower railing.

blies. Then, cut and apply the scalloped trim to the outside of the railing.

The lower and upper railings are not applied to the gazebo entry. To finish assembling this section, install railing supports to the posts (if you haven't already) and then add a 2 × 4 top rail, followed by a pair of braces (Illus. 13-29).

Illus. 13-29 (right). The braces are more than a decorative feature of the gazebo. They help strengthen the structure.

Step 12: Make the Seats Make eight seat supports, each one consisting of a pair of 2 × 4's and a 4 × 4 (Illus. 13-30). The seat supports are nailed to the inside of the posts, and sit on the deck. The seats are made by attaching 2 × 6 stock to the top of the seat supports with 12d galvanized finishing nails (Illus. 13-31). The seats form a pattern like the deck. Trim the edge of the seats with 1 × 4 stock (Illus. 13-32).

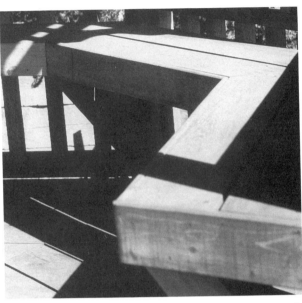

Illus. 13-32. The edges of the seat are covered with 1 × 4 stock.

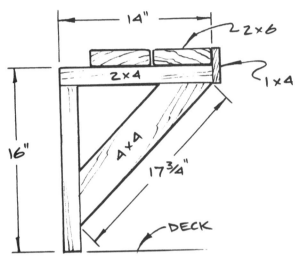

Illus. 13-30. The dimensions for the seat supports.

Step 13: Make the Entry Step If you want to indent steps into the deck, don't add a band joist at the entry side. Add a 4 × 4 where the steps end. The 4 × 4 forms the riser for the last tread and also serves to support the deck at this point (Illus. 13-33).

Illus. 13-31. A sturdy bench wraps around the inside of the gazebo to provide plenty of seating space.

Illus. 13-33. The entry step offers easy access to the gazebo.

You can locate the support while you are adding the deck. In doing so, you can place the support directly under the deck piece.

Step 14: Make the Cupola (Optional) The cupola aligns with the inside of the roof frame octagon. Cut two pieces of exterior-grade plywood to size (Illus. 13-34). To make the cupola posts, bevel eight pieces of 2 × 2 stock to 22½ degrees, and then cut the parts to 10-inch lengths. Nail the cupola posts between the plywood plates. The bottom plate is cut out to allow airflow through the top of the gazebo (Illus. 13-35). Cut ⅜-inch-thick strips from "2 ×" stock to form the bands around the perimeter of the cupola and the exterior trim. The trim, which is beveled to 22½ degrees along one edge, covers the joints between the bands and the cupola posts (Illus. 13-36).

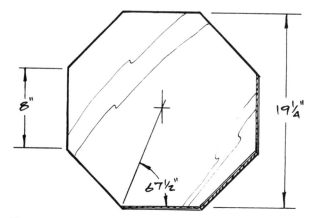

Illus. 13-34. The cupola aligns with the inside of the roof frame octagon.

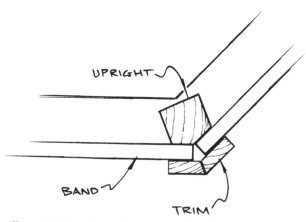

Illus. 13-36. The trim covers the joints between the bands and the cupola posts.

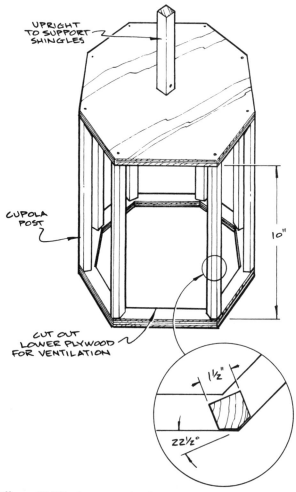

Illus. 13-35. Cut out the bottom plate of the cupola to allow air to flow through the top of the gazebo.

Illus. 13-37. Cut and fit cedar shingles to make the cupola roof.

Next, nail an upright to the top of the plywood, and then add cedar shingles to form the cupola roof (Illus. 13-37). To prevent bugs and birds from nesting in the cupola, add screening as needed.

The cupola trim covers the joint between the cupola and the gazebo roof shingles. Using a band saw, resaw stock as needed to make the trim (Illus. 13-38). Cut the trim parts to length, mitering their ends to 22½ degrees. Attach the trim by driving galvanized nails through the trim and into the cupola banding.

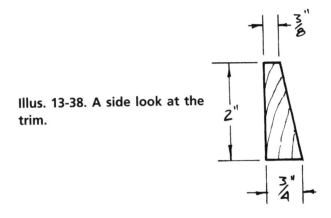

Illus. 13-38. A side look at the trim.

Chapter 14. Children's Playhouse/Outdoor Toy Storage Shed

As kids, we made playhouses from cardboard boxes. The boxes were not very big or strong, and once you closed the flap that served as a window, it got so dark that you could forget about reading any comic book. By comparison, this project (Illus. 14-1) is the Park Avenue penthouse that we would have wished for back then.

Spacious, dry, airy, and well lit, this playhouse makes an attractive addition to the yard. Its large plastic windows (Illus. 14-2) also allow you to easily keep an eye on your children. And the lou-vers provide plenty of fresh air to the interior, so it never gets musty (Illus. 14-3).

When the children are not using the playhouse, it doubles as a storage shed for outdoor toys. Wagons, bikes, sleds, skateboards, and other items that clutter the backyard can have a dry place to call home.

Following are the steps for building the children's playhouse/outdoor-toy storage shed:

Step 1: Make the Frame Start by making the playhouse frame (Illus. 14-4), which consists of

Illus. 14-1. This sophisticated children's playhouse is large and attractive. It has big plastic windows and louvers that provide plenty of air to the interior. It can also double as a storage shed. Pages 121–128 show the playhouse in full color.

PLAYHOUSE MATERIALS LIST (All Dimensions Actual)

Part	Size	Material	Quantity
Framing	1½ in. × 3½ in. × 12 ft.	Fir	4
Framing	1½ in. × 3 in. × 12 ft.	Fir	12
Louver	¾ in. × 3½ in. × 10 ft.	Cedar	9
Upright	¾ in. × 1½ in. × 10 ft.	Cedar	3
Sheathing	⅜ in. × 4 ft. × 8 ft.	Exterior Plywood	2½ sheets
Floor and Roof	¾ in. × 4 ft. × 8 ft.	Exterior Plywood	2 sheets
Siding	¾ × 5½ in.	Tongue-and-Groove Red Cedar	130 feet
Window	¼ in. × 5 ft. × 5 ft.	Acrylic Sheet	2
Footing	8 in. × 8 in. × 16 in.	Concrete Block	4
Butt Hinge	3 × 3 in.	Brass	2

Illus. 14-2. Large acrylic windows on two sides of the playhouse make it easier to keep a watchful eye on the children.

MISCELLANEOUS MATERIALS

The following materials are also needed to build the children's playhouse/outdoor toy storage shed: 4d, 10d, and 16d galvanized nails; 6d and 8d galvanized finishing nails; 3-inch × number-16 flathead wood screws; hinges; silicone sealant, copper tubing, fiberglass tape and gel; one gallon of siding stain; and one quart of exterior gloss enamel paint.

Illus. 14-3. Wooden louvers keep out rain, yet allow plenty of ventilation. This is a view from the inside of the playhouse.

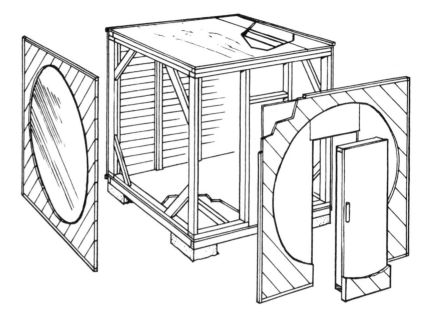

Illus. 14-4. An exploded view of the children's playhouse.

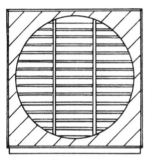

LOUVER SIDE

Illus. 14-5. The louver, window, and door side frames.

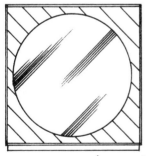

WINDOW SIDE (2 REQ'D)

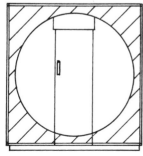

DOOR SIDE

a floor frame, a roof frame, a louver-side frame, a door-side frame, and two window-side frames (Illus. 14-5–14-8). The floor frame is made from 2 × 4 stock, and the remaining frames are made from 2 × 3 stock.

Begin by assembling the floor frame and covering it with ¾-inch-thick plywood. Note that the plywood is recessed ⅜ of an inch from the edge of the floor frame (Illus. 14-9). Space the joists 16 inches on-center. Make sure one of the joists is located to serve as a nailing surface for the edge of the 48-inch-wide plywood (also refer to Illus. 14-19).

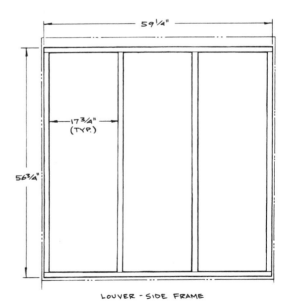

LOUVER - SIDE FRAME

Illus. 14-6. The dimensions for the louver-side frames.

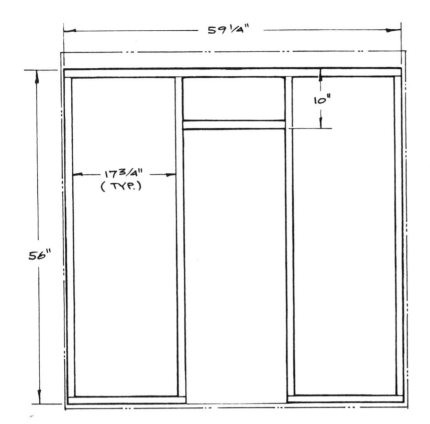

Illus. 14-7. The dimensions for the door-side frame.

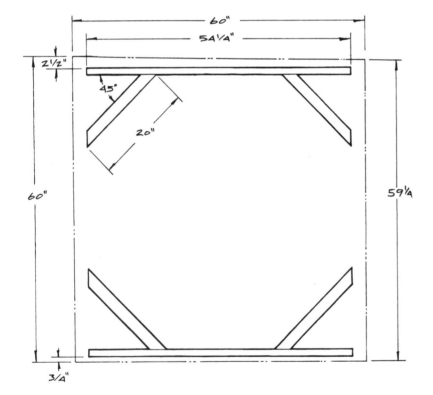

Illus. 14-8. The dimensions for the window-side frame.

Illus. 14-9 (right). The plywood that covers the floor frame is recessed ⅜ inch from the edge of the floor frame.

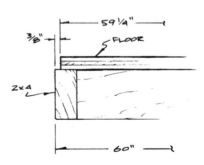

Next, assemble the roof-frame parts and then add the ¾-inch-thick plywood roof sheathing. Note that the plywood overlaps the roof frame by ⅜ of an inch all around (Illus. 14-10). Space the rafters 16 inches on-center. Make certain one of the rafters is positioned to serve as a nailing surface for the edge of the 48-inch-wide plywood (also refer to Illus. 14-19).

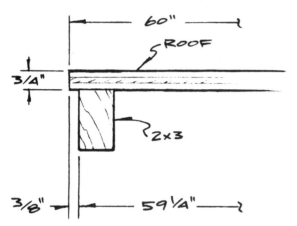

Illus. 14-10. The plywood roof sheathing.

Make the door-side and louver-side frames next. In order to pitch the roof, which allows water to drain, the door-side frame is made ¾ of an inch shorter than the louver-side frame.

Now, position the floor frame on your foundation and check to make sure the frame is level. For a relatively lightweight project like this, four 8 × 8 × 16-inch concrete blocks (one block at each corner) can serve as a simple foundation. Set the bottom of the blocks 4 to 5 inches into the ground.

Next, attach the door and louver-side frames to the floor frame with 16d galvanized common nails. Locate both of these frames so that they are flush with the edges of the plywood. Drive the nails through the bottom plates and into the 2 × 4 floor framing.

Cut the bottom plates to length for the two window-side frames. Nail them in position (flush with the edges of the plywood) with 16d galvanized common nails. Cut the lower diagonal braces to length, mitering their ends to 45 degrees. Using 3-inch-long × number-16 flathead wood screws, attach one end of the brace to the bottom plate and the other end to the frame walls. As shown in Illus. 14-8, the braces must be cut to 20 inches long. Before attaching the braces, use a carpenter's level to make sure the walls are square and plumb.

Next, cut the top plates for the window-side frames to length. The easiest way we found to nail the top plates in place is to nail temporary support blocks under where the top plates are to be located on the wall frames. Rest the top plates on the support blocks and toenail the plates in place. Remove the support blocks once the top plates are secured, and then enlist the aid of a helper to lift the roof frame into position on the walls. To secure the roof, use 10d galvanized common nails and toenail through the 2 × 3 roof framing into the top plate of the door- and louver-side walls. Also attach the upper diagonal braces. Like the bottom braces, the upper braces are 20 inches long.

Step 2: Add the Sheathing The four side frames are sheathed in ⅜-inch-thick exterior-grade plywood (Illus. 14-11). The best side of the plywood should face the interior on the louver and window sides. On the door side, the best face should be to the exterior. For safety, the rough side that faces the interior should be sanded smooth and free of splinters. Use 4d galvanized common nails to secure the sheathing to the framing.

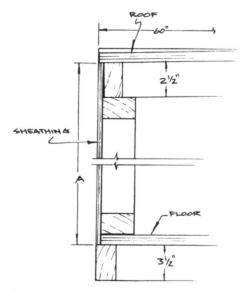

Illus. 14-11. The four side frames are sheathed in ⅜-inch-thick exterior-grade plywood.

The louver-side frame and the two window-side frames are sheathed with plywood cut to a width of 12 inches (Illus. 14-12). Add the sheath-

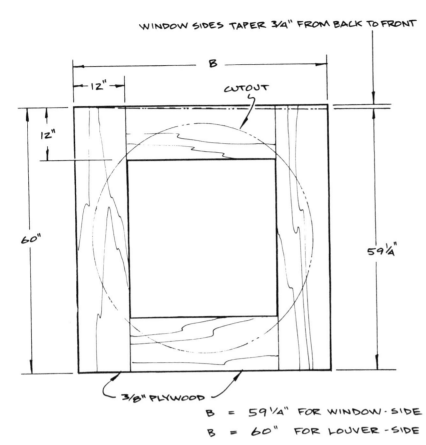

WINDOW SIDES TAPER ¾" FROM BACK TO FRONT

Illus. 14-12. Twelve-inch-wide plywood is used to sheath the louver- and window-side frames.

B = 59¼" FOR WINDOW-SIDE
B = 60" FOR LOUVER-SIDE

ing to the window sides first. Because the door-side frame is ¾ inch shorter than the louver-side frame, the top edge of the window-side sheathing must taper from 60 inches (at the back) to 59¼ inches (at the front). Also, note that the sheathing width (shown as dimension B in Illus. 14-12) for the window side is ¾ inch narrower than the louver side. The door-side frame is sheathed around the door, saving the cutout for the door itself. Temporarily tack the door cutout in place until the siding is added.

You'll need a shop-made compass in order to lay out all the circles. The compass beam is one such compass. It is simply a piece of narrow

stock that measures about 30 inches long. At one end of the beam, create a pivot point by driving a 10d nail through the beam. The point of the nail should stick out about ¼ of an inch or so. Now, measure 25 inches from the center of the pivot point and bore a hole big enough to accept the point of a pencil. Then, bore a second pencil hole ½ inch from the first one, or 25½ inches from the center of the pivot point (Illus. 14-13).

Temporarily nail a piece of scrap plywood at approximately the center of one of the walls. Then, at each corner of the same wall, tack four finishing nails in place, leaving about ¼ inch of

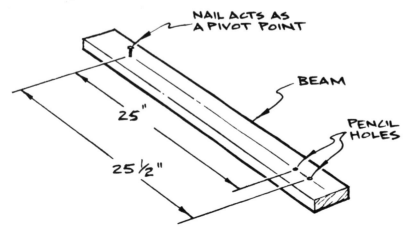

Illus. 14-13. Laying out the circles with a shop-made compass beam.

the nail exposed. Using the finishing nails as anchors, stretch a couple of lengths of string diagonally across the wall. The point where the two diagonals intersect is the center of the wall. Mark the wall centerpoint on the plywood (Illus. 14-14).

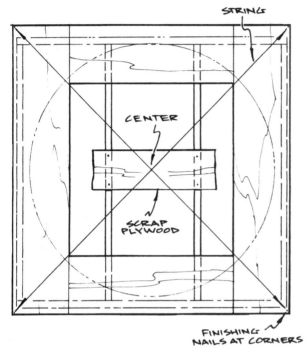

Illus. 14-14. Marking the wall centerpoint on the plywood.

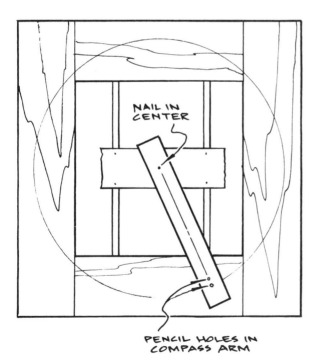

Illus. 14-15. Scribe a circle on all four walls.

Place the pivot point of the compass beam on the centerpoint mark. Insert a pencil into the hole farthest from the pivot point (the 25½-inch radius), and then scribe a circle. Repeat this procedure for all four walls (Illus. 14-15).

Using a saber saw, cut out the circles on the louver side and the two window sides. *Do not* cut out the circle on the door side. When cutting the louvered side, you'll have to stop the cuts each time the blade meets the two 2 × 3 vertical frame members. Use a sharp chisel to cut away the portion of the sheathing that remains above the two 2 × 3's.

Step 3: Apply the Siding We used 1 × 6 red-cedar-tongue-and-groove boards for the siding. Redwood is also a good choice. Pine is acceptable, although it doesn't offer as much natural decay resistance as cedar or redwood.

Begin by adding the siding to the louvered side and the two window sides. Don't do the door side yet. Cut and attach the siding to the 2 × 3 framing with 8d galvanized finishing nails. For safety's sake, make sure that no nails penetrate the wall sheathing and are exposed on the inside of the playhouse. Cut the siding flush with the outside corners of the sheathing to allow room for the ¾ × ¾-inch edging that's added later. Don't follow the slope of the roof as you work along the window-side roof line. Instead, adjust the siding length so that the top edge of the side is horizontal.

Use a nailset to countersink all the nails.

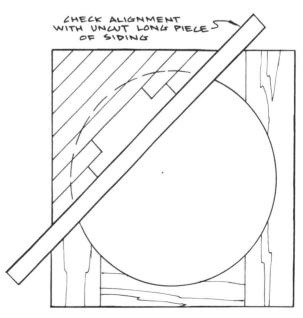

Illus. 14-16. Use a long piece of siding to check the alignment of the short pieces.

There is no need to run the siding all the way across the open circle. Instead, cut the siding just long enough to extend inside the circumference of the circle. A long piece of siding comes in handy for checking the alignment of the short pieces (Illus. 14-16).

Now, use the compass to scribe a circle on the siding, but this time use the hole nearest the pivot point (the 25-inch radius). Once the circle is scribed, cut out the circle with the saber saw.

It's a bit more difficult to apply siding to the door side of the playhouse. That's because the sheathing interferes with the saber-saw cut. When you reach the marked circle on the door side, temporarily tack each piece of siding in place and then scribe the radius using the compass beam. Next, remove the piece and cut the curve with the saber saw. Finally, reattach the piece with 8d finishing nails. You'll need to repeat this for each piece on the circle.

When the siding is done, rip some of the cedar siding stock into ¾ × ¾-inch pieces for the edging. Cut the edging to length and attach it to the ends of the siding with 8d galvanized finishing nails.

Step 4: Make the Louvers The louvers are made from 1 × 4 stock. Bevel both edges of the

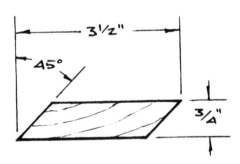

Illus. 14-17. A cross section of the louver.

stock to 45 degrees (Illus. 14-17) and then cut the stock to 17⅝ inches long so that it can fit between the 2 × 3 vertical studs. You'll need a total of 51 louvers for the playhouse.

The six uprights are made from 1 × 2 stock. Cut them to length so they extend from the plywood floor to the top of the wall framing. You'll need to notch the edges of the two outside uprights in order to fit around the braces. Glue and nail the louvers to the uprights, allowing the uprights to overhang the louvers by ¾ inch. All the louvers, except for the bottom one, are spaced 3⅛ inches apart (Illus. 14-18).

The three louver/upright subassemblies can now be inserted between the studs from the inside. Secure them in place by driving 6d finishing nails through the uprights and into the studs (Illus. 14-19).

Step 5: Make the Windows Use ¼-inch-thick acrylic sheet (Plexiglas) to make the plastic windows. Scribe the circle with your compass, using the pencil hole farthest from the pivot point (the 25½-inch radius). To avoid damaging the sheet with the sharp pivot point, use hot glue to attach a small block of wood at the centerpoint of the acrylic sheet. After the circle has been scribed, the wood can be easily removed. Use the saber saw to cut the circle just inside the scribed line.

You'll need a helper for the next step. Bend the plastic slightly to pass it to the inside of the cube. Run a bead of silicone around the inside edge of the siding, and then press the acrylic sheet into place (Illus. 14-20).

Step 6: Assemble the Door Now, remove the door and stiffen it with 2 × 3 backers, and then hinge it in place. To provide clearance for the door to close, allow ½ inch between the backer and the wall frame (Illus. 14-21). Also, bevel the

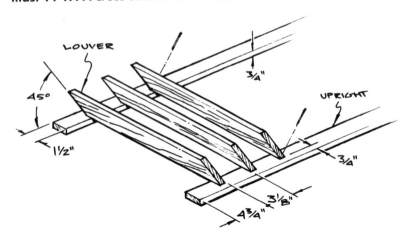

Illus. 14-18. The placement of the louvers.

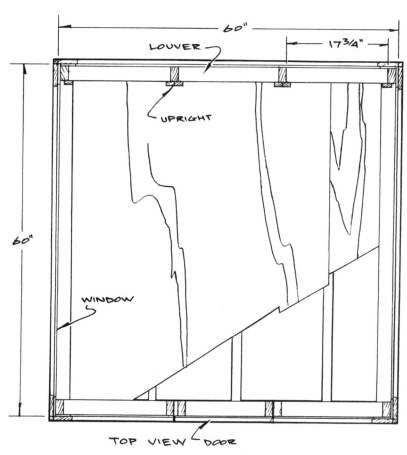

Illus. 14-19. The three louver/upright subassemblies are inserted between the studs from the inside.

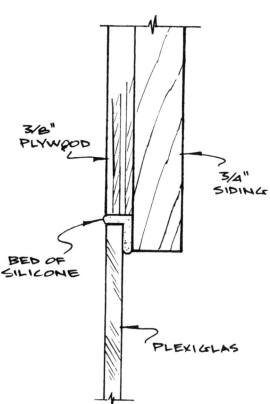

Illus. 14-20. A cross section of the Plexiglas pressed into place.

exterior siding at the hinge side so that the door does not bind (Illus. 14-22).

A simple door pull can be made from 1-inch-diameter dowel cut to a length of five inches. Use a hand plane to create a ½-inch-wide flat area on one surface of the dowel and then secure the dowel in place by driving a pair of screws from the inside of the door into the flat area.

Step 7: Add Tubing for the Roof Drain A length of tubing must be added to allow water to drain from the roof. Drill two holes to accept copper tubing—one at the low side of the roof and the other directly below it in the floor. Cut the tube at one end as shown in Illus. 14-23. Bend the pieces over and insert the tube in the holes. File off any sharp spots.

Step 8: Seal the Roof Use fiberglass tape and gel to seal all the seams on the roof. Cover the exposed copper flanges of the tube with the fiberglass tape, and run the tape down into the tube slightly.

Step 9: Paint and Stain the Gazebo Paint the exposed plywood a bright color using exterior gloss enamel. Apply a clear or tinted siding stain to the tongue-and-groove siding.

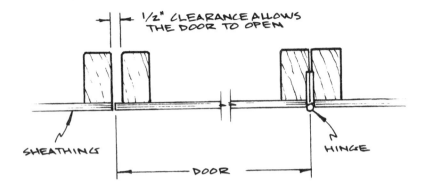

Illus. 14-21. Allow ½-inch clearance between the door backer and the wall frame.

Illus. 14-22. The exterior siding at the hinge side of the door should be beveled so that the door does not bind.

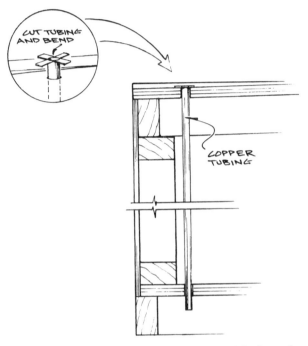

Illus. 14-23. A length of tubing is added to the roof to allow water to drain from it.

GLOSSARY

Air-Dried Lumber Lumber that is dried by exposing it to the outside air.

Anchor Bolt A bolt that holds structural members in place. One end of the bolt is embedded in concrete, and the other end is exposed to accept a washer and nut. Also called a J-bolt.

Appearance Lumber Lumber that is used for appearance applications.

Barge Rafter The rafters that form the outer face of a gable overhang. Also called a fascia or verge rafter.

Batter Board Temporary wood frame that is used in conjunction with a mason's line to lay out foundation corners.

Beam A structural member with a nominal thickness of 5 inches or more, and a width that is more than 2 inches greater than the thickness (6 × 10 or 8 × 12, for example).

Bird's-Mouth A triangular cutout in a rafter that allows the rafter to rest flat on the wall top cap.

Blocking Members that are installed between floor joists and wall studs to strengthen the frame and provide additional nailing surfaces.

Board *See* Board Lumber.

Board Foot A unit of measure equaling a board that is 1 foot square and 1 inch thick (144 square inches).

Board Lumber Lumber graded primarily for appearance. Also called boards.

Bottom Plate A horizontal wall member that provides a base for attaching all the vertical members. Also called a sole plate.

Butt End The thickest end of a wood shingle.

Ceiling Joists Horizontal boards, installed on edge, that serve as the primary supporting members of the ceiling.

Centered Pattern Roofing pattern for three-tab asphalt shingles. The shingle cutouts are centered on the tabs of the course directly below.

Closed Gable End A gable roof without an overhang on the ends.

Collar Beam A horizontal member that connects the rafters on opposite sides of the ridge. Also called collar tie.

Collar Tie *See* Collar Beam.

Corner Post A vertical supporting member at the end of a wall. Used when it is necessary to create inside corners for finishing walls with Sheetrock, sheathing, paneling or other materials.

Cripple A short stud located between the header and the top plate or between the rough sill and the bottom plate.

Deck The boards or plywood panels that are attached to the top edge of the floor joists. Also called the subfloor or platform.

Dimension Lumber Lumber milled to either 2- or 4-inch nominal thickness and in widths of more than 2 inches.

Double-Header A pair of headers nailed together to provide additional strength.

Double Plate The structural member formed by joining together the top cap and the top plate.

Dressed Dimension   The thickness and width of a piece of lumber after it has been dressed (planed smooth).

Dressed Lumber   Lumber that has been planed smooth. Also called surfaced lumber.

Dry Lumber   Lumber with a moisture content that is 19 percent or less. Also called seasoned lumber.

End Joist   The floor joist that is located at each end of the floor frame. Also called a stringer joist.

End Rafter   The rafter at the end of a roof.

End Stud   The stud located at the end of a wall.

Exposure   The distance between adjacent courses of shingles.

Fascia Board   A member covering the ends of the rafters at the eaves. Also sometimes used to cover the face of a fascia rafter.

Fascia Rafter   The rafter that forms the outer face of a gable overhang. Also called a verge or barge rafter.

Fill-In Bracing   A diagonal member attached to a wall frame to provide additional strength.

Floor Joist   A horizontal board, installed on edge, that serves as the primary supporting member of the floor frame.

Framing Lumber   Lumber that is to be used as structural members.

Gable Overhang   A gable roof with an overhang on each end.

Gable Stud   A vertical member that is added between the top cap and the end rafters.

Grade (Plywood)   1: The quality of the front and back veneers for American Plywood Association (APA) sanded plywood. 2: The suggested use of APA Performance-Rated Plywood.

Grade Mark   A stamp applied to plywood that provides useful information such as the grade and the exposure durability.

Grade Stamp   A stamp applied to the lumber that provides useful information such as the lumber grade, wood species, and moisture content.

Grading   The process of inspecting lumber for defects.

Green Lumber   Lumber with a moisture content of greater than 19 percent. Also called unseasoned lumber.

Header   A horizontal member that supports the weight of a structure over an opening such as a door or window. Also called a lintel.

Header Joist   A horizontal board, installed on edge, that is secured to the ends of the floor joists.

In-the-Rough Lumber   Lumber freshly cut from logs. The lumber has a rough surface caused by the big, fast-cutting mill saw blades.

Jamb   The two sides and top of a door or window frame.

J-bolt   *See* Anchor Bolt.

Joist   A horizontal board, installed on edge, that serves as the primary supporting member of the floor frame or ceiling.

Joist Hanger   A metal bracket used to support floor or ceiling joists.

Kiln-Dried Lumber   Lumber dried in a huge oven, called a kiln, that controls the temperature and humidity of the wood.

King Stud   The stud located on each side of a door or window rough opening.

Let-In Bracing   A diagonal member attached to a wall frame to provide additional strength.

Lintel   A horizontal member that supports the weight of a structure over an opening such as a door or window. Also called a header.

Lumber Wood cut to specific thicknesses, widths, and lengths.

Moisture Content The weight of the water in wood expressed as a percentage of the weight of wood from which all the water has been removed.

Mudsill A horizontal member, secured to the top of the foundation, that supports the subfloor. Also called the sill plate.

Nominal Dimension The thickness and width dimensions of a piece of lumber immediately after it is cut from a log.

Outrigger Horizontal members that connect the end and fascia rafters.

Penny The term, indicated by the letter "d," used to specify the length of common, casing, finishing, and several other types of nails.

Platform The boards or plywood panels that are attached to the top edge of the floor joists. Also called the subfloor or deck.

Plug A repair made to a small defect in plywood veneer. Also called a patch.

Plumb Exactly vertical.

Plumb Bob A pointed metal weight used in conjunction with a plumb line.

Plumb Line A line or string from which a plumb bob is suspended. It is used to check the verticality of an object.

Post Cap A wooden member that is bolted (with an anchor bolt) to the top of a post foundation. The floor frame is nailed to the post cap.

Quality Mark An ink stamp or end tag label that is applied to pressure-treated lumber. The quality mark provides important information about the lumber, including the type of preservative used and the water retention level.

Rafter A sloping frame member that spans from the ridge to the wall top cap.

Rafter Line A line running parallel to the edge of a rafter, extending from the corner of the bird's-mouth to the centerline of the ridgeboard thickness.

Ridge A long horizontal board at the highest point of a roof. Also called a ridgeboard.

Ridgeboard *See* Ridge.

Roof Pitch The ratio of the rise to the span.

Roof Rise 1: On a *gable roof*, the distance from the top of the wall top cap to the end of the rafter line at the ridge. 2: On a *shed roof*, the difference in elevation between the front wall top cap and the back wall top cap.

Roof Run 1: On a *gable roof*, the distance from the outside of the framed walls to the center of the ridge. 2: On a *shed roof*, the roof span minus the thickness of one wall.

Roof Slope The ratio of the rise to the run.

Roof Span 1: On a *gable roof*, the width of a building measured between the outside of the framed walls. 2: On a *shed roof*, the distance between the outside of the front wall and the outside of the back wall.

Rough Sill The horizontal frame member that creates a supporting base for the window.

Seasoned Lumber Lumber with a moisture content that is 19 percent or less. Also called dry lumber.

Shank The unthreaded portion of a screw.

Shingle Joint The space between adjacent wood shingles that allows the shingles to expand when wet.

Sill The bottom member of an outside door frame or window.

Sill Plate A horizontal member, secured to the top of the foundation, that supports the subfloor. Also called the mudsill.

Sole Plate   A horizontal wall member that provides a base for attaching all the vertical members. Also called a bottom plate.

Square   When roofing, the amount of roofing shingles needed to cover 100 square feet of roof.

Stringer Joist   The floor joist that is located at each end of the floor frame. Also called an end joist.

Stud   The vertical wall member that extends from the bottom plate to the top plate.

Subfloor   The board or plywood panels that are attached to the top edge of the floor joists. Also called the platform or deck.

Surfaced Lumber   Lumber that has been planed smooth. Also called dressed lumber.

Threshold   A wooden or metal strip that fills the space between the underside of a door and the top of the sill.

Timber   Lumber that has a nominal thickness of 5×5 inches and greater.

Top Cap   A horizontal wall member, attached to the top of the top plate, that serves to provide additional support to the roof and helps to tie the wall frames together.

Top Plate   A horizontal wall member that is attached to the top of the vertical wall members.

Trimmers   Short studs located on either side of a door or window rough opening that support the header.

Unseasoned Lumber   Lumber with a moisture content greater than 19 percent. Also called green lumber.

Veneer   A thin sheet of wood. Also called a ply.

Verge Rafter   The rafter that forms the outer face of a gable overhang. Also called a fascia or barge rafter.

METRIC CHART

mm—millimetres　　　**cm—centimetres**

Inches to Millimetres and Centimetres

inches	mm	cm	inches	cm	inches	cm
⅛	3	0.3	9	22.9	30	76.2
¼	6	0.6	10	25.4	31	78.7
⅜	10	1.0	11	27.9	32	81.3
½	13	1.3	12	30.5	33	83.8
⅝	16	1.6	13	33.0	34	86.4
¾	19	1.9	14	35.6	35	88.9
⅞	22	2.2	15	38.1	36	91.4
1	25	2.5	16	40.6	37	94.0
1¼	32	3.2	17	43.2	38	96.5
1½	38	3.8	18	45.7	39	99.1
1¾	44	4.4	19	48.3	40	101.6
2	51	5.1	20	50.8	41	104.1
2½	64	6.4	21	53.3	42	106.7
3	76	7.6	22	55.9	43	109.2
3½	89	8.9	23	58.4	44	111.8
4	102	10.2	24	61.0	45	114.3
4½	114	11.4	25	63.5	46	116.8
5	127	12.7	26	66.0	47	119.4
6	152	15.2	27	68.6	48	121.9
7	178	17.8	28	71.1	49	124.5
8	203	20.3	29	73.7	50	127.0

Index

Pages in *bold italics* are in color